Praise for *Stillness*

"Engaging and reminiscent of *Eat, Pray, Love*."
—JACK ADAM WEBER, activist, poet and author of *In Love: Celebrating the Seasons of Intimate Relationship*

"Fascinating!"
—STAGE ACTOR OF STANHOPE, London, & international director of education for Nexxus Products Company

"For anyone who is going through a spiritual awakening (or close to someone who is), *Stillness and Wilderness* will bring you peace in knowing that you are not alone and that the light is guiding you just where you need to be. Elisabeth shares with her readers the intimate ups and downs of her sudden and intense awakening in its raw and authentic form. Spiritual awakenings are divine blessings. Along with the bliss, peace and vast opening that accompanies an awakening often comes pain, confusion, loss and even despair. While no two travelers along life's path will share the same experience, it is sacred, nonetheless. *Stillness and Wilderness* will guide you towards your well-being and spirit."
—SCOTT SALZMAN, Bright Spot Solutions

"Spirit through nature has changed Elisabeth forever. I was especially moved to read her story of Divine Mother's healing through the hummingbird."
—NAYASWAMI NARAYAN, spiritual co-director of Ananda, Los Angeles

"This memoir is an account of the author's recovery from a period of intense darkness and despair, to finding meaning and wholeness. The author's journey to her destination is a highly personal and vulnerable one, as she shares her innermost thoughts and emotions. Many will relate to aspects of her journey."
—BOOKLIFE PRIZE

Stillness
and
Wilderness

Lauren,
To Divine soul
shine your light,
Much Love,
Elisabeth

Stillness
and
Wilderness

A Bold Ride from Despair to
Deep Wisdom and Love

ELISABETH LAVA

Dedication

In honor of all those who suffered the pain of depression and anxiety to the point of suicide, the family and loved ones affected, and to all those who still suffer, regardless of the cause, depth, or frequency.

If you **W**alk through the **hole** in your heart, you will return to **Whol**eness, to be complete once again and again.

The names of most people in this book have been changed to protect their identity.

Heartfelt thanks to the long list of women in my life who have shared the space for tears from heartbreaks in order to mend and heal together: Sheri, Shelley, Wendy, Patti, Lynton, Tamara, Sandi, Ellen, Kim, and Gale.

For "Maxwell," "Kevin," "Drew," and "David."

You were all part of the divine plan for my awakening. Without intending to harm me, you broke my heart open repeatedly, forcing me to dive deep inside my soul to heal old wounds, to awaken, and to allow my true Self to emerge.

I bow reverently at the feet of the ultimate teacher for my soul, revealed in this story. I was brought to my knees repeatedly to be brought to you and have been again and again since the end of this storyline. I dedicate this book to you.

Contents

Part III: Ascending to the Summit of Life

Photo © René Perolt

About the Author

ELISABETH LAVA is a traveling mystic, a mobile transformational and holistic health, life, and spiritual coach, a Certified Spiritual Emergence Coach®, a worksite wellness consultant, a yoga instructor, and an advocate, champion, and spokesperson for access to mental health services and reducing stigma surrounding mental health challenges. She loves coaching those who want to change their life to help others or the planet in bigger ways and supports each client to do so in a way that nurtures their own health and soul. She is a former dancer, veterinarian, deadly disease investigator, and competitive triathlete who still loves cycling, yoga, van life, and horses. She intertwines these passions into her services. Elisabeth has completed federal public information officer training and has spoken to mass media and at large conferences while working in public health for twenty years. She speaks on the importance of addressing access to mental health services in all settings. Elisabeth plans to live in the San Juan Mountains of southwestern Colorado the majority of each year to create a spiritual site for group meditation and yoga that honors all spiritual paths and a trauma sensitive healing program and space. Proceeds from this book will help create this healing space and program.

Spiritual Emergence Coach® is used with permission through Integrative Mental Health for You.

For more information,
visit **BeeTrueYou.com** or www.elisabethlava.com

Preface

This book is broken into three sections with symbolism from both Buddhism and cycling. Without Buddhists, I would not have had an awakening, would not have understood that I was having an awakening, and would not have found my spiritual path. Cycling introduced me to three key souls in this story and allowed me to integrate events into the book you now hold.

Wilderness in the title signifies not only the pristine wilderness where I was immersed when my awakening began but also signifies embracing the mystery of the mystical and spiritual moments of the path that unfolded from 2018 through 2020.

For those souls who experience a sudden or intense awakening, I hope this book supports you in knowing you are neither alone nor irrational. Finding the right counselor with strong spiritual competencies may assist you in navigating and overcoming the fear associated with such an awakening. Just know an awakening can be the start of the deeply profound inner transformation of becoming your truest Self—and it might give you the tools to help others do so, as well.

As many souls are yearning for a continued healing awakening and aspiring to become a part of something larger, join me to opening and arriving at wholeness.

Heartbreak and cycling led me to an awakening . . .

Part I:

Descent Into the Darkness

The crossed Buddhist vajra represents the four noble truths of Buddhism:

1. The truth of suffering (Dukkha)
2. The truth of the origin of suffering (Samudāya)
3. The truth of the cessation of suffering (Nirodha)
4. The truth of the path to the cessation of suffering (Magga)

Sunrise over the Cimarron Range, San Juan Mountains,
near Ridgway, Colorado.

CHAPTER 1:

Raven's Laughter

"To fly, we have to have resistance."
—MAYA LIN

It was an angelic sunrise for a morning filled with sorrow overshadowing my heart. My soul felt as if it were dying. As the first sun rays extended across the jagged edges of the Cimarron Mountains and entered through the large, east-facing picture window into the master bedroom—a moment that would normally make me feel joyful and peaceful—I woke to an engulfing wave that swallowed me with wailing, grief, and sorrow. I could not move, let alone get out of bed.

Movers were on their way to empty my house, a house I had purchased and shared with Kevin, the sweetest, kindest, most loving soul I had ever known. He had moved out just a few weeks before. This was the lowest point in my life. Selling and moving out of the house we shared felt like driving a nail into the coffin of our relationship. Kevin and I had been together for five years—five years of a mostly blissful relationship in my heart. There was no turning back, however. This move marked the end of the best chapter of my life.

The phone rang. It was the movers. "Hi, Dan here from the moving company. We will be there in about thirty minutes. Are you ready?"

I choked on my tears and cleared my hoarse throat. "I'll do my best. Call me back if you have any trouble finding the house."

I sent an email to my two sisters that read in part, "I've never been like this. I can't get out of bed. I'm frozen in grief. Help."

My sister Heidi called me immediately. She had also been through hell and back in her personal life, and I've always admired her fortitude. Heidi said, "I'm so sorry, little sis. It's going to be all right. I know this must be rough. You are strong and resilient. You will get through this."

The strength she referred to was about the life events I had already experienced, from growing up with a sibling with a severe mental illness to graduating from veterinary school and surviving twelve years of marriage to an emotionally abusive narcissist. I had performed on stage as a ballerina with a professional company while in high school under the watchful eye of a Bulgarian teacher who whacked students with sticks to correct our mistakes with tough love, completed many iron distance triathlons include the world championship in Hawaii, and moved to a new area alone where I knew no one to restart my life from scratch several times. But this time, my resilience had run out.

After hanging up with Heidi, I called Ulli, a cheerful local German friend. I'm not sure why I called her, as we were not that close. My parents are German immigrants, so German friends were a natural part of my life. Ulli had played the harp at my wedding eighteen years before. Now she knew just what to do. She began to sing in German to me "Die Gedanken sind frei" (which means "thoughts are free," and includes a lyric about renouncing sorrows), to lift my spirits.

Those two connections with Heidi and Ulli gave me the courage to get out of bed. I shuffled downstairs, having slept for only three hours. A disarray of boxes and wrapping materials was strewn everywhere in the living room. Kevin had helped me the day before, but he was now on a work trip. I had no energy to pack more. My fingertips were thickened with calluses from three days of handling boxes and every item I owned. *Oh God*, I thought. *I'm not ready.*

The phone rang again. "It's Dan the mover. Are you okay? You sounded rather upset. We can move you tomorrow or later this week if you want."

Such a kind offer, I thought, but I refused in a panicked tone, "Thanks, but no. It must happen today. The house has been sold. The new owners are moving in tomorrow. I'm struggling to pack the last few items. I know our contract doesn't include packing, just moving. But if you're willing, I might need some help packing up the last items."

"We'll get it done, ma'am. It's a hundred per hour for packing," Dan replied.

"I'll do my best. Drive safe."

As I hung up the phone I thought, *I have almost nothing left in me.*

I gazed at the beautiful view across the landscaped backyard that extended to the escarpment and cliff, with the rays of morning sunshine now streaming brightly across the Cimarrons. It was a crisp September day. The swing Kevin and I had shared during so many sunsets, watching alpenglow on those unique mountains, now swung empty, in an updraft breeze that buffeted the edge of the cliffs. I worked long hours at the local health department, resulting in few evenings with enough time to enjoy the bench and views together.

When the moving truck began backing up the narrow, steep drive, I scrambled to clear the front doorway of boxes. A young man hopped up the stairs to the front door and extended his hand warmly, "Hi, I'm John. Don't worry. We'll get you loaded up and onto your next home."

"It's a rental in Ouray," I said, wiping my eyes. "I haven't rented in over twenty years. But at least I'll be closer to work."

As the two movers went into the house to assess the scene, I stepped out onto the back patio to pack up some outdoor items. Over the past year, Kevin and I had gazed at the Milky Way and witnessed hundreds of shooting stars in the dark San Juan Mountains sky while soaking in the hot tub. So many moments of complete peace and joy, once shared here, were now fading into the past. As I swaddled bubble wrap around a piece of tile from an outdoor table, two large ravens[1] circled overhead. I peered up and realized these were the same two ravens Kevin and I had witnessed many mornings, as they perched on the juniper snag extending off the edge of the escarpment. Those two ravens sat side by side, on many mornings watching the sunrise, and we had assumed they were a mated pair . . . lovers.

Now the two ravens were repeatedly squawking with cackles that sounded like laughter. As I squinted and observed them circling over me multiple times, they swung into larger and larger circles, eventually drifting the arcs of their flight toward the escarpment edge. With one final *ka* they flew away from each other. My hair stood up on my neck

---

1. As an omen, ravens can encourage us to dive deeper and to look within to seek the way to put in motion change we might need. Ravens are described in spiritual literature as helping transitions and transformations move along smoothly by casting light into the darkness.

with the eerie symbolism, and a hollowness echoed in my chest. Their evil laughter felt directed at me—laughter that I had gotten my way. I was moving off Log Hill, ridding myself of an expensive house and mortgage. I'd always said that's what I wanted. I had also wanted the simpler life of being closer to my job due to my long work hours, but not our two souls parting ways. This marked the most exquisitely painful end to a relationship—one I'd thought would last the rest of my life.

As the hours of final packing wore on, John noticed the look of despair spreading across my face. "We can just pile all this into one huge heap in the backyard, have a bonfire, and head to the local brewery if you like."

I looked up and cracked a smile at him, "Oh I'd love that. Simplicity. But half of the furniture is Kevin's." Kevin had moved into a furnished house just down the road on Log Hill. I had offered to store and temporarily use what he couldn't take for now.

I glanced down at the carpeted stairs where I had sat for hours trying to figure out how to bring Kevin back into my life —not letting go, not accepting, and tearing myself apart over mistakes I had made. I'd also had moments there of visualizing how I was going to take my life. Visions of razor blades to my wrists had emerged on their own, without calculated planning, and seemed to erupt from fear deep within.

Kevin had been so loving to me in this home. I knew moving away from this house that Kevin and I shared was the right step. There were too many memories in that house for me to heal and move forward in my life.

The rest of the day was a blur as the movers dumped the boxes into the empty rental house near Ouray. I unpacked the kitchen and bathroom cartons, wrapped the mattress in sheets, and collapsed in a fog in middle of the night. I was determined to leave the next day, heading to Arizona for Thanksgiving to escape the cold and see old friends.

The next day, after three hours of sleep, I was jolted awake by the sound of a truck driving within a few feet of my new rental's master bedroom window in Ouray. I had become spoiled by the quiet on Log Hill. *That's it*, I thought, *I'm buying that land.*

Sometime before, I had fallen in love with a nearby wild piece of land surrounded by national forest that was quiet, sunny, yet still close to town. I had visions of building a very small home there—and a place for meditation and healing.

Two ravens on a snag overhang the east-facing escarpment of Log Hill.

When I brought it up, Kevin had been extremely resistant and became angry. He knew it would be challenging to build from scratch. He wanted to move into a preexisting house in a developed neighborhood with a paved driveway, fancy finishes, and a landscaped yard. I wanted a more natural setting in the mountains, to eventually share with those in need of healing in peace. That perhaps was one of the indicators that could have told me our relationship would not go the distance.

My cell phone vibrated.

"How are you? Are you still planning on driving to Arizona today?"

It was Sharon, a dear friend from Gunnison (another regional mountain town), whose camper in Sedona I was going to stay in overnight. As I tried to sit up, all the muscles on the back side of my legs cramped. I writhed in pain. "I'm going to try. But I don't know if I can get out of bed. My body is seizing."

With no family close by and nowhere to go for Thanksgiving, I had accepted the invitation of some friends in Arizona, a twelve-hour drive away from Ouray. I thought warm sunshine and seeing old friends might be soothing for my soul.

I knew now that the relationship with Kevin had been peaceful, but also suffocating. Kevin wanted to be with me every waking moment when I was not at work. His travel was limited, despite having a job as a traveling salesman. Consequently, there had not been much time to develop friendships in my four years living in the area. Ouray is a sleepy little hamlet of only a thousand year-round residents in southwestern Colorado.

"Girlfriend, don't you think you should rest some first?"

Sharon's voice was filled with worry, but I said, "Thanksgiving is tomorrow. It's not good for me to be alone right now. Besides, a dear German girlfriend of mine has invited me to Thanksgiving dinner with her family. I used to spend Thanksgiving with them every year when I lived in Arizona. This will be good for me."

"Okay, I understand. When you get to our camper in Sedona, the keys are in the side door by the propane tanks. Make yourself at home, but lie low, all right? We aren't supposed to let non-family stay there." Sharon and her husband were renting an RV spot at a gorgeous campsite along Oak Creek in Sedona.

"I really appreciate it," I said. "It will be great to wake up tomorrow in Sedona. I can even just sleep in my car. I have a futon thrown in the back."

"Why would you do that?"

"I don't know if I'll make it all the way there tonight. I might have to pull over and sleep somewhere on along the highway in the desert tonight."

"What? Please don't do that. I don't know if it's safe."

"I'll be fine. It will just be good to get out of here."

"All right, well, text or call me if you have questions."

I departed for Arizona later than I planned, due to the challenges of packing for a trip while still having my household in boxes. As I drove into the night across the Navajo Nation, a beige-orange moon rose over the horizon.

I had hours to reflect on why I seemed to attract men like Kevin who could not share unconditional, long-term love. I still hoped to find a compatible partner one day who could, but I knew I had a long road of healing ahead of me. I had given all the love I could to my former husband and Kevin, but it never seemed to be enough.

In the wee hours of the night, I pulled into the campground in Sedona along a creek surrounded by sycamore trees with freshly fallen, large, crispy leaves cloaking the ground. I turned my headlights to the parking light level so as not to disturb the sleeping campers while I drove around the loops multiple times looking for the site. On the third lap, I finally turned on a fork of the loop and was relieved to recognize their camper, which was tucked into a secluded corner. Exhausted, I could not muster the energy to search for the camper keys that they had hidden for moments like this. I crawled into the back of my Toyota FJ and collapsed for the night onto a foam mattress pad that I had added as a possible last resort way of napping on my journey.

Insights and Ruminations: Darkness had draped over my soul. I was running away from the darkness, as I didn't have the spiritual tools to face it at the time. I could only sense from the ravens' flight overhead that there was some divine play at work. While driving through the night, I reflected how Kevin

could not handle my need to bicycle for hours or my intense drive and long hours at work. To him, I worked and played too hard. I was trying to do all I could as a government leader on a shoestring budget to improve the health of the community and the population in the jurisdiction for which I was responsible, but I didn't know how to balance that work with self-care and a relationship. Now I was facing how that had been—and still was—affecting me. And yet Kevin had refused to discuss his flaws when we had attempted to revitalize the relationship. As I drove in the most exhausted state of my life feeling like a shell of a person, I sensed I did have guardian angels protecting me.

CHAPTER 2:

Spirals Begin

"Transformation is always a spiral development."
—RAVI RAVINDRA

I pedaled my bike up narrow Oak Creek Canyon and rounded the last two switchbacks, ascending away from Sedona and heading toward Flagstaff. I had just enjoyed three days during the Thanksgiving weekend filled with old friends from the Phoenix metro area. Hikes and bike rides in the warm sunshine with people who understood me had been very soothing. I stood up on my pedals to climb the last stretch to the overlook of the upper portion of Oak Creek Canyon, thinking, *This is it—I've shaken those blues. This trip and bike ride are just what my soul needed.*

I pulled into the overlook parking lot above the canyon and was pleasantly surprised by the Navajo women at their tables with their displays of gorgeous jewelry. I clicked out of my pedals and *clippety-clopped* in my bike shoes, admiring the beauty at each table. I asked the women about every piece of jewelry that spoke to me, and they each seemed to have some symbolic meaning related to my current state.

"What does this symbol mean?" I asked, as I softly touched a shimmering silver spiral with a green iridescent stone in the center.

"It's the wind," one of the women replied. "Out with what does not serve you; in with what does serve you."

Perfect symbol for transition in my life, I thought.

"Lovely. How much?" I asked, digging around in my back pocket and presenting payment.

I put the necklace on, clicked into my pedals, and careened around the sharp corners back toward Sedona, a magical, healing place that perfectly punctuated my trip of healing.

Insights and Ruminations: The Navajo women had offered nuggets of guidance as they explained the various symbolism of their jewelry. Up to that point, the only spiritual moments I'd had in my life were from being immersed in the wonder and splendor of nature in the western United States. Now something new was coming.

CHAPTER 3:

Return to Darkness within the Veil of Isolation

---◆◆---

All humans need love, respect, and attention.
—MIKE FARRELL, HUMAN RIGHTS ACTIVIST, ACTOR

Loosening my steely grip on the steering wheel after driving in a snowstorm over Lizard Head Pass and Dallas Divide while returning from Phoenix, I pulled into the ice-crusted driveway of the rental property in Ouray. The house was tucked into the narrowest and darkest part of the glacially carved canyon just north of the hamlet, known as the Switzerland of America. I was lucky to have found this modern, warm-in-the-winter home. Most of the houses in Ouray had been built either at the turn of the century or in the 1970s. I had lived with Kevin for three years in a '70s rental house that was drafty and frigid, but at least then I had a warm man to keep me toasty. Now I was returning to a warm house, alone. There was no man or roommate present to warm my heart. And in December, the sun dipped behind the cliffs each day at half past noon.

It's okay, I thought. *This is a fresh start. Everything is going to be just fine, and I am so blessed. This is the closest I've ever lived to work, only a mile away. I can walk or ride my bike everywhere.*

13

Boulder in backyard of rental house in Ouray,
a possibility of a quick end to my misery

But as I unpacked from the trip and after my first days back at work, the walls seemed to close in on me. The dark thoughts returned.

I found it difficult to focus. My new chapter seemed daunting. Despite the brief vacation, I was drained, and the days at government work seemed to grow more challenging. Most nights, I would go to the gym and soak in the hot springs. Returning to an empty house filled with boxes and no one to talk to just served as a reminder of my mistakes, so I avoided being there. The nights were long. I was sleeping only two hours a night due to fear-filled thoughts of how I had made mistakes in the relationship. The words were on repeat in my mind: *I had the gentlest, kindest soul, and I lost him. I'm such a fool.*

I worried about not being able to make true friends in the local area.

"Sorry, John and I are headed out of town for a month," one friend said.

Another said, "I work on the weekends giving massage, so our schedules are completely opposite. I'm sorry. Maybe we can get together for lunch one day in the future. Maybe this summer."

Yet another: "I'm celebrating my retirement, and Don and I are headed on a three-week road trip to celebrate. Maybe we can get together when we return."

Everyone was paired up, it seemed, and their lives were so full that they couldn't t make time for me. Would I ever find a kind, gentle man with whom I could share the beauty that surrounded me? I supervised those with whom I worked, so spending time together as friends was unwise. Multiple attempts to get together with women my age and with similar outdoor interests failed. The long, demanding hours of my work and the sparsely populated region made it unlikely for me to find a soulmate again. I was losing faith.

Don't take it so personally, I told myself. It was the same when I had Kevin in my life. We did so much together and rarely spent time with others, except for the occasional dinner guests we hosted. But now, I was out of the couple loop. *Couples invite over other couples. Now I'm the fifth wheel. I have no children, so bonding with other mothers is just not an option.* I kept in contact with close friends in Arizona and Denver, but with no moments shared outside of work and no touch from a fellow human, I craved affection, hugs, and just to know someone cared.

Conversations with my family were infrequent and strained.

"Well, you are just like Dad," one sister told me. "You can be harsh at moments, Elisabeth."

"Wait, what do you want?" another sister asked. "I can't talk right now. I'm running late and have to pick up the boys."

"Why did you get involved with a man who could not provide?" my father wanted to know. "And your need for exercise: no man is going to tolerate that!"

Tears flowed down my face and onto my pillow and chest as I lay in bed each night, feeling so alone. My heart was breaking even more as I felt that no one genuinely cared for me. Each morning, I would gaze out the south-facing window to the stark mountainside, which had precipitous, deep red and brown cliff faces. A house down the street had been crushed by a huge boulder that had careened down the mountain. As I lay in bed, I could see the approximate track the boulder, a third of the size of the house, had taken down the cliffs. Fortunately, no one had been in the house at the time. *One evening, another boulder could drop down into* this *house,* I thought. *There is a rather large boulder in the backyard already. There is that huge old spruce on the west side. Maybe that would protect the house and me. Hmmm, on the other hand, maybe that would be a perfect way to go. So be it. That would take me out of my misery.* I tossed and turned with these ideas for hours, a brief pause from my painful, nightly writhing in fear.

One morning that winter at our quaint health department, my amazing assistant Vivian briskly walked into my office and rattled off what seemed like twenty tasks to be accomplished that day. It was overwhelming.

"Of those twenty tasks, which two are the top priorities?" I asked, my voice cracking.

Surprise and disappointment spread across her face. "What? Um, I'll have to think about that." She went silent and then walked away.

In subsequent days, I struggled to complete tasks, the list of to-dos growing longer as more and more deadlines approached. Each day as I left the ranch-style office/house facing the ancient volcanic caldera known as the Amphitheatre, I would gaze at the last of the light or at the moon cresting over the jagged peaks, a view that would usually fill me with gratitude for a day of rewarding activity in a setting of stark beauty. But, as the days grew shorter and my energy faded more and more, even that vision did not give me joy.

Vivian tried to lift my spirits. "I am so looking forward to life in my fifties," she said, smiling and wrinkling her forehead. "It will be so wonderful, don't you agree?"

We are close in age, both working hard to help the community behind the scenes. She had noticed the bagginess of my clothes, as I had started to shrink from the stress of depression.

"I want the old Elisabeth back," she finally said, as she dropped her chin and cocked her head in confusion.

"I'm trying, I really am. I'm sorry," I said as I looked down onto my desk in shame.

It became obvious to me and others that I needed counseling. Our health educator had worked hard with county government leaders to establish an employee assistance program, which included three counseling sessions per year. Little did I know that I would be utilizing the program I had pushed for so soon after it was established.

"I'm exercising, taking hot baths or soaking in the hot springs, journaling, talking to old friends on the phone, but it's not enough," I said to my counselor, Tom. "So, what do I do when thoughts of Kevin arise?"

"After six o'clock, just push him out of your head," he said with a reassuring smile.

"Is that it? Is it supposed to be that simple? Okay, I'll try, but I don't know if that will be enough."

"Let's make a plan for you," Tom said, pulling a chair for me alongside his. "Come sit next to me as I write what we decide on together."

As I looked up to the screen, under "diagnosis", I saw the words: "clinically depressed." I was stunned. *Wow, I am clinically depressed. I've been blue or felt sad at times, but this is serious. Oh, no.*

Those sessions were great for venting my emotions and thoughts. Just having someone listen without judgment did help, but that bit of relief only seemed to last into the evening of the session. It was not enough to stop the downward spiral of depression I was on. Winter turned into early spring, and I was still struggling.

Showing up to an all-hands-on-deck staff meeting at work, I waited along with other department heads for another meeting to be over. I hadn't brought my laptop. As the clock ticked away for almost forty-five minutes, I could at least catch up with email on my phone. Without the laptop, though, I could not work on deadlines that were approaching. When the meeting I came for finally began, I struggled to read what was projected on the wall screen. A new financial management system was being set up for department heads, and we were there to learn about it. I couldn't follow or focus. I was exhausted, had no username or password for the system, couldn't see most of what was on the screen, and could not stop thoughts about what I had to complete when I finally got back to the office.

After thirty minutes, I raised my hand. "I'm sorry, I'm not able to focus much. Is anyone else struggling with the font size on the projection screen? I can't make it out. I guess I should have opted in for the vision plan this year."

Cathy, the county leader who was demonstrating, was clearly annoyed by my interruption, and I became even more overwhelmed with worries of not being able to meet my deadlines. I quietly tapped on my watch and then pointed to the door, and mouthed, "I'm sorry I have to go."

A flood of relief came over me as I walked out in the fresh air to my car. *I've got to get back to the office, or I'll be there until eight o'clock. again*, I mulled.

As I typed away on my laptop back at my office, the phone rang.

"It's Cathy. She's on hold for you."

I picked up. "Hi, yes. How may I help you, Cathy?"

"You had no right! Do you know how hard I worked to put that system together and prepare that presentation? That was so disrespectful of you."

And the reprimand went on. I tried explaining my level of stress, but ended up muttering as I swallowed hard, "Yes ma'am, I understand. I apologize," over and over again. When I hung up the phone, I thought, *That's it. I'm done. I don't need this anymore. I'm going to quit and leave this dark hole of an office and canyon. I'm going to be free and go to a warm, sunny place to heal.* I took a few breaths. *But I need this job. It puts a roof over my head and food in my belly. This is not worth it. Just breathe.* I highly respected Cathy, and I knew the interaction was mostly due to both of us being stressed out from all the demands of government work with limited resources.

The next day, Vivian stormed into my office.

"I'm *not* going over there!" she said as she tossed some interoffice mail on my desk.

"Where? You mean the courthouse? Why not?"

"The tension over there is so thick, you could cut it with a knife. *You* take the paperwork over there today. I'm not doing it," Vivian retorted.

"Okay, I'll go," I said as the hair on my skin stood on end due to anxiety of facing that level of tension from others.

Then Cathy called me to ask, "Why did you cancel your department credit card? You're not supposed to do that. You are supposed to notify me instead."

"I was in Arizona, visiting friends on vacation, when the credit card company called to check on some charges. I didn't recognize them and neither did my staff. I did what I thought I was supposed to. The bank is sending a new card that we should receive any day."

"You don't have the authority to do that."

I didn't know how to respond, so after a long pause, I said, "Sorry. I'll notify you next time."

The next day, I was standing at the county clerk's counter to register my personal vehicle. I felt a tap on my shoulder.

"When you are done here, I need you to come to my office," said Samantha, the human resources director, with a serious tone.

"Yes, ma'am. I'll stop by," I swallowed hard. *Oh my God, I'm getting in trouble again. What did I do wrong this time?* My stomach knotted and tears welled up.

Kelly, a fellow government employee behind the counter, furrowed her brow and said, "Is everything okay, Elisabeth?"

"I can't seem to do anything right anymore, I guess," I replied with a lump in my throat.

Kelly gave me a reassuring smile.

Finishing my personal business, I scurried down the hallway to the HR office. I felt like a kid going to the principal's office, with impending doom creeping over my shoulders.

"I feel like peeling my skin off. I can't handle the stress of work anymore!" I shrilled as I walked into the human resources director's office.

"Whoa, whoa, whoa. What's going on? Take a deep breath and have a seat." Samantha waved her hands toward a chair and closed her office door.

"I've been feeling anxious for the past few days, and I just can't handle work anymore. I'm tired of getting in trouble. I'm trying really hard, I am," I said with my voice quivering. I explained how the end of the relationship, selling the house and moving, working long hours and falling behind, and lack of sleep had piled up into a wall that I could not get around.

"Take time off, as much as you need, Elisabeth," Samantha said softly as she looked at me with concerned eyes.

When I returned to my office, Samantha had sent me an email, outlining how much vacation and sick leave I had accumulated, with an offer to consider how much time I needed to recover. *Wow, I thought, that's unreal how much time I have accrued. Looks like I'm finally going to be forced to take more time away from the office than is customary, but even if I take it all, I don't know if I can dig my spirit out of this deep hole.* My thoughts raced. Worries about taking a long time off and then trying to catch up again welled up inside my chest. Finding time on the calendar with no required meetings or deadlines was virtually impossible as the health department director, but I managed to schedule a vacation for the following month. I felt fulfilled in helping others, but I had neglected my own need for rest.

Recovery in Nature Receded

During two weeks of camping in the Utah red desert near Moab in March, I found peace and reprieve from the depression. Exercise, sleep, and a perfect blend of spending time alone and with friends from Denver were all just what I needed. But when I returned, so did the depression. During a counseling session, Tom asked, "What do you think was different on vacation than while at work?"

"Fresh air, exercise, sunshine, no stress."

"When you exercise, you breathe more. I want you to try to take more conscious breaths."

"And if that doesn't work, then what?" I furrowed my brow with doubt.

"Have you considered FMLA?"

"You mean the Family Medical Leave Act?"

I had learned about FMLA at work and was stunned this was being suggested. I thought it was only intended for severe illnesses such as hospitalizations and for caring for family who are ill. When I got home, I called my brother-in-law Michael, a family physician.

"I'm sorry you aren't feeling well," Michael said. "How long has this been going on? Have you tried antidepressants?"

"I don't want to be on drugs," I lamented.

I could hear him shaking his head over the phone. "Your limbic system has been overstimulated for too long. You sometimes need medication to get out of a hole. It will just be for a little while but be prepared as it takes time to feel an effect. You should try to stay on it for a few months."

I swallowed hard. "Okay, I'll make an appointment with my new primary care doctor." My last doctor had left, and I'd never seen this new one. "But I'm afraid with my first visit being about this, and mentioning drugs and then FMLA, she will think I'm just working the system."

Michael explained the paperwork and process to me, and I thought I could handle it.

Another stressor was the five-year anniversary of being at my job, which was only a few months off, but seemed like an eternity. I called Kimberly, my friend who is an expert in human resources. "Damn it. Every time I get close to being fully vested for retirement, I seem to have to leave a job. I'm so close."

"Yes, but if you are on FMLA when you reach that five-year mark, your retirement will become fully vested," she assured me. "You are protected!"

"I hope I don't have to go that route, but that's a relief."

When I went in for my doctor's appointment, the medical assistant asked, "Who's your emergency contact? You left that part blank."

"I don't have anyone," I said frowning. "I mean, my parents are alive, but they are elderly, and I wouldn't want to burden them. Besides, they might not understand what you tell them if something happens to me. They're hard of hearing."

"Don't worry," she said. "You know, good things happen quickly, too, not just bad things in life."

"That doesn't seem to be my experience lately."

At the end of my appointment, the doctor smiled. "This is the most frequently used antidepressant. Very trusted, works well. Please do try this. Give it a chance, and if this doesn't help, I'll fill out the FMLA paperwork for your job." She tore the prescription off the pad and gazed at me reassuringly.

After reading about withdrawal symptoms and side effects, I became fearful of starting the meds. I was currently training for a half iron distance triathlon. *Stomach side effects, great. I already have diarrhea from stress as it is, and this is going to mess even further with my delicate gut. And the side effects from withdrawing seem to be just as bad as how I feel now!* As I read the package insert and bottle label, I choked down the pill as a couple of tears rolled down my face. *Why can't I be stronger than this? I've got to figure out how to get out of this on my own, without meds.* I looked in the mirror and wiped my tears away. *I'm not going to take any more of those pills.*

As I lay in bed that night, I tossed and turned, full of tumultuous worries and reflections.

What if I can't work at this job anymore, then what?

Okay, Elisabeth, what do you really want to do?

Hmmm. Well, I wanted to be a physical therapist to help people one-on-one. But I became a horse veterinarian as a compromise to my father's demand to become a physician and follow in his footsteps. I love providing one-on-one health screenings for those worried about sexually transmitted diseases and blood pressure checks. Maybe I could do broader health screenings or education.

While in veterinary school and then while practicing as a vet, I realized I wanted a more balanced life than was possible while being the local roving emergency room for horses, cattle, sheep, pigs, and goats. Even though I loved being outdoors and living in rural areas while practicing as a large animal veterinarian, I shifted into public health, which was a better fit in fulfilling my desire to help people just as much as the animals. My government jobs forced me to move to large cities which was not good for my soul but was required due to the nature of being a veterinarian in a state health department. Working in public health as a veterinarian was the best way for me to serve for the greater good with my education. However, working in government for decades responding to deadly diseases did not allow me to live a balanced life either.

When I glanced at the time on my phone, it was three in the morning. My entire body ached, and every joint was throbbing. I checked social media apps to distract myself. An ad popped up with a spiral symbol.

Hmmm. Just like my spiral necklace.

I clicked on the ad and read about an online health and wellness coaching program.

Wow, this seems perfect. Maybe this is what I should do. Start my own business as a health and wellness coach.

This was the moment when I knew I could shift my career into alignment with my needs for fulfillment and work-life balance. Being a health coach was in perfect alignment with my desire to help others one-on-one, control my schedule, and work remotely. Over the coming months, as I emerged from depression, I reviewed the credentials and training methodologies at the Institute for Integrative Nutrition (IIN) program and was impressed. In September, I enrolled with IIN to become a certified health and wellness coach.

Insights and Ruminations: I was repeatedly experiencing a dark night of the soul that would become darker over time due to isolation. Within the depth of yet another night of darkness for my spirit, divine guidance appeared without my looking for it. A glimmer of hope emerged for a different future. The first lecture of the course began: "We are spiritual beings having a human experience" —Pierre Teilhard de Chardin, Jesuit Catholic priest, paleontologist, geologist.

Many serendipities would occur related to the coursework talks and my interactions with others.

CHAPTER 4:

Spring and Possible Love
Return the Light

"Whoever shows up is exactly what we need,
hidden in their trouble."
—Mark Nepo

I stood in tree pose and gazed out the window toward staggering, snow-cloaked peaks. A golden eagle darted past in a dive for prey. *Wow, was that an omen?* To some, sighting an eagle symbolizes it's time to look inward with a careful eye. Allow your heart to guide you, and opportunities you never dreamed were possible will present themselves when you least expect it.

I dedicated my yoga practice that morning to Lynn, a new friend who had shared that she was so tired of not having a partner. After yoga, I drove an hour from my home to meet Lynn to ski in Telluride that afternoon in early April.

"It's been over three years, and I guess I'm getting impatient and a little sad," Lynn sputtered in frustration as we rode up the lift on closing day in Telluride. "Maybe I'm just getting too old to attract the right person."

We were dressed in costume with colorful wigs, tutus, and sequined shorts over ski clothes to celebrate the last hurrah on the ski slopes and the change of season. I clanked the sharp edges of my skis together to knock off the slushy spring snow, watching the chunks plummet fifty feet below us.

"Nonsense! You're gorgeous and have such vibrancy and richness to offer!" I said with a hollowness in my chest. "The right man will come along at the right time, when you least expect it."

Her fear of being alone for the rest of her life resonated with me, so while it was hard to believe when I was saying it to myself, it felt good to try to support her. Lynn and I chatted about using online dating sites due to the isolation of the mountains and the sparse population. Lynn said she wasn't bold enough and the idea of meeting someone that way gave her the creeps. There is a saying that mountain girls espouse to each other when the topic of finding a suitable male partner arises: "The odds are good, but the goods are odd."

After completing an online yoga class earlier that morning with Shiva Rea's Samudra Global School of Living Yoga teacher program, I started to shut down my computer when an email popped up from a dating app. *Argh. I don't really think I should look at that. I've got my career issues that I need to sort out, before any more men.* But curiosity got the better of me. I clicked on the profile. *Hmm. He is a cyclist, loves to travel, seems intelligent, successful, fit, and in touch with who he is and what he wants. Well, he sure does look like a good fit on paper. He says he is stable and well adjusted. Darn it, I can't read the message from him to communicate unless I pay.* I tapped my fingers on my chin. *All right, I'll think about meeting him if the conversation goes well. It's good to meet new people. Broadens my horizons, and occasionally these men turn into great friends.* I hurried off to get my credit card.

The man, Drew, was traveling in his van through Colorado in search of a place to call home. *Cool, a guy who likes to cycle and explore,* I thought as I typed back with a big grin on my face—I liked his sense of adventure. Our dating app messages in April turned into texts, which turned into long phone conversations while he traveled in his van to visit his sons in Washington and then Southern California. I heard the trials of his older gray Sprinter van (named "Flipper") breaking down with dozens of parts installed and thousands of dollars spent. We kept each other company on the phone as he waited for tow trucks and repairs and drove long distances to visit his sons, while I was living a very isolated life. We bonded over the phone that month and finally decided to meet near Moab, Utah.

Rendezvous in Moab

"What the heck? This drop pin on the map on my phone is not taking me to where you described!" he sputtered. "There is no sign of your trailer."

"Oh boy. Well, I hope my trailer is still there. I'm so sorry. The idea was for me to get there first, and I could have navigated you in better."

It took quite a while for us to figure out that Drew had turned Flipper down a road that was indeed on the way to the drop pin but was one road to the north of the campsite. I had left my retro camp trailer (named "Ladybug"—we both named our vehicles. Cute!) where I had camped the weekend before with a bunch of girlfriends, most of whom hailed from Steamboat or Durango in Colorado. It's funny how Moab would draw friends together from afar together *and* was the place where men seemed to emerge in my life. I had shared one of my favorite camp spot locations with Drew. But I had been warned by a friend to set healthy boundaries.

"What? You're going to meet him there all alone?" exclaimed my girlfriend Patti. "Just go for a mountain bike ride with him. Meet him at a trailhead instead."

"I've talked to him enough."

Drew had been showering me with so much attention on the phone and had started to refer me as his girlfriend. I had told him I was starting to get freaked out about his charisma and was having some déjà vu that felt like the way my ex-husband had swept me off my feet during a time of transition. So he dialed back the girlfriend language to calling me a cycling buddy. Our mutual love of cycling was part of our chemistry.

"He has reassured me that he won't interfere with my path, wherever that takes me in life, and that he is harmless. I've talked to him enough that I think it will be fine."

"Oh, Elisabeth," Patti said, "I worry about you."

Due to delays of a busy day at work, I arrived at eleven thirty at night to meet Drew. I had told him to go to sleep and I would see him in the morning, but he'd said he would wait up. When I pulled up on the dusty red rock landscape, he opened the side door of his van. It

Rainbow above the red earth of Moab, Utah.

was cool and dark in the remote desert for May, so he waved me in. As I stepped into the van, he was so ecstatic and poked me in the ribs. "You are real! We finally get to meet." Tan, smooth skin covered his pronounced, happy cheekbones and wide, muscular shoulders and arms. His long light gray bangs flopped in front of crystal blue eyes that sparkled with joy. I was a bit taken aback because his energy was so high for late at night, but his joy was very welcome.

"Yeah. It's wonderful to finally meet you and in one of my favorite spots on Earth."

We chatted until midnight, made plans to ride trails near camp the next morning, hugged and said goodnight.

The next day, with only one day mountain biking together, we were giggling in delight at our shared love of cycling and dispersed camping in raw nature. We were well matched in technical and fitness levels on the bike. I felt like I had come home in being with him due to his playfulness and wit. Conversation was so easy and fun due to his high intelligence and humor. After just two nights at camp, we decided to hit the road to take in the most scenic route possible to St. George and visit a few national monuments and parts along the way.

Drew and I happened to be going in the same direction and ended up traveling together for twelve days. I followed Drew in Flipper, pulling Lady Bug behind my SUV. Drew suggested that I leave my rig in Moab and throw my gear into his van. I was a bit shocked and responded that I liked having my own rig and that I had a ton of gear in tow for a triathlon.

Drew was a strong cyclist, handsome, successful in the health and fitness field, adventurous, sweet, and funny. He was intelligent, articulate, fun to relax and play with, and easy to talk to. He had all the criteria I had been hoping for in a man and more personality traits that attracted me. Drew emanated joy and playfulness that was extremely infectious. He had mentioned he was "Buddhish" in mindset.

I was on my way to St. George to participate in a Half Ironman triathlon. Despite being depressed for months and running on an average of two to three hours of sleep a night, I somehow had mustered fitness while spending two weeks alone in February and March in Moab. I had spent most of those two weeks alone, cycling, running, doing yoga on giant orange, red, and pink slabs of slick rock, and relaxing in the warm sun. I was finally able to sleep. The red desert surrounding Moab always provided solace and healing for me. And living only three hours away by car, it was a relatively easy escape from the cold that still gripped the deep canyons of the San Juan Mountains.

Drew was on his way to celebrate a graduation ceremony with his family—his son had completed his graduate degree at a university in Southern California. We shared long bike rides and remote and quiet campsites, cooked meals together, had long conversations, and hiked through Bryce Canyon and Zion National Parks as we made our way southwest toward St. George.

One morning while dispersed camping in a remote pine forest after a romantic, sensual moment, I swooned and gazed at him dreamily as he monologued about watching the ego, as he had learned to do after reading Eckhart Tolle's books. After an articulate stretch of speech and reflections on Eckhart's teachings, he asked me, "What do you think?"

I shook off my endorphin-engulfed peaceful state and responded, "Umm. Yes, I agree." All he stated made sense to me, but I honestly didn't know what else to say. I saw a tiny eye roll from Drew, and he switched the subject.

A week later, as I crossed the finish line of the St. George Half Ironman, I saw no one I knew. *Wow, that was harder and hotter than I thought. No Drew. I hope he is okay. I'm sure traffic and the logistics of making his way around the course and town with this big event is challenging and frustrating*, I thought as I stumbled past the finish line chute area and headed in the direction of the food and massage tent.

"No cell phone? How am I supposed to find you?" he said as he ruffled his brow earlier that morning. There was no way I could carry a cell phone in a triathlon, and there was no safe place to store valuables in the transition area.

"Oh, this is a tough course, and I don't do well in the heat. I've been struggling in my training, so it may take me six hours to complete the race. How about this: If I don't see you at the finish line, let's meet at the lovely waterfalls and ponds you can walk through, around one o'clock?" I suggested smiling with reassurance. I also asked him to be my emergency contact—there was no one else to list as a reliable contact in case of emergency.

"Gladly. I'd be honored to be your emergency contact," Drew replied emphatically with raised eyebrows and a kind smile.

As soon as I saw him after I finished, I walked straight to him, and we wrapped each other with a big hug. I melted in exhaustion and in the love I felt in his arms.

"I'm so sorry I missed you at the finish," he said, as I laid my sweaty and crusty cheek across his tan, muscular shoulder. "How was it?"

"No worries. You don't need to apologize. I'm sure it was mayhem out there with traffic and roadblocks."

"Yes, it was crazy. I have your phone."

"That's okay, I need to eat and lie down in the shade for a moment. It's over ninety degrees, and I'm still overheated. Do you mind holding onto it for just a bit longer?"

As we lay in the cool grass in the shade, he reached into his pocket, "Your phone is blowing up."

"What do you mean?"

"Here, take a look. You have a fan club, I see."

"Oh, please. I just have a few friends. I've been in this sport a long time. What the . . .? Scott says I won in my age group. That can't be. That's got to be a mistake. I'll believe it when I see the results." I searched in the athlete tracker app, and there it was. "Well, I'm a baby in this age group. I'm turning fifty at the end of this year. I've heard about aging up advantage but never experienced it. I guess that's what happens when you start getting old." I grinned at him as I looked up from my phone.

As Drew walked back to the van to pick up me and my equipment, his phone fell out of his pocket into one of the manmade ponds designed to walk through on hot days. That suddenly nonfunctional cell phone turned into a communication problem as our time together wound down and we parted ways in the days to follow.

Drew loaded me up in his van and insisted I relax on his bed while he tried to line up a new phone and ran errands to prepare for a nice dinner at camp. I was overheated and so grateful to have a trusted new strong soul in my life to look after me in my vulnerable state after the event. Upon returning to camp, I hung a hammock and swayed in the breeze as the sunset. Drew draped his strong arms around me as I swung in the hammock, giving me the most beautiful embrace and kiss. He knocked my socks off with an amazing dinner as sunset turned to dusk.

A few nights later, Drew became frustrated when dinner was late due to my constant need for more exploring and fun. As I stepped into his van and asked if he had any butter I could use for scallops, he stepped on my foot and pushed more weight on it.

"Um, ow, wow," I said. "Never mind. I'll leave." I scurried back to my camper and continued to cook the scallops.

When he entered Ladybug, I sheepishly said, "Oh, you want to eat dinner in here? That's good because I was afraid to reenter Flipper van."

Drew looked confused and then reflected and softened.

After dinner and a couple of glasses of wine, I asked him what he was looking for.

"Companionship."

"Not a relationship? Not someone to truly connect with?"

"Not yet!" He raised his eyebrows, and his jaw muscles flexed.

"Well, I want to find someone to connect deeply with and have a lasting relationship," I barely eked out. I doubted that he was going to ask me. We had discussed our desires for a long-term relationship prior to meeting, and I was stunned as this exchange was in stark contrast to our previous deep conversations.

"Commitment leads to expectations, and expectations lead to disappointment!" His voice had started to rise in anger.

"Oh, okay, okay, okay. I'm sorry. I didn't realize. We don't know each other very well, so how can I expect anything?"

"I don't want to find someone or get married for at least another year or two. And besides, I need to protect you from me," he said softly as he gave me an eerie, dark side glance.

"What do you mean by that, Drew? I don't understand."

"I'm tired. It's time to go to bed."

And just like that, the discussion was over.

The next morning, I found a tiny glass jar on the step of my camper, Ladybug. It was filled with butter and written on the top was "Butter for Bee-bee."

I felt the butter was an apology for his anger the night before, a kind apology provided through gesture. I had never received that in the twelve years of my toxic marriage, so I was appreciative. Kevin had very rarely lost his temper. *Well, Drew knows when his anger is out of proportion, and he apologizes sweetly. Okay, I can manage this.*

For our last hurrah, we moved camp from Sand Hollow Lake, whose stunning views to the north of the desert mountains of Zion National Park that were sugar-coated with snow when we first arrived, then back east to Gooseberry Mesa, where both of us had yearned to camp and mountain bike. The quiet dispersed campsite we found on Gooseberry Mesa was just large enough to fit our two rigs and had expansive views toward the multihued cliffs of Zion and beyond, which was perfect for sunsets.

On the last mountain bike ride together, we paused to turn around and eat a snack. As Drew peered over a purple desert flower, he asked, "Bee-bee[2], do you know the name of this flower? The bees sure do like it." Drew had already given me the pet name of *Bee-bee* before we met, after long discussions on the phone, which was endearing but also a bit disturbing since we were still getting to know each other.

"Mmmm. No, I don't think so. The vegetation in this area is different than other deserts that I've visited closer to home." Talk of bees made me think of bee stings and how they are risky to some. "That reminds me," I said, "are you allergic to anything? We should probably know that about each other, don't you think?"

After a long pause, he looked off into the distance. "The only thing I'm allergic to," he said finally, "is commitment and expectations."

I couldn't move. My legs felt as if they were sinking into the sand around me, and a cloak of sadness weighed on my shoulders. I could not speak.

"Come on Bee-bee, it's time to head back to camp. Let's go."

I stood in silence for what felt like an eternity, due to the exquisite pain in my heart. "Well, you shouldn't have been calling me pet names then, and you certainly should not have called me your girlfriend. Just for that, no mercy, mister."

I jammed my feet into the pedals and hammered past him. I had flashbacks from about halfway through our trip, and tears rolled down my face as I flew down the trail and across the desert. Drew had started detaching by first half-jokingly mentioning he had thought about leaving a note on my dash and driving away in the middle of the night, but I didn't believe he meant it.

I could not handle those last statements from Drew while we were on the trail together. I had not anticipated being treated as if I were just around for a good time for a couple of weeks.

2. Bees signify a reminder to trust in miracles and are for those whose greatest wishes are for all living things to coexist in peace and love.

When I returned to our campsite on my bike in a raging rush after his comment about allergies and commitment, I hurriedly rounded up the camp chairs from the campfire ring we had enjoyed under the stars the night before, shoved them into the back of Ladybug, loaded my bike, rolled up the floor mats, and tried desperately get my campfire wood into Ladybug before he got there. I was determined to be gone before he got back to give him a taste of his own medicine. I toyed with letting the air out of one of his tires so he'd be stuck for a while. He pulled up as I was frantically shoving the last items into the camper.

"Whee! That was fun, wasn't it, Bee-bee?"

I didn't respond.

"Please don't be mad at me, Bee-bee. Let's crack open one of those bombers of beer from Ridgway and play whatever music you like to dance to." He hugged me and tried to lift me off the ground.

"You want to hear music. Okay, I'll play you some music." I jumped into Ladybug for my Bluetooth speaker and began to play "How to Be a Heartbreaker" by Marina and the Diamonds. I began to dance next to him and grabbed him by the collar of his sweaty bicycle jersey. "Do you hear these lyrics, Drew?" I sang as I teased him with hip grinds, as if that were all he wanted.

The lyrics were almost step-by-step instructions from a cookbook recipe on how to break someone's heart, and he met all the ingredients and timing. The lyrics perfectly matched his behavior on loving and then running. As I drank the smooth dark beer from the Colorado Boy Brewery, and breathed deliberately, I calmed down but was still reeling with sadness, anger, and confusion. We packed to leave, and I shifted focus to what was next—driving back to Colorado. As I followed his van down the dusty road away from our campsite, I continued to breathe deeply to calm myself.

"Pull over at the little park, where we have to go our separate ways," he texted me.

What? Let's just wave at each other out of the windows as we turn in opposite directions at the intersection and call it the end. I don't understand why he wants to pull over, I thought. But I followed his van toward Hurricane near St. George.

He pulled into the park and waved his arm for me to follow. When I crawled back into Ladybug to check that the fridge was fully closed, he jumped in behind me with a mixture of joy and sadness on his handsome face.

"Okay, Bee-bee, I don't like long good-byes," he said, wrapping his arms around my waist. "I'll come visit you in Ouray, like I said I would."

Early in the trip while still in Moab, I had asked him at a critical moment, "Before we go any further, will you promise me something?"

"Depends. What?" he asked with a grin.

"Will you come visit me in Ouray?"

"Of course, I'll come visit you in Ouray. Why wouldn't I?"

I cocked my head, raised an eyebrow, "Do you promise?"

"Yes."

And then, in this little park in Hurricane, he pulled out a few small memento gifts for me. A jar filled with rice covered with stickers of where we had traveled together. I swirled in confusion. "Thanks, I don't have anything for you. I'm sorry."

With what he'd said leading up to the last day and the last deeply hurtful comment, I had started a poem for him but had not bothered to finish it. I could sense his detaching.

As I drove back along Highway 63, along the same route we had shared together, I reflected on the confusing moments and reassured myself.

He promised he'd come visit. I'll just enjoy the drive back, visit Danelle, and prepare for his visit. Danelle was an old friend from my college triathlon days.

Insights and Ruminations: I was in denial that Drew, with whom I had I fallen in love, would suddenly run away when my aching spirit needed so much trust and love to heal. And yet, he'd shared guidance before departing—without intending to do so. It was painful to hear his feedback on my frantically paced mind and body, but as it sank in, I knew he was right. My spirit needed guidance while everything known in my life was beginning to fall away. It is recommended that the reader pause and listen to the heartbreaker song mentioned above for a more vivid experience of the emotions, yet with an air of levity, felt within this chapter closing. https://www.youtube.com/watch?v=vKNcuTWzTVw

Rainbow outside of Zion National Park, Utah

Painting from my talented mother, Wilson Peak from
Wilson Mesa, San Juan Mountains, Colorado

CHAPTER 5:

Broken Promises

———— •.• ————

"Ego is a good servant but a bad master."
—MME. JEANNE DE SALZMAN

Six months had passed since I had moved from Log Hill into the
rental house in Ouray. I had never finished unpacking from my
move. Nothing hung on the walls. Any large task had become too
daunting after a long day or week at work. When I returned home
from the trip with Drew in late May, I spoke with my friend Sharon.

"He's going to visit!" I gushed with joy.

"Oh, who? The guy from Wisconsin? So, you like him?"

"Yes, his name is Drew. We had a great almost two weeks together
after bonding over the phone for a month. He'd never even heard of
the San Juan Mountains. I purposely didn't tell him how beautiful it
is here. I just told him it's unique. I wanted him to be surprised and
experience the awe without any build-up of expectations."

"Okay, I'll come over to help you hang all of those gorgeous paintings your mother had. We'll make it look like a cozy home. It will help
you anyway, Elisabeth."

"Oh, that would be fun. I'm finally ready. I'll try to get as much
of the rest unpacked, so hanging the paintings is my reward. That's
how I always try to unpack."

Drew's attempts to contact me waned. I kept in touch with him enough for me to know he was journeying back from California and through Utah. He seemed to be slowing as he approached Colorado.

The day he was supposed to arrive, he called me from Grand Junction.

"Did you read my email?" Drew asked with tension growing in his voice.

"Umm, no, I'm sorry, I didn't know you sent me an email. I don't look at my computer before going to work. It's my time to go for a walk or run outside before I have to sit at a computer all day."

Drew sighed with anger. "I sent you an email because you aren't a very good listener."

"Oh, I'm sorry. Do you want me to pull up the email while I'm on the phone with you?"

"No, you can't read an email and listen to me at the same time." His tone began to fill with anger.

"Okay, sorry. I'll close my email and try to listen."

Drew began to provide a litany of reasons why he could not make the two-hour detour from Grand Junction to see me.

"I'm so sad you aren't going to visit me. You promised."

"I'm not moving to Ouray!" he shrilled.

"I just wanted to show you the beauty here," I said. But my mind raced realizing I was hoping for him to fall in love with the mountains here—and me, once he got to know me better.

"I don't want to be close to anybody!" he yelled.

"Geographically or emotionally?" I responded.

Drew paused, and I heard him take a breath.

"Good question," he replied with a bit of introspection, and I could hear a smirk in his voice. Then he yelled, "You are just like my ex-wife. Lastborn baby of the family and always making me feel guilty!"

"I'm sorry, but when you said you don't want commitment, all I could envision was you jumping in bed with the next pretty lady you crossed paths with."

"I was never committed to you! It is going to be this way, or it ends now!" he shrilled.

"You know what, Drew, you are a heartbreaker!" I yelled back and hung up, wishing I could make a slamming sound like an old landline phone.

Sharon had walked with me away from the office as I talked to Drew, as I had sensed it was going to be a strained conversation, but I didn't know it would turn out this way. "He's not coming. He started yelling at me." I began to cry.

I sent scathing texts and an email that evening. I was so hurt. Coming out of depression was going to be even harder now. My ego was bruised. I felt betrayed and used.

Over the following days, I took more time to read and reread Drew's email that he intended for me to read before the discussion that had turned heated.

I think that the entirety of the trip is what will always remain with me. It was two wonderful weeks of riding, dining, touring, intimacy, and adventure! Sure hope we can do it all over again someday soon! Even slopping through the morning snow and running to and from the van in Zion. But of course, those super sweet campsites in Capitol Reef, Gooseberry Mesa, and Moab will be treasures forevermore.

I'm sorry that you're feeling vulnerable. I've done my best to try to not endanger you and hope getting close to you hasn't done that. Maybe it's a good thing that I snore. A lot.

If there's something specific I can do to help you with that, just say it! I wish I could say that I'm head over heels in love with you, but I'm not even sure that's possible with all of the other things in my head and life right now.

I like you. A lot. And I love spending time with you: You're the best ever cycling buddy; interesting and engaging to talk to; and you have a healthy attitude about life and living!

But we're also running on different frequencies right now. Maybe it won't always be that way, though people really don't change much. We tend to just be ourselves most of the time. It's taken me a few years to slow down my body and, especially, to slow down my mind. The mind wants to do, do, do things, function, operate, move: settle this, plan that, secure a future, lock down precious things.

Somehow, some way, I've managed to shed much of that, caring less or little about whatever happens next. Eckhart Tolle, Chinese monks, and deeply spiritual Buddhists seek only to be. And it's hard. I still teeter into the frenzied rat race of American expectations every now and then, but spend more time seeking and finding contentment, peace, and calm.

Not only does the frequency of the mind change, but the way the body responds when the mind finally settles a bit is the true elixir. While there were plenty of seamless and natural moments together, there were definitely more than a few collisions between my slowing and awakening consciousness and your crazy-paced mind and body. I try not to judge much, if anything at all. There's nothing wrong with crazy-paced mindfulness and drive; indeed, that's highly respected by most folks, myself included. However, it's not me, and being near that energy was draining and stressful for me at times. What's more important is that you might not be able to change that much. You've been both blessed and somewhat cursed by an exceptional intellect. It would be both very unnatural and somewhat wrong to try to change that. Further, the conflict between my awakening consciousness (inner purpose) and that outer purpose would be an unhealthy place for both of us.

Then there's the route(s) we are on. I'm going to be a granddad before the summer's over, and it's a role I'm trying not to get too excited about. Expectations. I do know, however, that I was proud to be a good parent, and would like to fit into the life of this kid, however best it works out. And that might not be living in Idaho, Utah, or Colorado. There are places in California that have felt very much like home during time spent here the past few years, this trip included. I lived in California twice earlier in my life (once as a student for a year @UCSB; then as a young professional for seven years in the Bay Area).

It was only when I left Madison as a young graduate that I felt sadder about leaving a place. There's a lot of energy (and some sensibility) pulling me back here.

Only you can feel anything, vulnerability withstanding. It's up to you to decide that you aren't vulnerable and aren't worried about whatever happens next. I'd like to be part of what happens next, but I can't and won't make any commitments. Commitments lead to expectations, and expectations are frequently the source of disappointment, frustration, and unhappiness. No one likes to disappoint or be disappointed. Whatever happens next happens next, and I can't put a filter on that.

I'm sorry.

I'd still very much like to see and spend some time with you in Ouray, but certainly understand if you see all of this as terms unacceptable at this point. Perhaps it's something to think about. I once promised to do my best to not hurt you, even if that meant keeping you away from me, and I still hope to fulfill that rare promise made.

In any case, I am at a crossroads like no other today (over ninety days on the road). I have lots of thinking to do myself. The past five weeks on the road have been a whirlwind of events, with those fantastic, epic two weeks together punctuating the ride! Above all else, thanks for drenching me with attention and affection.

I don't have a bucket list. Expectations, you know.

What the heck is he talking about? Awakening Consciousness. Expectations. And why is attachment so negative in his mind? Hmmm. I'm going to have to research Buddhism and men.

I stumbled across a scathing article on *Huffington Post* by Mariana Caplan, PhD, called "The Problem with Zen Boyfriends." Caplan shares, "What defines a Zen boyfriend is the manner in which he skillfully uses spiritual ideals and practices as an excuse for his terror of, and refusal to be in, any type of real relationship with a woman." This article was written by a frustrated woman about her experience with men using Buddhism as an excuse to evade commitment, and I could feel anger rising as I read on. *Argh. This non-attachment idea and using it as an excuse to avoid commitment. . .* I clenched my teeth.

Drew had sent me an insulting email about "The Universal Hot Crazy Matrix" video, where a pseudo professor draws a graph on a whiteboard, espousing the direct relationship between hotness and craziness in women.

Ha! This article is what I'm going to send in rebuttal to his insulting email, I thought.

I wrote to Drew, "I've seen that video before. A male friend of mine shared it with me several years ago. It can be amusing for women as well, depending on context, such as when a man refers to it after chasing a hot woman merely for her looks who then left him in shambles. I've seen it happen many times—testosterone-driven lust that results in the man being hurt instead of the woman. Otherwise, it's women bashing. Ladies do tend to overanalyze and frustrate men with that over-analysis for sure. I'm quite sane, not that it matters to you. Just crazy for adventures in nature. So here is a link to my friendly touché, on Zen boyfriends, which I alluded to when we were in Utah. If that describes you, which it might, I don't ever want to get involved with you again, anyway. But I'd like to see you just as a friend."

Insights and Ruminations: *I later realized that I didn't want to face the many red flags because of my strong need for love and approval. I seethed with thoughts, such as, What is this bullshit Buddhism? as I tried to make sense of the pain that drew me back into depression. But quieting the mind, letting go of expectations of the future, and letting go to just "be" instead of "doing" was exactly what I needed. As I learned from a Patanjali Kundalini Yoga Care counselor, Shakti was soon going to force me to stop doing so much and instead just "be." In Hinduism, Shakti is the feminine divine energy or Divine Mother who calls for absolute surrender. I wanted to change my life so I could do just that for a while but was too afraid of stepping off that cliff into the unknown of a different life. I had been so cerebral and worked hard all my life, driven by the need for my father's approval, which I would soon realize was impossible to obtain and was preventing me from becoming my true Self.*

CHAPTER 6:

The Pain-Body

———— ·•· ————

"Forgive others, not because they deserve
forgiveness, but because you deserve peace."
—JOHNATHAN LOCKWOOD HUIE

Turning open the blinds in Ladybug, I gazed across the bright green grass of the meadow. It was Memorial Day weekend, and I had come to camp alone to enjoy the already rideable trails around Crested Butte. Two girlfriends of mine who love to mountain bike as much as I do, Sharon and Gail, lived in Gunnison, a college town to the south. I also knew a couple in Crested Butte whom I had enjoyed visiting, camping, and cycling with over the past few years. *Strange how I have more dear friends here than I do in the southwestern Colorado hamlets of Ouray, Ridgway, or Telluride. And the trails are so epic here. And it's sooooo green.* I breathed in the fragrance of early summer. I was embracing the freedom in my life and the access to the beauty as summer began, still squeezing in trips into deep nature on long weekends.

I had no phone reception at camp, which was normally just the way I like it, but I had not realized it would be that way before arriving. Thus, it was a challenge coordinating with my friends. As I rode up a steep section of Deer Creek, I heard a familiar voice.

43

"Is that you? How funny. I was just asking Mike, 'Who is that? She sure looks fit.' And then you turned your head. Ha, ha."

"Sharon! Mike! Funny how things work out, isn't it?"

Toward the end of the loop, we parted ways, and I rolled into town alone. My phone began to vibrate and ping with sounds of text alerts. It was another man from a fitness-based dating app. His name was River.

"I can't wait to meet you. Can we talk this weekend?" River crackled through my cell phone as I rested on a sidewalk in Crested Butte.

"I'm just in town briefly and have to ride back to camp before it gets too late. Let's talk Sunday on my way home, okay?"

"Oh, come on, just a quick chat, pretty lady?"

River was handsome, charismatic, successful according to his self-description, and a fit cyclist. Several more texts, and I gave in. As I sat down onto the still-warm sidewalk near the visitor center, I called him. We talked for about forty-five minutes, filled with views on life and laughter.

"I'll buy you dinner this week, say Tuesday after work? I'll drive to Ouray on Tuesday."

"Well, that's sweet of you, but I have to cram five days of work into three this week. So that means long days, and I don't know when I'll be able to get out of work. I don't want to disappoint you or keep you waiting. Let's wait until next weekend."

River texted me through the weekend, my phone lighting up each time I rolled through Crested Butte. As I backed Ladybug into the driveway in Ouray on Memorial Day evening, my phone rang again.

"So it's settled, I'll see you tomorrow."

"Um, remember what I told you? I don't think that's going to work for me. Listen, it's dark and it's hard to back a trailer into a narrow spot in the dark. My friend Sharon is helping me, but I have to hear her to do this without crashing into the house."

"Okay, let's talk in the morning."

Well, it's nice to have a handsome, fit, successful, charismatic guy who really wants to visit me in Ouray, but . . .

"A little more to the left, that's good. Just two more feet. Okay, that's far enough," exclaimed Sharon.

"Thanks so much, Sharon. You are such a dear friend."

Morning Following Memorial Day Camping Trip

I woke on Tuesday morning to my cell phone ringing. It was River again. He was convincing.

"This way, if you get to know me, you can visit me in Durango, or I can stay with you in Ouray next weekend."

"Um, slow down partner. I'm just worried I won't even get out of work early enough to meet you. Drive safe, okay? I better get ready to leave for work."

River arrived at my office after everyone else had left and I was finishing up. The last person to leave did not lock the door behind them. I heard footsteps as I was typing away on my laptop.

"Hello? Who's there?"

"Hi!" River said as he walked into my office. He was tan, handsome, had a strong build, and was sharply dressed, but he looked nervous.

"Hello, how was the drive? Um, I'm sort of caught off guard."

"Well, you said I could stop by if I was bored."

"Yes, well, I'm a bit embarrassed, my office is a mess."

"Well, am I good looking?" he spread his arms wide.

"Um, of course you are. I won't be able to meet you until I finish up here." I directed River to the closest bar with outdoor seating. "They have great beer, and the best views of the Amphitheatre mountain formation. Can I meet you there in about twenty to thirty minutes?"

He seemed a bit dismayed but left the office a few minutes later. Later that evening . . .

It's 9:30 p.m. as I sob in my bed in a fetal position, having stripped off my clothes to rid the feeling of him on top of me. I texted him: "Why did you attack me? If it was just out of alcohol and the need for skin to skin, I'm not that kind of girl! I told you that I'm a lady who wants a loving relationship. Not just sex."

4:43 a.m. the next morning, I had a flash of his tears over dinner before he started making advances. So, I texted: "I just can't handle going that insanely fast. I tried telling you that before we met. You don't know me yet. I hope you are okay."

He replied, "Good morning. I'm okay, just got back to Durango. Sorry about last night, yes alcohol and skin never work well together, do they? My apologies."

"Drink and skin can be wonderful together in moderation and when in control or when two people know each other. Last night was scary for me. I sense you are a decent man just going through a lot. Counseling is good. Keep going. So am I."

"I'm sorry you were scared."

Insights and Ruminations: Healthy boundaries were difficult for me to set and were even more challenging to establish and maintain while in and out of depression. River served to remind me once again of the importance of setting healthy boundaries. I had just read quotes from Eckhart Tolle about the pain body attacking others when this interaction with River occurred.

CHAPTER 7:

Healing Moments into Pain-Body 2

———— •ı• ————

*"And when ye stand praying, forgive, if ye have
ought against any: that your Father also which is
in heaven may forgive you your trespasses."*
—MARK 11:25, HOLY BIBLE

Gleefully Sharon took large steps from one impression to the next,
and she smiled like a little girl. "Forty-five, forty-six . . . a few more
still here, ooh, and more over there! Wow, how many did you count?"

"I lost count, as they are somewhat scattered, but there seems to
be a few more than we heard about!"

I smiled as I hopped from one dinosaur print to the next. Sharon
and I had learned about the dinosaur tracks from a local legendary
runner. It was now early June, a few days after my encounter with
River. Sharon and I had hiked from the trailhead that was only a few
hundred yards down the street from the house I was renting. We were
on a pale red-and-pink slab of rock that was attached to the same red
cliffs towering almost immediately above my neighborhood.

"I can't believe this is the first time I've hiked this trail," I said.
"What a treat. I am so blessed. How come it takes you to come visit
me to get me out to appreciate what's just around the corner?"

"That's because you've just been too sad or running away in your
camper. You are blessed. Sixty-three! I can't believe this isn't roped

*Dinosaur tracks discovered on a hike
in the San Juan Mountains.*

Hike near Ouray, Colorado.

off or preserved somehow. We need to try to find a paleontologist or some scientist to check these out and protect what's here," she said.

I snapped a photo of Sharon stepping from the last set of tracks as we headed back to the main trail.

As we clambered over a downed tree and then rounded a bend, the view to the south opened up.

"Oh, my goodness!" I exclaimed. "I had no idea how stunning it would be up here. Heaven. Heaven on Earth is where I live!" I extended my arms out and twirled.

We paused to take some candid shots of each other as we explored another cliff edge with the aspen leaves shimmering the brilliant light green of early summer growth, along the small meadow next to the cliff. The light glinted off the snow-capped peaks of early summer in contrast to the dramatic red hues of the San Juans.

"Do you have money with you?" I asked, as a bead of sweat rolled down my back. "I think I have a twenty-dollar bill in my pack. Maybe we should descend into town at the other end and have dinner. What do you think?"

"Yes, that sounds great. I'm game!"

At dusk, with our bellies full and a dusting of trail dirt on our boots and legs, we walked along the Uncompahgre River, back to the house, to complete the trail circle.

"Tell me what happened, Elisabeth," Sharon softly said as we made our way home.

I knew what she meant. "I don't really want to talk about it much," I said, as we picked up the pace in the chill of night approaching. "It's not good to relive it."

"But maybe it will be good to get it off your chest?" Sharon prodded.

"Well, I fought him off enough to protect myself from true harm, and I haven't heard back from him, so that's all that matters."

I proceeded to share a little with Sharon but didn't go into detail. As we rounded a corner, we saw two dark figures along the edge of the river trail. Sharon put her arm around mine and pulled herself close to me.

"Don't worry, Sharon. I think it's just a couple who can't hear us," I said, trying to comfort her. The spring runoff had begun, and the river was rushing with rapids wrapping around big boulders below us.

"Hello, hello!" I chirped loudly, hoping to ensure the people ahead of us were aware of our approach. I lifted my hiking pole forward with the tip angled in the direction of the figures. Sharon pulled me closer, her grip tightening on my arm.

"It's okay, Sharon, I'm sure they are harmless."

The two figures separated, revealing two large men. One slid his hand over his forehead, stepping sideways as if to deflect our eyes.

"Hello there. Nice evening on the river, huh?" I said as we walked by.

Sharon's grip grew tighter. I glanced over my shoulder and whispered, "I'll keep an eye on them." A few minutes passed by and I looked back again. The two men remained in the same spot next to the river. "They aren't coming this way, Sharon. Everything is fine."

She released my arm and began to cry. "I am so sorry I'm such a burden!" Sharon had not heard back from her husband who was supposed to pick her up that evening or at least the next day, but he was not returning her calls. They had had an argument the day she left home.

"Oh, Sharon, you aren't a burden. I'm glad I can help." I stepped towards her and began to slip one hand over her neck and shoulders.

Wham! Something very hard hit me in the face. I stopped in my tracks and sank to the ground, feeling broken teeth in my mouth.

"Oh my God! Oh my God! Ahhh!" Sharon shrilled just a few inches from my face as I held my swelling upper lip and my glutes hit the ground. "Oh my God. I'm so sorry; I thought you were those men attacking us!"

I couldn't handle her screams and gently pushed her away from me, as I was shocked and needed space. I pushed myself off the ground.

"I need to ice my face," I said as I walked in the direction of the house.

Sharon began to sob and remained frozen.

I don't understand what just happened, but I need to try to hold these fragments of teeth in my mouth and get ice on my face—ASAP, I thought. I glanced over my shoulder and saw Sharon hunched over in her own dismay and grief.

A few minutes passed, and Sharon passed me on the path, walking twice as fast as I was. "I am a horrible person. I'm going home!"

What? That's interesting. She has no car and nowhere else to stay. What is she thinking? I can't keep up with her, nor will I try, I thought as I felt my face throbbing.

Sharon disappeared in the approaching night. When I arrived at the house, I beelined straight for the freezer and placed a soothing ice pack on my upper lip. No Sharon.

"Oh, for goodness sake. Where did she go?" I thought as I rummaged for my cell phone. I texted her, "Where did you go? I'm not mad. I'm just in shock and in pain." A few minutes passed and I heard a knock on the front door. I opened the door to find Sharon sitting on the front stoop, still crying.

"I'm a horrible person."

I put my right arm around her and rocked her to console her as my left hand still clenched the ice pack to my face.

After a few minutes, we shifted inside as Sharon dried her tears and I went into the bathroom to assess the damage. Two bruises were taking shape on my upper lip and two of my lower teeth were broken. The remaining pieces were too tiny and splintered to be worth keeping. I found some crown glue to cover the sharp edges of my teeth as air coming across the exposed tooth was painful.

"Well, it could have been worse," she said. "It's not as bad as I thought it would be. I could have hit your eye." She smiled. We began to laugh.

"I suppose you are right," I said as I tried to smile. "What the heck did you hit me with? That was harder than a fist."

Sharon pulled out a small canvas bag and revealed a small glass food container that she had carried on the hike.

"Oh goodness. Well, you can definitely defend yourself! I wouldn't mess with you."

We both chuckled. Sharon was relieved that I laughed, but deep inside I knew the preceding moments in combination with the attempted sexual assault meant something was seriously wrong in my life. I had never had anyone ever attack me, on purpose or by accident. I had an eerie feeling crawl up my spine. I didn't know what to make of it.

The next day, I awoke to a distinct awareness that the universe was indeed sending me a message. It felt like a deep voice that echoed in my chest. The universe was telling me to isolate myself further. I thought, *If I'm sad when I isolate myself further, I can't blame anyone else for my pain. There must be a reason why Drew mentioned Eckhart Tolle to me. Reading some good books will help me get grounded again.*

The next day at the local library, I loaded up on *Power of Now* and *A New Earth*, both in hard copy and on CD, as well as several books on meditation and mindfulness. The librarian smiled as she pushed her long, shiny, red hair over her shoulder. "I see you are diving deep on a journey," she said. "Good for you." She made a few other suggestions of authors as she scanned in the tall stack of books I had laid in front of her.

As I drove back and forth between Ouray and Telluride to see my parents who were in town for part of the summer, I listened to Eckhart's soothing voice. My parents are immigrants from Germany, so Eckhart's accent was soothing to me. I didn't realize his teachings were spiritual in nature, and I probably would not have been open to his teachings earlier in my life. As soon as I heard the opening of the *Power of Now*, Eckhart's story of transformation out of depression hooked me. *I am not my thoughts. That makes sense. Practicing being present in the moment to stop beating myself up about the past and worries about the future. I'll try this. Kevin told me I was too emotional. I'll stop my negative thoughts before they become emotions. Perfect.*

Insights and Ruminations: I had never experienced such a string of negative experiences, and my spirit was baffled and determined to figure out the reason. Many months later, the librarian said she was looking for a place to live, and I offered to share part of my rental house with her. That's when I learned she is a spiritual counselor. I had to completely forgive Sharon and set healthy boundaries to be friends again with yet another soul who had not meant to hurt me. Sharon was the most present friend at that moment, choosing to spend time with me at the lowest point of my life in hopes of lifting my spirits with only positive intentions. I knew she was a truly beautiful soul struggling with challenging times as well. She continued to be an exceptionally reliable friend later in life.

CHAPTER 8:

Nature Tries to Wake Me

-----•••-----

"In creation it appears that God sleeps in the minerals, dreams in the flowers, awakens in the animals, and in man knows that He is awake." ∞
—PARAMAHANSA YOGANANDA

The next morning, I sat in an old wooden Adirondack chair nestled on the small front stone step of the rental house in Ouray, while the bees buzzed about the pink blooms on the fruit tree. Summer had arrived early, and the hummingbirds were zipping around on a gorgeous warm morning. But I was too sad to do much more than sit and breathe with my head tilted down, eyes closed, while I ached inside. I was ruminating on the "pain-body attracting other pain-bodies" phenomenon that Eckhart writes about, which I realized I had just experienced in rapid succession.

What is going on? I've never had such a succession of negative events. I know about the law of attraction, and I seem to be attracting negative experiences. The universe must be trying to tell me to be very alone and to figure out how to stop the negative internal emotions that I must be vibrating outward.

While I was arched over with my eyes closed, a hummingbird hovered by my face. The little bird fluttered against my forehead several times for several minutes. I felt the gentle bird's wings brush up against my skin on the side of my forehead. I was in such a dark place in my head and heart that I barely noticed at first. By the time I finally and fully sensed the lovely little creature, it hovered a bit further away from me and paused. I glanced at the bird as it gazed at me, and then it flew up and away. I looked at my clothes and hat. No bright colors that might attract the hummingbird; I was wearing gray and cream-colored clothing. *Hmmm. That's odd.* I looked up at the beauty of the summer for the first time that day.

Hummingbirds were my first memory of Colorado and particularly of Ouray, in the early 1970s when my family visited there in a Winnebago. During previous springs in Ouray, I had always announced with glee to my coworkers when I heard the first hummingbird sound. I tended to hear it while working in my office with the windows open. This time, I was too buried in emotions to notice until the one individual hummingbird decided to give me a face-to-face encounter.

Insights and Ruminations: In the TED Talk by Dr. Lisa Miller of Columbia University, there is an eerie parallel between her experiences of the Divine sending messages while at the depth of her depression due to being unable to bear a child. They came through a small duck, a TV station stuck on an infomercial on adopting children from overseas, and a stranger on a bus sharing insight with perfect timing. When one is willing to surrender and stay open in the midst of a dark night of the soul, the Divine will provide guidance. Check it out here: https://www .youtube.com/watch?v=7c5t6FkvUG0

CHAPTER 9:

Shift Begins

———— •·• ————

"She had a wild, wandering soul but when she loved,
she loved with chaos and that made all the difference."
—ARIANA DANCU

W hile the next few days and a couple of weeks drifted by, I calmed and sent Drew a softer email and poem:

I feel very blessed that I was able to spend that time with you on our adventure. I was feeling hurt as I was developing strong feelings for you, while you didn't seem to for me.

It would have been unrealistic for me to expect something from you after just spending twelve days together on one trip. And you have the transition ahead of you, and you cannot control where that path will go. My primary motivation for your visit was, and still is, a desire to share the joy of the beauty.

But I became very fond of you and would like to at least be friends. It would be fun to get to know you better. At least, I think it will . . . or would.

Here's something I wrote a while back.

I wrote part of this in my head during the triathlon, jotted down a bit of it while you drove us in Flipper around St. George after the race. Thank you for taking care of me after the event . . . it meant more to me than you know. And I think I did so well because you fueled me so well in the days leading up to it.

I planned to write this poem the following night, but the torture of the likelihood of you detaching while I felt stronger for you had started to set in. Some of the inspiration for this has escaped me now . . . due to how confusing that time was for me, especially toward the end. I'm a better poet than this when inspiration remains.

Remember how early in the trip, I touched your head, asking if perhaps you were ready only in your head but not in your heart, as I touched your chest?

And "from wheels in motion for a long time to move to Colorado," and "I have a girlfriend" (when referring to me), to "protecting you . . . even if from me," to moving to California, to perhaps not even leaving Wisconsin, to comparing me to your ex-wife, and "not being close to anyone," I was on a roller-coaster ride.

Roller Coaster Ride
So a "girlfriend" and/or guide you did/do seek.
You were oh so sweet
My heart began faster to beat

Meeting you had become a real treat.
I hoped our adventures were not complete.

In my knees, you made me weak
For three weeks before we met, across many miles—we did speak
Which made me comfortable to quickly kiss your cheek.
Oh my, this recovering triathlon geek . . .
Foolishly expecting something more from being together for just
*   under two weeks.*
Where I live, I wanted you to just take a peek,
But instead my face began to leak
My heart began to crack and creak.

I'm not sure how to end the poem at the moment. Sorry, I'm not trying to make you feel guilty. I just can't think of the next rhyme. I'll send you more if it comes to me and if you'd like to receive it.

I hope your moments in Wisconsin are treating you well and that your wishes are shaped further . . . that you gain more clarity and that your path brings you the direction you hope to go.

I'm trying to accept and embrace the path that life is taking me . . . despite not being what I envisioned, it's an amazing life.

Have fun purging, skating, and dodging mosquitoes.

The evening after I sent that, Drew left a voicemail explaining his status in selling his belongings and real estate. His last sentence was, "And then I'm coming to Ouray for a bike ride, and then . . . " The rest of the voicemail was cut off. My voicemail box was full.

There was little to no communication from Drew after that for weeks.

Insights and Ruminations: I believe Jesus Christ's teaching about forgiving is referring not only to forgiving others, but to forgiving ourselves and exercising self-compassion, which allows us to fully love ourselves and others, regardless of the past.

Part II:

Getting Back on the Bike

and Finding the Light

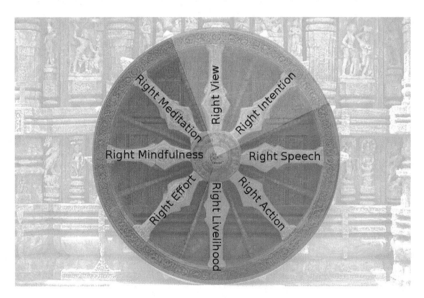

*The eight-spoked wheel is the dharma chakra, representing
the Buddhist dharma of the eightfold path to enlightenment.*

Paintings and cross on wall of grotto
decorated by locals near Playa Escondido, Baja.

CHAPTER 10:

First Ecstasy, Ananda;
Spiritual Awakening Begins

---·•·---

*Any kind of suffering in this life is preparing our soul to
achieve a higher purpose and directing you towards a higher level
of consciousness. Few people understand this, but it is true.*
—Prashasti

I gradually increased my awareness a little more each day by practicing being present while washing my hands and taking a shower,
feeling the warm water, smelling the soap, listening to the trickle of
the water . . . all while keeping my mind clear of thoughts.

On a day in mid-June, with each conversation through the day, I
became fully present while listening to others. I focused on absorbing
emotions and words while keeping consistent eye contact and delaying
my thoughts of a response until the other person was finished with
their sharing. Natural gaps in conversation emerged that normally
would cause me to feel awkward, but I welcomed them as I formulated
my response after allowing myself to reflect on what was shared.

At work, I enjoyed simple moments, such as pausing to watch a
stellar jay hop from branch to branch just outside my office window.
While I was gathering equipment for a field trip in my public health
duties, I was not thinking of yesterday or tomorrow—just that

moment. As I closed the door of my car before departing, I took a deep breath, appreciated my fluffy seat cover, and enjoyed the feeling of the soft steering wheel cover on my fingers. As I drove from Ouray toward the base of Log Hill, I gazed in full appreciation at the snow-capped peaks of the Sneffels Range. When I arrived at my destination and pulled into the driveway, I took a deep breath and admired the exterior of the house, the pinyon pine forest, and the striking view of the snow-capped, jagged mountains. As I spoke and listened to the couple inside, who had reported becoming ill with a rare tick-borne disease, I didn't worry about what time it was or what was next after this home visit. I was simply fully present. They expressed appreciation of my investigation and my recommendations to prevent further illnesses—and the time I spent with them. As I waved good-bye, I felt gratitude that my knowledge could help them.

I drove up Log Hill in the late afternoon early summer sun, toward the home of Amy and John. It was John's birthday, and I was invited for the celebration. As I drove past the northern edge of their thirty-five acres, I noticed the vertical stacks of rocks, cairns created as mindful artwork from the stones found on the land. Prayer flags flapped in the wind, hung from tall wooden poles on the west side of their driveway. *Oh, I'm so lucky I was invited*, I thought. *They are such a lovely couple.* Amy is a massage therapist, and both were members of a *sangha*, a local group who meditate together. The same methods I had used to be fully present in conversations with coworkers and during the field investigation were easy to employ with this social circle. All of those present seemed to be gentle souls. I never had to elevate my voice once, as soft-toned voices seemed to float around the living room. With only a half a glass of wine consumed but a long day behind me, I hugged Amy good-bye and wished John a happy birthday as I walked out to the car just after dusk. For the first time since I had moved into the rental house, I was not sad when I arrived home.

In the morning, I gently awoke naturally in *supta baddha kona-sana*, a yoga pose with the soles of my feet together and knees splayed out to either side, and with my palms facing the ceiling by my sides. It was around 6:20, early for me, as it was the weekend. As I became aware that I was waking, I felt weightless. The euphoria of pure bliss washed over me. No thoughts. No worries. No emotions. Just warm, soothing, gentle vibrational energy. I was in ecstasy and felt as if I were having a low-level orgasm that was not localized but instead was running throughout my entire body. And yet at the same time, I felt as if I were not in my body. (For the reader to experience a sense of the beauty of the ecstasy, pause and listen to "Hymn" by Ashana and Thomas Barquee from the album *Jewels of Silence* https://www.sound-ofashana.com/album/jewels-of-silence/ and "Shivaratri" by Benjy Wertheimer and John de Kadt from the album *One River* https://www.youtube.com/watch?v=xG-3NpC30xA.) I must have glanced at my alarm clock to be aware of the time, but I don't remember opening my eyes or turning my head to look.

The ecstasy continued for over two hours.

I became aware enough that I knew it was nearing time to get ready to go to my yoga class.

I don't want to miss yoga this morning, I thought. *It's the first day Yoga Shala is holding class in the new location. It's an auspicious moment, especially since Katie is teaching. Well, I'll just gently and slowly get ready and see if I can avoid disrupting this feeling.*

I slowly changed, drank some warm water, and gathered my yoga mat, a change of clothes, and my keys. I gently held onto the steering wheel as I drove north down the gradual hill to Ridgway, still feeling euphoric. *Hmmm, it seems like it is safe to be driving while I feel like this.* As I stepped into the entryway of the yoga studio, the euphoria disappeared.

After class, I spoke in the parking lot to a fellow yogi named Autumn—who was stunningly beautiful—and in that moment, Kevin happened to walk by.

"Hi Elisabeth. How are you?" He smiled.

"Hi Kevin. This is Autumn. Autumn, this is Kevin. Nice chatting with you, Autumn. Bye," I said as I loaded my yoga paraphernalia into my SUV. Out of the corner of my eye, I saw Kevin swallow hard as he gazed with large eyes at Autumn.

As I drove home, I thought, *I wonder what that blissed-out feeling this morning was all about. It was weird and lovely.* But the memory of the euphoria slipped away as I allowed myself to sink into blue thoughts about the end of my relationship with Kevin and how he had just looked with desire at another woman.

Insights and Ruminations: Without realizing it, I was emerging out of the dark night of the soul and back into the light. I was experiencing the most profound and auspicious moment of my soul's journey, which I inadvertently interrupted to attend a yoga class.

CHAPTER 11:

Drew Returns

*"The second chakra contains the universal truth: Honor
one another; the one-on-one honor code. Why do people not heal?
Why can't they get their spirit back? They suffer from the illusion
that people had come into their lives for destructive reasons."*
—CAROLINE MYSS

As I drove over Dallas Divide on my way to visit my parents on
Wilson Mesa and listened to Eckhart Tolle on CD, I looked down
at my gas gauge. *Darn it*, I thought. *Well, since I forgot to fill up in
Ridgway, I'll stop in Sawpit to get gas.*

My parents owned a home near Telluride that my father had
designed and built in the early 1990s. My father had envisioned retir-
ing in the house, but my mother didn't like the long winters. Once I
began working in the San Juan Mountains region of Colorado a few
years ago, I was able to see my parents more in five years than I had in
all the years since I'd left the Southeast when I was nineteen years old.
Every weekend that I had off, I tried visiting them when they were in
the area in the summer and fall. It was late June, and I had thrown my
stand-up paddleboard (SUP) in the car so I could stop at Trout Lake for
a few hours before meeting up with my parents. I had shed tears of joy
at Ridgway Reservoir a few days prior while paddling as I used Tolle's
techniques to focus on the beauty of where I lived. The techniques

Stillness in the wilderness of the San Juan Mountains.

helped me let go of my blues. I remembered how I'd spent a moment absorbing the light shimmering off the top of the water at sunset.

In Sawpit for gas and a sandwich, I saw Flipper the van whiz by. I took a deep breath. *Drew. That man. And he didn't tell me he was going to be here. Typical.* My jaws clenched. I was furious as Drew had promised he would visit me before we become entangled on our trip through Utah. His last voice message said he would be coming through the area, but he then ghosted me. Drew had blown up my phone with texts and photos before we met, and we had bonded so well during our trip, so I found his silence so sad and disappointing.

"Is everything okay?" asked the kind woman behind the register as she took my card.

"Oh, just dandy. Thanks so much."

I got on the road toward Telluride and immediately ascertained there were two cars between me and Flipper, which pulled Drew's unique trailer full of bikes.

It's Bluegrass Festival, the most crowded weekend of the year. He thinks he is just going to roll into town, get a camp spot and a ticket to the concert weekend. He has no clue. I clenched the steering wheel in frustration. *Well, I'm not going to follow him.*

As the only road into the dead-end majestic alpine box canyon town (which never can handle the masses of people who want to pour in for the Bluegrass Festival), all incoming traffic is stopped to evaluate whether people have a place to stay. If you can show proof of residence or lodging, you get a pass on your windshield and are waved in. If not, you get a short-term colored windshield sign with an expiration time of when you must be out of town. This roadblock and screening were to prevent droves of people trying to disperse camp in and around town, which is illegal. Drew and Flipper were waved to pull over into one of two lanes in the large dirt shoulder. The two cars between us were waved through. I was waved to pull immediately next to Flipper. I glanced over at Drew. He didn't see me.

"I'm just going to buy a few items at the grocery store and head back out of town," I explained to the volunteer.

"Here you go. I'll give you a couple of hours." She passed me a purple flyer to put on my windshield.

"Thanks, I won't be there that long." I rolled down my passenger window and watched Drew turning on the charm to the female volunteer.

I waved with a wry smile, as if to say, "Hi, you crappy person who wanted me so bad and now wants to hide. Have fun trying to figure it out!"—if all that can be squeezed into a two-second wave, eye roll, and jolting away.

I walked into the store, and as I picked out some produce, I took a few breaths. *All right, be nice. He has no clue how to find his way around here. It would be kind of you to help him experience the area. Otherwise, he will have to drive a long way to find camping and he likely won't get to enjoy Telluride.* I took some more deep breaths and calmed myself. I texted him, "I'll help you find camping if you want. You came the busiest weekend of the year. There's not much dispersed camping in the area. The only two developed sites will be full."

No response.

As I drove out of town, Drew was gassing up at the Shell in the middle of the valley, the most expensive gas on the Western Slope of Colorado. I pulled in next to him. He was staring into the sky, cell phone in hand, spaced out.

"Need or want some help?" I asked as I pulled alongside of him.

"Do I look like I need any help?!" he yelled.

Shell-shocked, I pulled forward, made a U-turn, and pulled back around to leave. Drew stepped forward toward my car as I started to drive by. His shoulders and chin dropped.

"I'm just trying to help. If you don't want it, that's fine," my foot poised to floor the gas pedal if he yelled again.

"Why aren't you back there in town?" he asked in an accusatory tone. "Aren't you going to the music?" He seemed to be accusing me of stalking him and panicked to see me.

"I don't like crowds. I just got some food. I'm headed to a lake up on Lizard Head Pass. It's one of my favorite spots on Earth." I described some campsites but needed to show him on a map or his cell phone. He leaned forward, and we discussed them as we looked at his phone.

"Don't touch my phone screen!" he said, his voice starting to rise.

"Umm, sorry. I'm not sure how to be efficient showing you otherwise."

After a few minutes, he calmed down as we discussed options.

"You can join me at the lake if you want. Do you have a surfboard or SUP with you?"

"No."

"Well, I can swim while you SUP if you want."

"I'll think about it, but I have some office work to do anyway. You know, most women would do something violent after what I did to you."

"All right. Suit yourself."

I drove away and to the lake. As I paddled my SUP across the smooth-as-glass water, I thought, *His anger and shock . . . I think he felt guilty and was hoping to not run into me. He is not coming. I bet he kept driving over the pass and beyond. Cracks me up. He keeps running away. For some reason, I think he can't handle that the universe wanted us to bump into each other. I really wanted to spend some time with him to better understand my experiences since I last saw him.*

I then swam for forty minutes in the frigid waters. The crystal-clear cold water always does wonders to clear my mind of all thoughts. As I changed in the car, I smiled that he didn't show up, shrugged my shoulders, and started the drive to my parents' place to meet them for dinner. As I entered into a bit of cell reception, my cell phone pinged loudly with texts from Drew.

"Here's a drop pin of where I camped. Come join me. I'll cook you dinner."

What? I thought he drove far, far away! I pulled over and called my parents. "Is it okay if I arrive after dinner? I bumped into someone I know who is offering dinner at his campsite."

"Sure, no problem," my mom said warmly. "See you soon."

As I pulled my hat over my wet hair and shivered while sitting in Flipper, Drew tossed me a clear plastic bag. "Pick whatever you prefer out of there. There is an assortment of tea bags." I thumbed through the bags and paused.

"Umm, Drew, I see you are prepared this time," I smiled as I pulled a sealed condom wrapper out from the middle of the tea bags and then chuckled as I Frisbee-tossed the condom. The condom whizzed immediately in front of his chest.

"I haven't been with anyone since I last saw you. I'm fine being alone!" he retorted as he blushed, looking down as he prepared dinner.

I switched the topic. "I bought a van! I named her Snowflake as she is white and because I tend to head on trips when winter arrives." I told him. "A Ram Promaster. I couldn't find anyone to look at it with me and help me drive the van and my other car back. They sell so quickly. So, I rode my bike yesterday from Ouray to Durango over three mountain passes. The hot head wind heading into Durango was brutal."

Drew's eyes flashed with fear. He looked out a side window of his van. "This was just yesterday?"

"Yes. I guess that's the way you drove here. I was wearing all red."

His eyebrows raised. I wondered if he had seen me on the road.

"I wrote a poem in my mind while sitting in the dealership waiting for the paperwork. Want to hear it?" I asked.

"Um, sure . . ."

I recited:

I have no man
So I bought a van
And made an adventurous plan
Because now I can
Soaking up this earth and sun
Along the way, getting a tan
And deeper into this life I ran.

Drew gently smiled as he stirred some pasta in a pot.

"Can I ask you a question?" I wanted to break the conversation about the mountains and cycling.

He turned the handle of the side window of the van, pushed it out. "I warned my camping neighbor that this was a signal for them to come save me if you got this way."

"It's not what you think," I replied with reassurance. I knew he thought I was going to ask where he was going to settle or more about why he went silent on me and is afraid of commitment. "What made you read Eckhart? How did it affect you?"

Drew let go of the handle, his facial expression shifted from fear and humor to serious reflection. "Darkness of winter, being alone in the Midwest." I listened as he shared some of his inner transformation. He had spent many long, dark Midwestern nights in an isolated vacation cabin after the primary home sold during his recent divorce. I listened deeply, grateful he had softened. He became quiet and a bit forlorn, not wanting to say much more. From what he shared, I sensed that after Drew's divorce, when he was alone in a cabin in Wisconsin, he had grown depressed.

"I've been reading it. I'll be right back." I left Flipper and returned from my car with a bag full of books, including *The New Earth*, *The Little Book of Letting Go*, and others.

Drew looked surprised. "*New Earth*. That's my favorite book of all time."

"I think that's why we were supposed to meet. Eckhart and other readings have been huge for me. I'm learning so much." Drew's look of surprise and relief made me smile inside. "I love how Eckhart mentions the common threads of consciousness, presence, being, and God between Buddhism, Christianity, Hinduism, and the great philosophers. My favorite priest who quickly became bishop mentioned this in a sermon when I was an adolescent, which fleetingly gave me hope about organized religion. That there actually could be a religion that does not judge other religions . . . and it only made sense there has to be one God or power, shared by all faiths. But he moved onto greater things than our church, and I never heard him speak again."

"Now that you are aware of the ego, do you observe it in yourself?" Drew asked. "I see it all the time in me!" He looked fearful as he shook his head and looked away from me and out a side window of his van.

"Yes, it is unsettling at times. It's helping me in other ways, too. I was coming out of depression when I met you, and the doctor wanted to put me on medication, but I wanted to find another way. The withdrawal symptoms listed on the bottle seemed as bad as the depression. So after taking one pill, I decided to try other techniques instead."

"Yeah, no medications," he said emphatically. "No medications!"

As dusk turned to night, we made plans for the next day to bicycle together—as friends. In the twilight, I drove to my parents' place feeling grateful to have shared some time with Drew as a friend. I focused on catching up with my parents when I arrived at their house and didn't mention much about Drew. The entire experience with him was still very confusing for me.

The Next Day in the San Juan Mountains

At the end of the day of cycling and jumping in the lake together to rinse off, Drew made an early dinner for us again. I became buzzed off a beer quickly after a full day in the sun. I gazed at the lake as I sat inside Drew's van. I felt a bit of anger rise inside as Drew prepared his rig for hitting the road once again.

"May I have my pink underwear back? I really don't want it hanging next to a string of other women's underwear," I said. I was echoing words he had uttered when we were camped together in May in Utah, where his sometimes-brutal comments pushed me away. He had admired my pastel landscape lights in my camper and stated he wanted to create something similar with Christmas lights and underwear from all the women he was going to sleep with.

Drew looked at me sternly and acted as if he didn't hear me. As we said our good-byes, Drew calmly said, "Elisabeth, I'm not ready to commit to anyone." As Drew drove away, a stream of tears ran down my cheeks.

Insights and Ruminations: It wasn't until many months later that I realized perhaps both Drew and I had experienced a "dark night of the soul"—when the ego and everything that ever held meaning in your life falls away. I had a few more dark nights after this time, when all the self-care I knew had failed, and my resiliency had run out. I felt so alone, like no one cared for me. Some people don't make it through these dark nights and take their own life. For those who are blessed to dig deeper into the darkness, an awakening may occur. My experience of the union of my soul with the Divine was just beginning. And a dark night of the soul due to a sense of divine withdrawal of favor would later be experienced by my soul. As the weeks and months passed, I sent Drew dozens of emails in hopes of maintaining a connection as I thought he might understand what I was experiencing, but he was not able to help me. Only through immersing myself in self-study, reading books, deep reflection, wandering the earth, meditating, meeting key guides, and finding my spiritual path did the insights and understandings set in.

Background on Dark Night of the Soul

The following excerpts of *Dark Night of the Soul* by St. John of the Cross describe the process of transformation from a medieval Catholic mystic's perspective:

> *In an obscure night*
> *Fevered with love's anxiety*
> *(O hapless, happy plight!)*
> *I went, none seeing me*
> *Forth from my house, where all things quiet be*

> "*... the soul tells the mode and manner in which it departs, as to its affection, from itself and from all things, dying through a true mortification to all of them and to itself, to arrive at a sweet and delicious life with God.*"

Theodore J. Nottingham relays within *The Journey of the Anointed One; Breakthrough to Spiritual Encounter*, that St. John interprets his own poem to mean:

> "*Even though this blessed night darkens the spirit, it does so only to impart light in all things. And even though it humbles us and reveals our miseries, it does so only to exalt us. And even though it impoverishes us and empties us of all our possessions and natural affections, it does so only that we may reach forward divinely to the enjoyment of everything in heaven and on Earth, all the while preserving a general freedom of spirit in them all.*"

Theodore J. Nottingham's interpretation says:

> "*According to mystic tradition, the darkness which is so oppressive to us can turn out to be light itself. The desolation of the soul becomes a purification from selfishness and desires in order to clear the ground for the reception of greater wisdom and joy. It can develop a new ability to perceive and understand; through unknowing we come to truly know.*"

CHAPTER 12:

Euphorias and Ecstasies

*"Depression is core to our development. Depression
and spiritual awakening are two sides of one door."*
—LISA MILLER, PhD, PROFESSOR OF PSYCHOLOGY AND EDUCATION,
COLUMBIA UNIVERSITY, FOUNDER OF SPIRITUALITY MIND BODY INSTITUTE

I pedaled my way up the steep climb toward Hastings Mesa in the baking afternoon sun beaming down on Sawpit. *Bottom of the last big climb*, I thought. *You have conquered the beast and most of the climbing. You can do this.* I wiped the sweat from my brow on this hot, late July day.

I was over sixty miles into the Telluride 100, a grueling hundred-mile mountain bike race with over sixteen thousand feet of climbing. I had completed it twice before and knew that, despite all the positive talk, this was truly the hardest part of the event. It was all I could do to turn the pedals. My heart was more fatigued than my muscles. But I felt stronger than the year before.

As I crested the first major portion of the climb, the view opened up across Hastings Mesa. *Ahhh, a bit of a reprieve. Maybe I can spin my legs out a bit on the rollers.* I soaked up the view of green alpine meadows. And then, I lost feeling in my legs, followed by my torso and upward. *Oh, this is weird. How am I supposed to push harder if I can't feel my legs? All I can feel is my hands on the grips and the bottom of my feet in my cycling shoes.* I worried I might cramp if I pushed too hard, but my effort was going to be difficult to gauge with the loss of sensations.

And then I felt as if I were floating above my body.

I approached the last turn to climb when two volunteers standing at a food aid station asked my name.

"Elisabeth, you have a friend who asked whether you were ahead or behind her," said the sweet gray-haired lady.

"Hmmm, how long ago did she pass here?"

They shrugged their shoulders.

Darn, I wonder when she passed me. Ack, she beat me last year, and I thought I was fitter than her this year. I peed so many times; she must have passed me when I was crouched in the bushes. That's it, sensation or no sensation, I'm going to push it hard. I started to pedal again. As I turned right to head up the northside of Last Dollar Road, I began to cramp. *Ugh, that is what I was afraid of. Back to moderate climbing speed.*

When I got to the top of Last Dollar Pass, I called to the volunteers there through a mud-spattered grin, "Do you have any electrolyte drinks left?"

"Nope, just water and whiskey. Oh, and we have hamburgers, too!" shot back a handsome young male volunteer.

"I'll try the whiskey and a bit of burger. My goal was to beat my friend, but now it's to break twelve hours." I guzzled down a large shot of purple whiskey to wash down a chunk of charbroiled burger and swung my arm over head in a circle. "Let's wrap this up, boys!"

The volunteers hooped and hollered at me in encouragement. I zoomed down the pass and pedaled as fast as I could to the finish, with no feeling in my legs all the way to the finish line. When I crossed the line, the small crowd of fellow finishers and their families cheered as I pumped my fist into the air. I didn't make it under twelve hours, but I was so elated and proud just to finish strong. My eyes met a fellow male racer whom I had met through Mindy, my very dear friend from Arizona. After Tobin, the Telluride 100 race organizer, placed a finisher's metal around my neck and shook my hand in congratulations, I rode my bike up to Mindy's friend.

"Elisabeth, you look so fresh. How is that possible?"

"I couldn't feel my legs for the past two hours until now, so maybe that's why. As the adrenalin and endorphins wear off, I'm sure I'll look destroyed."

Training and finishing such challenging endurance events gave me the courage to face other challenging parts of life.

Insights and Ruminations: *A counselor I would soon meet shared, "It's a good thing you are a tough endurance athlete and love to mountain bike, too. It gave you the skills to hang on for the wild ride you have been experiencing on this spiritual awakening." I had completed many iron distance triathlons, and the endurance mountain biking presented a new challenge that sometimes created the most wonderful euphoria due to the immersion with nature, endorphins, and the inherent requirement to be on the knife-edge of the present moment.*

CHAPTER 13:

Pushed by Tara's Spirit

*"Know that which pervades the entire body is indestructible.
No one is able to destroy the imperishable soul."*
—A.C. Bhaktivedanta Swami Prabhupada, *Bhagavad-Gita; As It Is*

As I crested another hill in my van on the Peak to Peak Highway, I soaked in the beautiful views of the early fall arriving in the Continental Divide. I was on my way to Scarlet's home. Her mother had passed away, and I knew she needed a visit from a friend. Scarlet was the best large-animal veterinary technician at the vet school I had attended more than twenty years earlier. She is a gritty, tenacious, humorous, empathic old soul . . . a beautiful horsewoman with a wicked quick wit who always knew how to make me smile through tough times in veterinary school. I was hoping I could return the favor.

When I got there, the two of us decided to go for a walk in the woods. I followed her tall, slender figure as we crushed the small leaves under our feet. The sun glinted off of the metallic tip of her prosthetic arm. Scarlet's strong, self-reliant soul despite the challenges of the pain and labeling since birth always inspired me and gave me strength. To take her mind off things, I asked her how she was feeling.

"I'm so sorry about your mother. I haven't lost my mother yet, so I can only imagine. It sounds like she was really suffering. I'm glad you were with her. You know her soul is free, right? You can write to her when you miss her. She will hear you." Scarlet looked over her shoulder as the first yellow aspen leaves of fall shimmered in the midday sun. While my words were meant to soothe, I could sense Scarlet wanted to focus on the beauty of the autumn day. I decided to shift the topic from the awkward moment of grief and filled her in on where I was emotionally with men. I told her my confusion with Drew.

"My other girlfriends tell me, 'You just haven't found the right man yet. It will all work out, Elisabeth.' And you know who I start to think about?" I asked.

"No, who?" Scarlet inquired.

"Tara. Do you remember my friend Tara? You and Tara are the first friends I reconnected with thanks to social media when I moved back to Colorado in 2009. She dated a guy in the San Juans for a bit when she lived in Telluride, but she said pickings were slim. Once she moved to Denver, she worked hard and played hard, but never really met a good guy. And then, she died in her early forties. That didn't work out well, did it?"

"Oh, that's right. When did she die, and how again?" Scarlet asked. "She fell, right?"

"She was hiking down from Paiute Peak in the Indian Peaks Wilderness with a guy friend. She slid down a field of snow and into some boulders. He tried reviving her but couldn't save her," I said. "I wish I had gone to her memorial gathering, but I couldn't get out of work. I think of her a ton. Most days when I go for a run in the San Juans, I think of how much she would have loved to still run in these mountains. She never did get to visit me after I moved to the San Juans."

Tara had been an earthy, sweet, fit, smart, hard-working, and loving soul.

"I had texted her Happy Birthday and told her I was going to call her the next day. It wasn't like her to not reply. And then I got the news a couple of days later."

As Scarlet and I relaxed after the hike near her house, I checked my phone. An email popped up from a long-ago boyfriend—Maxwell.

My thoughts raced. *Noooooo . . . How does he know I'm in the Front Range? I can't meet him right now. I'm too raw, too vulnerable. He has hurt me twice. He'll hurt me again. And my libido is raging right now. But oh, does he know how to love. He gave me the first true pleasure as a woman. Maybe he was sent to me to appease these intense urges I am experiencing.*

I looked up from my phone and muttered, "Maxwell. What should I do, Scarlet?"

"What?" she said, shrugging her slender shoulders. "He's reaching out now?"

"Scarlet, this sort of weird coincidence keeps occurring for me. How does he know? I'm rarely here. And now? I can't."

Scarlet fell silent and looked as surprised as I was, as she knew about Maxwell and how our relationship had ended.

It had been over six years since we dated.

Maxwell wrote:

I hope this finds you well and happy. I will keep this as simple as I can, but I do want to clear the air and apologize for what was a very naive decision on my part. Last spring your profile showed up as "someone you should follow" on Instagram. I had no idea that you were on there, though I was pleasantly surprised to see it.

Innocently, I thought it was permission to look into your life, even just a little bit. At first, I resisted this, but on the third or fourth occasion that this notice surfaced, I did open up your account and looked at some of your postings.

At the time it didn't seem like an intrusion, but I am now realizing that that's exactly what it was. I had no right to look into your life, and certainly no business "liking" one of your posts.

So, again, I'm apologizing to you. I will not be so naive again.

My thoughts rushed through me again. *Nooooooo. Not now. It would be dangerous to see him, for both of us. He is such an amazing lover, and that type of amazing love is what my body needs right now, but not the emotional turmoil that comes along with it. Why now? I didn't check social media much and would not have minded him peeking into my life.*

After taking some deep breaths, I wrote back:

No intrusion. No worries.

Did you get my Facebook message a few weeks ago? I mentioned Eckhart Tolle's work and how I think his work might be helpful for you as well.

I hope you are healing.

I am now struggling mentally after some losses but coming out the other side—with spirituality I didn't have before.

It's a gift and blessing that I didn't anticipate.
I hope you are well.

Maxwell replied:

No, I did not! I just checked and there is a message there! I really wished I'd seen it two months ago; I absolutely would have responded.

I'm so sorry to hear that you've had losses recently. Truly. I also appreciate your candor. I was actually in Telluride and Ouray a few times this summer to take pictures, and I really wanted to reach out, as usual to apologize, but I just didn't feel it would be appropriate. I started to shoot landscape images a couple of years ago and have found it very comforting and rewarding.

I feel as if I'm doing my best in a very long time. I feel grounded again, and content.

I'd be happy to talk with you, if you needed someone to listen.

The next morning, I replied:

Glad you are doing great. Considering our history, I don't think it would be good for my healing to connect with you. I have been nothing but hurt by men. Love on their terms with no long-term true regard for my well-being.

My last real love is trying to be a kind friend, which is somewhat healing. But it's also part of the problem. I lost a truly wonderful, genuinely giving and kind person. Okay, seeing the pain-body rising up in me now. Transmuting it now. Ahhh. Eckhart Tolle methods are immensely helpful. Have you read his books?

I have a blessed life.

And there have been a couple of men in my past long ago who I let go who are kind souls, so that is my own fault. But I had my solid reasons that were related to both of our needs.

I just need to not let people into my life so quickly so that I can figure out who is grounded and truly has good intentions for others and not just for their own gain.

Oh well, I guess I am conversing with you after all. Ha.
Email is fine.
But I don't think it would be healthy for me to talk or see you.
I have looked at your photography on occasion. You have
a gift!
Keep it up!

Maxwell:

First, I can only apologize for being one of the men that hurt
you. Finding you was a dream come true, and I know I squan-
dered that opportunity and hurt you so horribly in the process.
I can completely understand why keeping a distance between
us is important. I don't actually know what I would do if I saw
you again. I was thinking about that last night, and I would
probably just cry and apologize for hurting you. But know that
from my perspective I only see happy memories with you. Pure,
kind, happy memories.

It's really interesting that you've brought up Eckhart
Tolle's work. He has come up in conversations with my thera-
pist the last six or so months. I'm still seeing the same therapist
from just after our breakup. So, given your mentioning him,
and the repeated conversations in therapy, I've ordered The
Power of Now. It seems like the themes are more relevant
than ever.

Thank you for the kind words on my photography. It truly
has opened up a path for me that I'd never imagined possible.
I'm flattered and humbled that you would see it and think
kindly about it.

Again, know that I only want happiness for you. I am so
utterly embarrassed that you met me when I was so hurt, and
I had no idea how hurt I was. I am here as your friend, now
as an artist, if you ever want to or need to reach out.

Always, and in all ways, you are such a light, Elisabeth.

Ohhhhh, I melted. Okay, I think it would be healing for both of
us to talk, walk, and just catch up, I thought as pondered how to shift
my response.

That evening:

Oh Maxwell. You are so sweet. It helps me to read and know this. Means a ton. No reception at my friend's place and I'm in my van—only one bar of Wi-Fi. So, I'll save the rest until tomorrow as it might not go through.

Maxwell is an extremely dedicated schoolteacher, with a passion to open young minds to a world of wisdom and the wide array of possibilities for the students' futures. Handsome, a slender, sleek, but towering in height runner, cyclist, and physical yogi, Maxwell appeared as a deep soul in my life for a few months, but he had pushed me away twice, the second time on the night before Valentine's Day. I still had flashbacks of him telling me on the phone that he could not be in relationship as I glanced at the romantic setting I had set for a candlelight dinner, which I held the next day for myself while I licked the wounds in my heart. He later told me it was due to still needing healing after a divorce only two years before we met. By the time he reached out eight months later, I was in a relationship with Kevin.

We arranged to meet the next evening at Evergreen at the lake for an evening stroll.

That day, I beat myself up physically to help suppress my other needs and to soak up the fading summer in the alpine mountains.

I rode my bike from Idledale to the top of Mt. Evans and back. I love the challenge of a hard road-bike ride, and Evergreen was my old stomping grounds. As I came around the first corner of the climb above the tree line, I thought, *Aw, this is one of the last spots I saw Tara.*

I had a flashback of that day I had run into Tara. I had ridden from Winter Park with friends up Squaw Pass. As I refueled at Echo Lake Lodge, it was warmer than usual with no threat of the typical late-day mountain thunderstorms common in the high peaks of Colorado. I had been caught in a freak snowstorm in the summer on the top of Mt. Evans in the past. It was a window I didn't want to miss. On that same corner a few years before, I had just considered turning around due to low blood sugar. I had run out of food. And then I saw Tara's smile and we hugged.

"You are going up, huh? Great day for it!"

"Oh, I don't think I can make it today."

"Why not?"

"I'm bonking, nothing left in my bento box or jersey pocket."

Tara reached into her pocket and handed me a full row of Cliff blocks.

"Oh, I can't take all that from you, Tara."

"Why not? I'm headed down. Take it. I insist."

I hugged her, "Let's get together soon, okay?"

"Okay, we will."

As I passed that point on the road, I felt her presence. I had chills going up my spine. She loved this mountain. Tara used to stay with me at my house in Evergreen the night before the run race to the top. It was such fun to have this rugged, hard-core fellow mountain lover stay with me. She was one of the toughest women I've known.

The last mile up the mountain is usually half torture, half exhilaration. The air is so thin at over fourteen thousand feet, my asthmatic lungs always struggle. I usually feel like I'm pedaling through quicksand. But as I approached the peak past the Summit Lake parking lot, I felt Tara again. It felt as if I were being pushed from behind by her spirit. My hair was standing up on my arms. As I rolled into the empty parking lot, I mumbled, "Thank you, Tara. I sense you. Oh, my God."

Later, Maxwell sauntered up to the door of my van with his head hanging sideways, showing off his freshly clipped sideburns. He raised his eyebrows and peered deeply into me.

"I have something for you," he said as he extended his arm. "A photo of the Wilson Range."

"Aw, you shouldn't have. I don't have anything for you, Maxwell. It will travel with me as I explore in Snowflake. Thanks." I pinned it in the van above my camp stove and kitchen galley. "Just to be up-front, Maxwell, I can't be in a relationship with anyone right now. I think you might know that. But it's so nice to see you." I felt an eerie feeling. Hadn't I heard similar words from Drew just a couple of months prior? Then we hugged.

"Thanks for meeting me," he said as we let go of the hug.

"Sure. I figure it could be healing for both of us."

We grabbed headlamps and water bottles—we had six years to catch up on.

He mentioned that he thought of me often.

"It's not me," I said. "Trust me. If you are still thinking about me after all this time, it's not me. You don't know me as well as you think. I'm intense. It's hard for my soul to take how intense I am." Drew's feedback on my fast-paced mind and body echoed in my soul. I paused on the trail as I waved my arms in the sunset rays gleaming across the glassy smooth waters of the lake. "Look, I have to figure out my own obsession with someone who doesn't want to be with me. I think it's because I have to heal on my own, from many painful experiences. I'm seeing a couple of counselors in Montrose to help me sort all of this out. And the euphorias! I'm so confused. I don't know what to make of them. Ever since reading and practicing full presence, I've experienced bliss that I still don't even know how to put into words. And that counselor didn't know how to respond when I told her about one of the euphorias." I had switched from my counselor Tom to a female counselor at the same practice, in part due to scheduling challenges, and part, as I wanted to try working with a woman.

Then he shared his path of healing with me. It sounded like he still needed more healing, as I did. "I felt your pain this summer, Elisabeth. I could sense that you were suffering."

"How? Did Susan tell you? I don't talk to her, but we are friends on social media . . ."

Susan happened to be a mutual friend through two degrees of separation, via Tara. A strange coincidence that I had learned of but had not mentioned to him until now.

"I just could sense your pain, Elisabeth."

I gazed into his eyes and then at the ground, surprised.

Over dinner we caught up on our career paths.

After dinner at the Latigo, we hugged and drove in different directions. I was proud of myself for not exchanging more than hugs.

Insights and Ruminations: Maxwell's sincere apology plus his acknowledgment of me as a kind and loving soul was in perfect timing for me to begin to heal. I believe the Divine could see my pain and delivered him as a messenger. Deep connections reappear to reassure me that no harm was intended, but that it was all part of a larger plan.

Months later, I visited a fellow cyclist friend who lives in Idledale, near Evergreen. She had lost her significant other who was also a cyclist. She also experienced the energy of the lost loved one, helping her up and over obstacles on her bicycle, in these same mountains.

Feeling uplifted after sensing Tara's spirit on top of Mt. Evans, Colorado. The road to the top of Mt. Evans at 14,265 feet, is the highest paved road in North America

CHAPTER 14:

Tara Mandala

———— •·• ————

*"Chakras are pulsating discs of focused energy
located along seven points within our body, which
impact our health, emotions, and spiritual state."*
—UNKNOWN

Raindrops pitter-pattered on Snowflake's windshield as I drove up the washboard-rippled dirt road in the pitch black. It was nearing midnight when I pulled up to the entrance of Tara Mandala. Snowflake's headlights reflected off the gold paint on the impressive red entrance gate towering overhead. *Oh my, there she is again. Tara. I wonder if she ever came here. She had prayer flags in her home.*

I had such strong urges on the drive that I had to pull over to control myself. I felt like turning around to get romantically involved with Maxwell when I knew it wasn't right. I had said good-bye to Maxwell in a swirl of suppressing my glowing root and sacral chakras that were maddening with the most uncontrollable sexual urges I had ever felt. *What the hell is going on with me? I've never felt like this. I can't stand it anymore. I've got to talk to someone about all of this.*

I didn't really understand chakras—yet. I had learned about chakras in the yoga teacher training that I had completed over a year ago. According to an article from Yoga International: "In yogic literature it refers to the seven vital centers in the subtle or astral body, the body of life energy underlying the physical body. Their opening allows for the unfoldment of higher states of consciousness leading to the awareness of the Supreme Self." (https://yogainternational.com/article/view/opening-the-chakras-new-myths-old-truths). As I learned more about chakra openings and kundalini, which is a force that can rise once the chakras open, I became aware that my body and soul were not adequately prepared and purified, and thus I was experiencing an aberrant and incomplete kundalini rising. This explained why I was having increased, corresponding urges or energy at each center.

The long-standing rigid scientist in me had dismissed chakras as a hoax that new age hippies embraced as they felt strange experiences while high on marijuana or other drugs. I was supposed to read Stephen Mitchell's translation of the Bhagavad Gita, but I shrugged it off at the time.

I had registered for a four-day fall equinox transformation retreat. When I registered, I was drawn to the title of the retreat, "Embodying the Hearth of Mandala, Fall Equinox Transformation," but I had no idea that I was headed to a Buddhist retreat tucked into the rolling hills south of Pagosa Springs, Colorado, until I received the details after registering.

No cell reception, perfect. I needed to detox my brain from social media, email, and outside distractions to sort out what I was experiencing. I turned off the engine and crawled under blankets in the van, relieved that I had arrived safely.

In the morning, the clouds in the sky were mystical. I walked back to the entrance gate to view the grounds from a distance.

Silence.

Those were the orders on the door of the dining hall at Tara Mandala for each morning, until group instruction began in the temple. I had missed check-in the night before and didn't understand where to go after breakfast. I saw three younger women who were obviously close friends enjoying breakfast together outside. They seemed to be struggling with the "no speaking" orders and were starting to whisper with a bit of sign language. I moved next to them.

"Sorry, but may I ask you ladies where we are supposed to report after breakfast, since you are seeming to not follow the silence rule? What's your name?" I whispered as softly as I could to one of them.

"Tara. Nice to meet you," she whispered back as she giggled.

Gateway to Tara Mandala, an international Buddhist community outside of Pagosa Springs, Colorado.

Prayer flags along the route from lodging and lunch hall to the main Tara Mandala temple.

"Oh, Tara, huh? Wow, how appropriate. Perhaps you are meant to be here. I can't believe you are the first person I met this weekend." I told the story of my friend and that I sensed she may have visited here in the past due to her Buddhist background and living in the San Juan Mountains for years. "Please remind me of the meaning of your name, Tara?" I whispered.

"Earth. Tara means Earth."[3]

I nodded, reflecting that "earthy" was definitely how I would describe my friend Tara, who had passed away, only to realize later that Earth is the element associated with the root or first chakra at the base of the spine.

Space to Allow for Spiritual Experience

Reporting to the large Buddhist temple in silence, I noticed that all the other participants' mats were already in place from the day before, in a tight arc along the perimeter of the interior circular walls. The only place I found any possible space was on either side of one purple mat. As I could not ask anyone what to do, I peered around for the owner of the mat. I sheepishly slid it closer to another mat to fit my mat within the circle of soulful sisters, knowing that it was a no-no to touch or move another yogini's mat, but didn't know what else to do. Only women were in attendance, except for Shiva's husband. Other retreatants filed in to settle on their mats, and I began to wonder where Shiva was and regretted that I had not made it in time the previous night for a proper orientation. I looked across the room and finally spotted Shiva giving a student a hug just before she walked toward me with a smile. She settled onto the mat which I had slid to the side. My cheeks flushed with embarrassment. I felt mortified. I whispered and introduced myself, apologizing for not being able to attend the night before. Before I could even utter an apology on moving her mat, she wrapped her arms around me and welcomed me. She turned to face the beaming faces of her students and began to speak.

Wow. She isn't offended and wouldn't even allow a moment for me to explain myself further.

---

3. Tara has many meanings depending on the spiritual tradition, including the equivalent to Shakti and the following explanation: Although the word Tārā means a star, the Tantras take its etymology to mean "that which leads to the other shore." "She who brings us to the other shore (Tārāti) is Tārā." (https://www.wisdomlib.org/definition/tara). Tara also is also defined as the Divine Mother aspect of God.

Later that day in the temple, Shiva Rea prepared us for 108 *pra-nams* (full body prostrations with hands passing through prayer at the heart center, as a form of prayer), divided into four rounds of twenty-seven pranams. The four sets were dedicated to the following: self, loved ones, the world, and the naked self that sees God in everything. She instructed us to ponder on each round, "May I offer . . ." I made a list of what I released on each outbreath and on each inbreath what to allow in and express . . . for myself, loved ones, and the world. After each round, we paused to write what was realized during the rounds of pranams. After our first round, I wrote, "Let go of fear of the unknown and awaken in the now, allowing unfolding of my path. Let go of reaching, urgency, neediness. Allow space for unfolding in freedom. Allow space for inner wisdom to be revealed. Allow space for spiritual self-discovery, spiritual openness, and spiritual awakening." After round two, among many other reflections, I wrote, "To impart the feeling that we are all one."

Shiva instructed us to then reflect on the four most healing qualities of earth, water, air, and fire. Under healing qualities of earth, I wrote: "grounding, supporting, connecting with natural landscape for full presence, clearing and cleansing of the mind, sense of awe, reminder of the impermanence of all things but also of rebirth, universal intelligence in full display, acceptance of what is . . . seasons, temperature."

Insights and Ruminations: When I registered for this transformation workshop, I had no idea I was going to be immersed in a Buddhist community and retreat center. I was so moved by how peaceful and caring the setting and souls on site were that I decided if I ever faced depression again, I would spend weeks or even months at such a site. Being fully present in the mountains after learning about Eckhart Tolle was bringing me out of depression. The retreat was extremely calming and grounding, and in hindsight, my soul was realizing I was at the start of an awakening, even though my mind didn't seem to fully grasp the power of these moments.

*The eight-spoked wheel appears on the porch
of the round Tara Mandala temple.*

Full moon rises during fall equinox at Tara Mandala.

CHAPTER 15:

Spiral Wellness

Artwork near Palm Desert,
near Santa Rosa Wilderness, California.

"The path isn't a straight line; it's a spiral.
You continually come back to things you
thought you understood and see deeper truths."
—BARRY H. GILLESPIE

"Hi. My name is Laura. What's your name?"
I looked up at a very warm face who suddenly was standing next to me as I finished lunch on the second day of the retreat at Tara Mandala.

"Hi Laura, I'm Elisabeth. Nice to meet you. Hmmm. You look very familiar."

"Yes, same here."

"Well, I never forget a face, but I'm bad with names. Before this weekend is over, perhaps I'll figure it out."

I asked Laura a few questions between the last bites of food to try to figure out where we might have seen each other before. Laura's large eyes twinkled from her lovely round face as she exuded gentleness and wisdom. I enjoyed her calm energy.

Later, as we rolled our yoga mats up from the old yurt floor in the last of the light of the day, I called out, "Laura, can I talk to you for just a bit? You said you're a counselor, right? I've been thinking. If you are a counselor and you are here, maybe you can help me. I mean, I don't want to invade your time and space during this retreat, but maybe we can talk in the future? My counselor in Montrose doesn't know what to make of the euphorias, and I don't want to share the strange sensations I'm having with her. I see a couple of counselors from the practice in Montrose at professional meetings. I'm an advocate for mental health and substance abuse issues. When I see them walk into a meeting, it just makes me want to slink away. I can't open up to them."

We started to walk down the dirt foot path toward the dining hall.

"I understand," she said. "It's a small world on the Western Slope. Tell me a bit and I'll see whether I'd be a good fit."

I threw my arms up in the air as she walked behind me in single file. "I feel like I'm going insane at times. Euphorias, seeing beams of light within me, and it seems I see things in a fourth dimension sometimes...."

"Hmmm. Well, how about I provide you a session as a *dana*, an offering? I think I might be able to help."

I spun around, "Oh, what do you mean?"

"It's a Buddhist tradition. An act of service. Karma."

I blushed. "Well, I'll pay you if you can help me."

She handed me a card the next day. It had a spiral logo design on a palm with the following text: "Laura Wade Jaster, MA, NCC, eRYT. Spiral Center for Transformation Practices"

"Spiral Center?" I read out loud.

"Yes."

Umm, wow, there's that spiral symbol again. Spiral symbols have been appearing at powerful moments ever since I signed up for the health coaching course.

Laura continued, "And since we both practice this type of yoga, maybe we've seen each other in Denver when I used to live there. I loved attending the Friday Night Yoga Club events that rotated between studios."

"I bet that's it. I have taught and attended those as well."

"Well, I'm so glad to have officially met you here!" I smiled, and we said our good-byes for the moment.

After the last gathering at the temple, on a beautiful, blue-bird-sky day, I walked alone down one of the soft, undulating dirt paths of the gentle hills back to the dining hall building. I heard rapid footsteps behind me. A small, smiling, handsome, and agile Asian man bounded down the trail in my direction. I stepped off the trail and smiled back.

"Well, hello! What's your name?" I asked. He was moving so fast, that I felt that blurting out a question might cause him to pause, so that I could meet him.

He abruptly stopped on the trail next to me. "I'm Jampa!" He exuded joy, happiness, and love.

"Hello, I'm Elisabeth. Do you work here?"

He flashed his big smile again. "I'm the Tibetan translator and librarian for Tara Mandala."

"Oh, how perfect. I'm on my way to the bookstore. I'm very curious about Buddhism now and don't know which book to buy. What do you recommend?"

"Don't fill your mind with too much. All you need to know are the four noble truths and *bodhicitta*. That is all you need to know! Be like a swan and drink only the milk from the mixture of milk and water."

"Yes, I kept hearing Shiva mention *bodhicitta* and didn't know what she meant. Well, thank you so much, Jampa. Wonderful to meet you."

Jampa began to bound joyously down the trail, as I was filled with wonder in the magic and comfort of Tara Mandala.

Filled with peace and joy from meeting so many grounded, spiritual, kind women, I drove home. Fall colors were approaching peak with yellow leaves turning a dark gold, and some aspen groves beginning to display deep oranges and occasional red leaves. As I approached the base of Coal Bank Pass north of Durango, I turned off my CD of Eckhart Tolle speaking about being fully present and flicked on some Sanskrit chanting music. Being fully present was easy and blissful due to the serene fall scene and the four days of no distractions from digital devices—or men.

As I turned the steering wheel of my van around the first switchback, a euphoria completely engulfed me. My skin tingled, and I struggled to feel the wheel.

Oh my, I'm driving. Well, I'll just keep driving and enjoy.

I felt high. Several switchbacks later, I saw a couple of mountain bike riders with their thumbs pointed to the sky and in the direction I was headed. *Oh, but I'm in a euphoria . . . Well, I want to help them, though.* My thoughts drifted from wanting to stay in the euphoria to seeing whether I could maintain the euphoria while picking people up. I pulled to the side of the road, and the young man smiled wildly as he jogged to the van, away from his female companion who held onto both of their mountain bikes. I leapt out of the van from the side door and flashed a smile back.

"Hi, there is only one other seat, but I think I can fit you both in."

Based on the happy but a bit cautious look on the young man's face, I realized I must look high. My euphoria vanished.

"Oh, are you sure?" he said.

We walked around the back, and I showed him how much room was in the back of the van.

"Well, just give me a lift to the top. I'll leave my bike with my girlfriend, get my car, and drive back down," he said. I felt him study me closely.

"Okay, if that works for you, let's go."

He walked back to his girlfriend and explained my offer. She smiled and waved in relief and gratitude, and he climbed into the van. Still swimming in the aftereffects of the euphoria, I didn't think to ask his name. I sensed that he didn't want to put his girlfriend in the van with me, as he seemed worried that I might be high.

"I'm so happy I can help some fellow cyclists. I just came from a four-day yoga retreat. Do you know the importance of the present moment?" I inquired as we zoomed up the hill.

"Yes, my girlfriend is taking some mindfulness courses."

"Fantastic! I'm thrilled to hear that." I smiled with the warmth and afterglow and bliss from full presence.

We chatted about the cycling route of the Colorado Trail that they had ridden from the top of Molas Pass down to Purgatory. I had done that once and knew of the spectacular beauty of that section of wilderness. After popping off the main trail, they had decided to thumb a ride back to their car on the top of Molas Pass. I had done the same in the past and was happy to return the favor.

Insights and Ruminations: At the start of the retreat, I was not yet aware that my experiences were spiritual in nature, but my intuition sent me there to discover this gift that was starting. During the retreat, we walked around the temple barefoot, connecting with the earth. My body, mind, and spirit immensely needed such grounding. Bodhicitta is the state of enlightened mind.

CHAPTER 16:

Kundalini Rising

———————

"In the Indian spiritual traditions of Yoga and Tantra, sudden energetic awakenings are depicted as kundalini awakening. Kundalini—derived from the Sanskrit word kunda, meaning 'to coil' or 'to spiral'—is an intense and explosive form of energy that lies dormant in the . . . lowest of the seven chakras." (excerpt)
—STEVE TAYLOR, *THE LEAP*

On our first counseling call a week later, Laura was excited to share with me the beauty of my experiences, despite my expressions of fear. "Elisabeth, this is what yogis and yoginis strive for, some for all their lives. Congratulations," Laura said. "But you have come to this through hardship, a different path."

"Congratulations?! I feel like I'm going insane. I don't know if *congratulations* is the right word."

"Have you heard of kundalini? There is a book called *Kundalini Rising* I want you to read."

"I've heard of kundalini yoga, but I've never tried it, as it seems likely to be too much sitting and too boring for me. What's a kundalini rising?"

In the remaining minutes of our session, Laura explained that I was experiencing chakras awakening, and she texted me later the names of this and another book to read.

Painting by Charlotte Zimmerman, eight-year-old friend, 2018.

"Spiral Wellness is the name of your counseling business webpage? So strange. Spirals keep appearing in my life at this time. What does the spiral symbol mean to you?" I asked.

"Spirals represent transformation. The full name of my business is Spiral Center for Transformative Practices," she said. "And as we progress in life, we are climbing a spiral staircase, coming back around again and again."

Insights and Ruminations: The Kundalini Rising book arrived in two days for $2.50 including shipping. Stunned, I realized that the universe knew I needed to read this. As I read passages from it and later from Leap by Steve Taylor, I began feeling relieved. I realized I was not going crazy but experiencing one of the greatest phenomena that one can in life. I began feeling joyous instead of confused, worried, and weird. Laura Wade Jaster became my primary counselor for the next two years to help me handle my rapid change in the perception of reality which initially caused much fear, and the quickly shifting nature of close relationships due to my internal changes.

CHAPTER 17:

Sensing Energy of Passed Loved Ones

———— •·• ————

"Your Loved Ones, though they have lost their physical body,
they have not lost their Spiritual Body."
—AMANDA LINETTE MEDER

My uncle Heinz had passed away in August 2018, and the service was held in early October. When Heinz was hospitalized during the summer, I had asked his daughter, my cousin Stephanie, for advice about what I could send. "Flowers? A book? I'm not sure what's best."

"Write a poem, Elisabeth. He's too sick to read, but a poem from you would mean a lot to him."

I finished the poem in my van while camping in the jagged mountains surrounding Fernie, in southern British Columbia, Canada, on the evening that he passed. As I drove back into cellular service range, I received the sad news via text from my mother. When I called her, she let me know that my father was also hospitalized. He had been in the intensive care unit for the past two days after a minor surgery caused sepsis, a widespread infection of the blood system. My father was stable, but she was worried.

I dialed the intensive care unit and was quickly transferred to my father. Without even saying hello, he immediately started repeating something I could not understand behind the gurgling I heard from his fluid-filled lungs.

"Dad, what are you saying. I'm sorry. Slow down, I can't understand you."

He coughed and then cleared his throat.

"You must write a book. You must write a book."

"Papi, why are you saying that?" I called my father Papi, which means Daddy in German.

"That horse you rode over the Continental Divide in a blizzard to save her. That was something. And that horse."

I was shocked and silent for a moment. I had kept that story a secret from my parents, as I thought they would think I was foolish and off my rocker. Many years prior, I had told my uncle Heinz but swore him to secrecy.

Heinz retorted, "This is a fabulous story. It must be told. Why haven't you told the rest of your family?"

I shook my head, rolled my eyes. "My father would think I'm insane and continue to worry about me."

After a few minutes of pressure from Heinz, I gave in. "Fine, you can tell it at my wedding, if that ever transpires. Then my father won't be so worried, as I'll have a man to watch over me."

I had completely forgotten about my statement to Heinz. At my wedding reception, he promptly stood up, tapped his wine glass, and told that story with a smirk and many sidelong glances at me. I had been mortified but amused at his mastery of the story. My parents and I had not discussed it any further since.

"Okay, Papi. One day. I'm actually writing something else right now."

I smiled inside and was surprised that all this time, I didn't know the story had impressed him. I think he saw a bit of his adventurous self in me. I inquired how he felt and whether he was being treated well.

"So, so. It's not the best."

"I'm praying for you, Papi. I love you." I hung up with a lump in my throat.

Next, I called Stephanie about her dad, my Uncle Heinz. "I'm so sorry, Steph. Your dad was one of my favorite people on Earth. I finished the poem last night finally. Darn it."

"Aw. That's quite the timing."

"He didn't get to read it, but it really wasn't my best. It takes me a long time to write a good poem," I said, full of sadness.

"You will have plenty of time to put the finishing touches on it in the coming weeks. It would be lovely if you could read the poem at his memorial service this fall."

"I'd be honored. Let me know if you need anything. I wish I could hug you over the phone."

I spoke to his wife, Aunt Johanna, as well. I gave her hugs over the phone the best I could.

I called my mother again and asked her how she was doing.

Her voice cracked, "I couldn't stay at home alone today. A friend had a coffee-and-cake gathering. It seemed very strange for me to attend, but it lifted me up to be around others."

"Mom, I'll head back to Colorado in case I need to fly back home. This is too much all at once for you. Call me if you need to talk. I have days of driving. I love you."

When I hung up the phone, my chin, shoulders, and heart dropped. *My poor mother. First, she loses her brother and then we might lose my father in short order. I better start the drive back. I might need to step on an airplane as soon as possible to be with my mother.* I had arrived in Canada only three days prior and was exhausted, but my entire being knew it was time to leave.

My parents are immigrants from Germany, who arrived in the 1950s separately on ships with few belongings and great hopes for adventure and possible better futures in America. Germany had been ravaged by the war, with many memories of loss, grieving, and moral trauma, particularly for my father. They met in Alabama when my father had just started practicing as a surgeon and my mother was working at a university library on the same campus where my father spent some of his professional time. On my drive back to Colorado, I reflected on how both my mother and father had modeled incredible resilience, strength, tenacity, and a diligent work ethic. I thought of how my father encouraged me to write a book, as he was reminded of Heinz's speech at my wedding, partly due to Uncle Heinz's passing away. And my parents loved the roasting yet loving poems I had written for their eightieth birthdays and golden anniversary. By the time I arrived back in Colorado, my father's condition had quickly turned around. He was out of intensive care unit, had been transferred into a rehabilitation unit, and was recovering quickly. It was a miracle that he survived the sepsis in his nineties. *Still strong as an ox, that man.* I shook my head with disbelief and relief as I pulled into the drive in Ouray.

Fall Memorial Service for Heinz Two Months Later

As the airplane to Boston leveled to cruising altitude, someone pressed the overhead button above their seat for assistance. It wasn't long before a flight attendant made the announcement, "If there is anyone on board with medical training such as a doctor or nurse, we have a medical emergency on board."

That's interesting, I thought. The last story Uncle Heinz had told me was about the exact same announcement and request made on an airplane in his senior year of medical school. He wanted to volunteer, but he had not yet graduated nor did he have a license. No one else offered, so he nervously and bravely offered and then helped a sick passenger. I had heard the story before, but Heinz had done his usual magic of spinning the story to be even more entertaining than the last time he had told it.

Then later in the flight, the pilot announced, "Ladies and gentlemen, we are going to have to divert to Chicago."

Oh my, I hope the sick person is going to be okay. Oh no, I'm supposed to meet Mother at the Boston airport. I'm afraid she will be confused all alone. My father had worked diligently to ensure that we landed in Boston at the same time, so I could help her arrive safely at the hotel.

As soon as we landed in Chicago, I tried calling my mother's cell phone. No answer. She had no voicemail set up, as usual. I sent her a few texts. I called my father and asked him to explain my delay if he spoke to her. Upon boarding another airplane in Chicago for the final leg to Boston, I was concerned my mother would be confused when I was not there to meet her in the Boston airport.

After landing in Boston, as I waited for my luggage at one thirty in the morning, I again tried calling my mother. It went straight to a recording that no voicemail was set up. I was worried as I tucked my phone back into my carry-on bag. As I looked up, there stood my mother.

"Mom, when did you arrive?" I sighed with relief.

"Just a few minutes ago. I just got my bag. I have a ride. I made friends with a nice woman when my flight was delayed as well. She is getting the car and is going to give us a ride." My mother smiled, and she hugged me warmly.

Wow, and I was worried about my mom. She is spry and smart as ever! Or someone other than me is looking out for her. I reached for my luggage as it popped out onto the carousel.

The next day at Uncle Heinz's memorial service, I stood at the podium and felt my cheeks turn bright red under the stress of being in front of an audience, mixed with grief. I cleared my throat and unfolded the paper.

"I started this poem for Heinz and his family during a very recent, transitional time in my life, on many levels, including spiritual. Much of the poem is in present tense, a tense which I somehow naturally began using for describing all those in my life who have transcended, for those I know who have passed beyond the world of form. To warn you, I am not a good poet, and you all will soon know it. But it is my honor to share my thoughts of dear Onkel Heinz."

Onkel Heinz's Path to the United States
*Once upon a time, there were two brothers named Heinz
    and Franz*
They both knew how to tell tall tales galore
The duo hailed from Germany, but they wanted to see more.
So, Franz to the US, he went across the ocean to explore
To see natural wonders, and medical training sites to tour.
You see, Franz had wanted to become a veterinarian
But his little brother's ambition he could not ignore,
As Heinz had decided to become a human doctor, for sure
Big brother Franz realized that profession won respect, even more
*Franz convinced Heinz to visit the US; that it was worth the
    travel chore.*

*And their sister, Waltraud, my mother, was brought along, to
    keep the lure of a man at bay.*
*When his tour of America was done, Heinz decided in the US
    to stay,*
While Franz loved his homeland too much to move away,
*Eventually Heinz fell in love with Johanna, a German beauty,
    anyone would say*
Back home to Deutschland, Franz fell in love with Ushi, hurray!
Both Johanna and Ushi, to marriage, said okay
So, to Eggelsberg, Austria, they made their way
And all four were married on that same glorious day.

Heinz: Medicine and Boston

Heinz officially emigrated to the US in 1963.
At the VA Medical Center, he became chief of anesthesiology
And at Harvard Medical School, he taught others to help gain an MD.
So, Boston became home, a wonderful place to be
All the culture and music, provided so much glee
And Johanna also did agree
Boston seemed to fit them both to a "T."
Lovers of classical music, they soaked up Boston Symphony.

Heinz's Heart

As a doctor, Heinz helped keep pain from patients at bay
Keeping patients alive but asleep, as they lay
He made sure for surgeons, patients still . . . to stay
But Heinz's intense focus and worry, eventually turned his hair
*   to gray*
And took a toll on his heart, to his dismay.
Eating healthy and frequent runs were his routine, almost every day
With his heart telling him to slow down, and a great pension from
*   the VA*
Early retirement made sense, to end stress and work's fray.
A new chapter of travel and freedom, "Qu'est-ce que c'est?"

Heinz's Humor

Oh, Heinz, a master storyteller, with a warm, quick wit
He is always poised to create a funny bit
As many laughs, Heinz can always manage to get.

Heinz's humor sure does come in handy
As the Lavas' mood, are often not very dandy.

And Lava tension frequently needs to be diffused;
Even my father, Elmar, he quickly amused.

Behind a veil of seriousness, with Heinz, one cannot hide
A brilliant comedian and sweet beauty by his side.
Making friends around the world, they did glide.
To be with Heinz is always a great ride

He gives everyone a smile, a mile and half wide.
Can't you still see his spirit, running along the beach, at low tide?

Heinz's traits are like a treasure trove
He is a gift all around and from above
Oh, Heinz we all do love.

I know that Heinz's energy and spirit are not gone
One can sense him, especially at dusk and at dawn
Like a ripple, his divine essence of passion, love, and kindness
Go on, and on, and . . . on.

I waved my hands and arms like waves to each side moving outward as I finished reading the last line, choking on tears as my voice cracked.

Later that evening, family gathered at Johanna and Heinz's flat overlooking the ocean as the sun set.

"I'm so tired and want to go back to the hotel," my mother whispered. "But Johanna said she wants to speak to me about the last day and hours of Heinz's life." She looked exhausted and torn.

"Oh, Mom, that sounds important for you to hear what she wants to share. Let's sit down on the couch." We made our way to a quiet corner of the room. "I'll bring you a glass of water. People are starting to leave. I'm sure it won't be too long."

My aunt finally came over. As she began to describe Heinz's last hours, I struggled to understand all of the German. Johanna saw the strain on my face and switched to English.

"He was glowing. It's the most beautiful thing I've ever witnessed," Johanna's face exuded sorrow and joy wrapped together.

Wow.

"What's wrong, Elisabeth?" Johanna asked.

"Umm. Have you read Eckhart Tolle's *Stillness Speaks*?"

"I've heard him speak online and know of his work, but I'm not sure what you mean."

"You described what Eckhart depicts when a portal opens up before death, when one lets go and completely opens to . . . well, it sounds as if Heinz was experiencing bliss and enlightenment."

We all fell silent due to the power of what Johanna shared. My aunt and mother were still in shock and exhausted from grief and travel.

After many good-bye hugs and kisses for Johanna, I put my mother's arm in the crook of my arm and walked her back to our hotel.

"I'm so glad you are here with me. I'm so tired," my mother said warmly.

"Me too, Mom."

As my return flight reached cruising altitude, the flight attendant came over the speaker again. "Is there anyone on board with medical training? We have a person on board who needs medical assistance."

Hmmm. Again? My mind flashed back to the last story Onkel Heinz had told me. I burst out in laughter and quickly covered my mouth with my hand, stifling my chuckle. I sensed the same *bhavana* or mood that Heinz created each time he was part of a family celebration, as he was always lightening the mood with his wit, jokes, and rich storytelling. I felt Heinz's smile and radiant humor surrounding me with a warm hug around my torso, as if receiving a thank you from Heinz for the poem.

Okay Heinz. I hear and sense you. I have a hot date in Boulder this evening, so please don't divert the plane this time, I said to Heinz in silence, with a tear rolling down one cheek. *I hope that poor person is okay.*

Insights and Ruminations: Of course, I don't know whether the humorous hug was all in my mind or if I was truly sensing his spirit. But I do know Heinz was somehow thanking me for my words that moved his family and loved ones.

CHAPTER 18:

All Are One and Beyond

―――――•◦•―――――

"God is the sum of all of that is—every voice, every heartbeat, every man, woman, and child, every animal, every insect, every boulder, planet, and mote of dust, including sentient beings far removed from time and space. 'What's not God?' might be asked to simplify the answer: 'Nothing.'"
—MIKE DOOLEY

Over the course of six months, I experienced several unifying sensations of "we are all one," beginning around the same time as my root chakra experience, and then intensifying in the subsequent months.

Sending and Feeling Love from Afar

In the span of three months, many deaths and serious illnesses occurred in my circle of family and friends. Two girlfriends' husbands passed: one of a massive stroke, the other of ALS, or Lou Gehrig's disease. A third girlfriend lost her parents, an aunt, and an uncle in a single private airplane crash. A fourth girlfriend's husband was diagnosed with a rare form of rectal cancer. And Onkel Heinz had lost his battle against cancer.

I sent texts, emails, and made a few phone calls, but it felt empty to send love that way. *Saying you are sending love and prayers doesn't work unless you are giving love in person,* I thought while I prepared before a run one morning. This thought had filtered through me before. I'd had

Dogs in Baja near Gray Whale Watching Site

no one to give me a hug when I struggled through depression in the past few weeks. Mindy called me frequently from Arizona to check on me. Mindy and I had met over fifteen years ago at a triathlon, and she was my most trusted friend to speak with over the years. A social worker who knew how to help struggling souls grow, she had emotionally supported me through some other dark times. But I needed human touch for healing and had become frustrated by just hearing from a couple of friends over the phone and a rare text from a couple of other friends asking me how I was. I quieted my mind to the present moment by focusing on the joy of gathering my gloves, shoes, and cap for my run.

Suddenly, I felt an intense warmth on top of my head, spreading over my shoulders and down through my upper torso, radiating from the center of my chest outward to the rest of my body. Feeling overwhelmed, I stumbled and fell to the floor of the entryway. *Oh my God, I just felt a message of love from someone. But who? My mother? I don't think I'll ever know, but maybe I'm just to experience a prayer or the message of love.*

We Are Light

> "*Through the crown chakra, we engage our intellect, receive those sudden flashes of illumination, and experience enlightenment.*"
> —ELIZABETH CLARE PROPHET

On a late October day, as I drove to Montrose to go grocery shopping and run other errands, I was listening to a chapter from *A New Earth* by Eckhart Tolle that includes passages on how the ego removes our sense of how we and the earth are all one. *Hmmm. Nice sentiment,* I reflected, a bit skeptical as I pondered. I was more intensely noticing the cottonwoods and the irrigated fields to the east of the highway. As my gaze shifted to the northwest toward Grand Mesa and beyond, a broad, bright beam of cream-colored light flashed across the horizon, across the entire landscape before me, then toward me, and hit me, and my head and upper torso flew back against the car seat. I sensed the light continuing behind me, wrapping around the earth, and then back into me.

Clenching the steering wheel, I snapped my head back in alignment with my spine and gasped. *What the hell was that? I'm driving! Yikes.*

We Are All One with Each Other and the Earth

After my experience of the veil of light, whenever I gaze into the eyes of others, I feel as if I'm gazing into my own eyes or looking into a mirror. A trip to Baja, Mexico, was my first international travel after these experiences began. Despite cultural and language barriers, engaging with people of all colors, textures, shapes, and sizes in a foreign, sometimes stark land did not intimidate me. Even at military checkpoints, traveling alone in my van, with uniformed soldiers rummaging through my things with automatic weapons strapped to their torsos, I felt almost no stress after I was able to gaze into their eyes. And in reality, the locals were sweeter than most Americans I have met, contrary to the warnings of danger in Baja.

THE MOON OVER MEXICO

by "Milt" Miltenberger, wandering artist in Baja

Insights and Ruminations: As many others have experienced and expressed after an awakening, every blade of grass, flake of snow, drop of rain, every animal and every person is radiantly beautiful. A realization arrives that nature and fellow humans are all manifestations of the same life force, all an expression of Shakti, the feminine divine power, and universal consciousness.

CHAPTER 19:

Chakra Experiences Intensify

*"Energizing the chakras is believed to help
the kundalini on its journey from the base of the
spine up toward the crown of the head."*
—CASSANDRA LORIUS

As I clipped into my pedals and sat on my seat, my lady parts began to throb even more. I took a deep breath. *I thought long bouts of exercise and putting this kind of pressure on my parts were supposed to suppress this. This is making it worse.* I stood on my pedals to climb up Red Mountain Pass near Ouray. *What is wrong with me? I now have sympathy for teenage boys. Argh, I need a cold shower!*

I called my close friend Mindy that night.

"Don't do it, Elisabeth!"

"What, why not?" I said. "My counselor Laura tells me that having some great sex will help me raise this kundalini energy experience up further through my chakras. I can't stand this anymore."

"Chakras? Raising Kunda-what? I don't understand. You are going to really mess with Maxwell's head. It will feel empty. Don't do what Drew did to you. It's not right."

"I don't know about that. Maxwell is a super soulful man. And it's so nice he's apologized to me. And I won't do what Drew did. I will be honest and up-front. Nothing beyond just a night or two. We both have needs." But I felt a sinking in my throat and stomach. I knew

Mindy was right. I took a few deep breaths, "Well, that's why I called you. I wanted you to talk some sense into me."

I needed an outlet for this sexual energy and didn't want to be hurt again or to hurt anyone else. I ran into a friend with whom I had performed in a dancing fashion show called "Wine and Whiskers" in recent years, and she encouraged me to sign up for the annual burlesque show in Ridgway.

"If you want to do it, you should."

"I'll wear a mask, and not take that much off. I don't want people I know to realize it's me."

"Last year, Susan only took off her shoes and the men loved it. It's all in the choreography, charm and tease."

Workshop and Rehearsal

"Five, six, seven, eight . . . loosen those hips, express yourself, drive them crazy, girls," Tara said as she sauntered barefoot across the wooden floor.

Another Tara. This is just too much of a coincidence. I strutted my stuff across the room.

"Uh-huh. Wow, Elisabeth. I see you have some confidence. You are going to seduce them for sure!"

I blushed and skittered off to the side.

As we ate a snack and rehydrated, I chatted with fellow burlesque ladies, some of whom I had performed with in Wine and Whiskers, including Ruby. I reached toward my toes and whispered to Ruby, "I just have a ridiculous amount of libido right now, and this is my channel for it."

"That's what vibrators and shower heads are for, Elisabeth," retorted one of the eavesdropping fellow dancers.

I blushed again and giggled nervously as I covered my mouth with my fingertips. I'd tried that. It wasn't enough.

"What's your stage name going to be?" Tara asked.

"Not sure yet. But I know I want to be in red[4], all bright red or orange." I had already envisioned my costume. I normally hate to wear

---

4. Red is the color associated with the first, lowest chakra, or root chakra, which according to Elizabeth Clare Prophet's *Your Seven Energy Centers*, ". . . enables us to connect with the earth and nature to stay grounded . . . Along with the seat-of-the-soul chakra, it governs our sexuality. Through the seat-of-the-soul chakra, we also receive our gut reactions and hunches and we liberate our soul to fulfill her life plan."

red, but for some reason, red was all I could think of. "Ruby, do you still have those red wings from Wine and Whiskers? Can I borrow them?"

"Sure, I'll bring 'em by your office."

"Um, I don't want anyone at the office to know I'm doing this."

"Fair enough. I'll text you and meet you outside."

As I rehearsed, I fantasized about my ex-boyfriend Kevin being in the audience and getting revenge.[5] He traveled most of the time for work, so I dismissed that daydream.

Backstage Moments

Three weeks later, at dress rehearsal, I met yet another Tara.

"Tara, oh, it's so interesting you are dancing in this show. I met you in December last year at your full moon cacao ceremony, just before the winter solstice. You let me in even though it was full, as you sensed how much I needed to be there. Do you remember?"

Tara seemed to draw a blank and she blinked without much emotion.

I filled the awkward silence, "Well, it's nice to meet you again. I keep meeting powerful, pivotal women named Tara. I have a friend Tara who passed a couple of years ago. I think of her often, and she keeps reminding me . . ." Tara gently smiled and became distracted by the other performers.

A few minutes later, Tara approached me, pointed and then touched my Navajo spiral necklace.

"That spiral necklace you are wearing. I do remember you. I remember because it's so beautiful. Spiral is the shape associated with my business, *Naked Tantra*."

"Hmmm, that is so interesting. Spirals and Taras keep appearing for me. I think I was supposed to do this so I could meet you and Tara the choreographer. Something very strange is happening to me. I can't explain it."

Tara gave me a little smile. "Come to my meditation class this Wednesday. It's free. We will be doing a root-to-heart chakra meditation."

"Well, my counselor Laura said I should practice more meditation. I've been experimenting on my own, but I really would love to try an in-person guided meditation. I've only done something similar once, and I fell asleep."

---

5. Revenge is the shadow side of the first chakra.

Group Meditation with Tara

"Tell me what you experienced. Each of you, please share if you are comfortable."

I had felt the usual, frustrating, overly active pelvic floor, which she reminded me was the root chakra. Then my sacral chakra was also throbbing. My third chakra, the solar plexus or *manipura* felt as if it were rising out of my upper belly. My masculine energy and intuition have always been strong, and I felt it during the meditation.

I started learning about the chakras two years before while in yoga teacher training, and I remembered feeling that from *manipura* before. But when I placed my hand on my heart, I couldn't even feel my heartbeat. Prior to being depressed, I could feel my heartbeat so easily. I felt embarrassed and a bit sad. I couldn't feel my heart.

When it was my turn, I said, "I couldn't feel much with my hand over my heart, but on my third breath, I felt an upward stream of energy like an electric bolt, with a shape of four long black-and-white lines, shoot from my heart, through the center of my upper body up to the center of my head, but the energy didn't seem to reach the top of my head. What do you think that was? Maybe a brief migraine symptom?" I shrugged my shoulders.

Tara replied as she lay on her stomach with her chin on her hands, "Not sure. Thanks for sharing."

Epiphanies and Chakra Openings

The next day, I slipped out early from a mental health conference in Telluride. I stepped from the crisp October air into the gondola to descend back into the ski town by myself. Focusing on the passing golden aspen trees and the snow-cloaked mountains, I purposefully didn't think about my next to-do, the drive ahead, the performance that evening. I stayed in full presence.

The gondola vibrations reverberated in my spine. The floating sensation turned into a feeling of my body being weightless. I could not feel anything touching me. No gondola seat. No glass in front of me. I felt as if I were floating through the air outside, just a drifting orb of energy. I allowed another very enjoyable euphoria to take over me, and then I walked along the red crushed-rock path along the stream toward my car. I could barely feel my legs.

Upon entering my car, I felt normal enough. I drove over Dallas Divide mountain pass, listening to Chapter 10 of *Stillness Speaks* by Eckhart Tolle, on the topic of death. "Some people glow and become translucent in the days, weeks, or months before death."

My jaw dropped. *That is what my Aunt Johanna described after my uncle's memorial service. I found it. This is what we discussed just last week. I'll have to get a copy of the book for Aunt Johanna and highlight this section as I promised. Wow, my Uncle Heinz was in complete surrender and experienced full bliss and awakening in those last hours. What a lucid, good passing.*

I clicked off the stereo and focused on the road and the golden aspen between the dark green spruce trees lining the edges of the road. It began to rain and sleet. Suddenly, I felt a warm, glowing sensation that turned into a pressure from the center of my chest, spreading outward.

Oh, what is this? I thought, confused. I gripped the steering wheel. *Wow, I've never felt such expansion. This feels like the opposite of a heart attack. Just keep driving . . .* I was alarmed and felt overwhelmed by this sensation for about ten minutes. A few minutes later, as I crested the pass, I thought, *Phew, what was all that about? I need to breathe. Burlesque. I'm nervous. But I'm wearing a mask tonight. No one will know who I am.*

As I prepared backstage at the Sherbino Theater, I received a text from Kevin.

"Are you going to burlesque tonight?"

I was stunned. He was now traveling so much for work that he was out of town about three weeks out of each month. While I had secretly hoped he would be in the audience, I didn't think it was likely. I typed back, "Maybe."

"Rick and I are going. Where are you?"

I showed the text chain to Ruby, who knew I was using the burlesque to feel more empowered as a woman after my breakup and had admitted my fantasies about making Kevin jealous.

"Classic. Perfect!" Ruby mused as she paused applying eyeliner. I was scheduled to be first on stage for the individual acts, most likely because I revealed the least. I kept more than the equivalent of a bikini in coverage on my body, removing a corset at the end of the act, revealing another corset underneath. Conflict had arisen within me while rehearsing—conflict between the wisdom that it was aimmoral to support objectifying women as sex objects and the empowerment of displaying my feminine side without becoming involved with a man at this stage of my life. My Catholic upbringing and shyness despite being on stage as a dancer in high school were also at play.

I waited behind the edges of two black velvet curtains until I heard the announcer belt out my stage name of "Hot Lava," and a couple of whistles erupted from the audience.

You can do this, Elisabeth. You've performed before as a ballerina, and you know once the music starts, your body will automatically make the moves due to the level of practice before tonight, despite the jitters.

The stagehands turned the lights as low as possible, so I could slip between the black curtains without being noticed by the audience. I wrapped my entire body with the shimmering red wings, turned my back to the audience, and low-level red lights began to beam on my back. Lady Marmalade's version of "Moulin Rouge" with singers Christina Aguilera, Lil' Kim, Mya, and Pink boomed over the speakers. I unfolded and opened one wing at a time as the red lights slowly brightened, and then waved the wings mimicking a butterfly emerging from a chrysalis. With a crescendo in the music, I twirled to face the audience with the wings flapping, revealing my provocative costume. The lights on the audience were brighter than I was accustomed to while performing on a large stage in a major ballet, which made me uneasy as I could see faces that I recognized and their expressions. Stomping and spinning on the historic wooden stage dating back to 1915 with my red-sequined platform shoes was immediately empowering, and I lost my stage fright. I felt like a female warrior and virago wrapped into a fiery ball of raw energy. My twenty years as an iron-distance triathlete and a prana vinyasa yogi had created a powerful frame and life-force, or prana, that was now in full, passionate expression.

I steadily removed a red feather boa, followed by each long, full arm-length red silk glove with my teeth and then by stepping on the tips of each prop. Bending at my hips until my head neared the floor, I slid my fingers from my toes to my chest, emphasizing my red fish-net-wrapped muscular legs. Unhooking the front of my corset with my back to the audience, I glanced over my shoulder and winked at the audience with my hips gyrating. I spun around to reveal another full-coverage corset as a tease to the audience, with no intention of revealing more. On the last few notes, I rolled toward the audience on my side onto the floor, ending with my elbow on the wooden stage, chin on my palm, and a final wink. The crowd roared as the lights went dark. I jumped up and scurried backstage before the lights came back up.

I did it. That was a blast. I feel like a strong beauty again.

After high-fiving fellow burlesque dancers backstage and catching my breath, I cheered the other dancers to pump them up before their acts. Two acts later, curiosity got to the best of me on whether Kevin recognized me. I texted him, "What did you think of Hot Lava?" A few more acts passed before he finally texted back, "That was you????"

Post-Performance Celebration

Fellow performers had informed me that everyone was headed to a neighborhood bar to celebrate and that a drink on the house was guaranteed. We were encouraged by the head of the show to mingle.

When I entered the bar, I saw Ruby, Tara, and other fellow performers dancing in celebration. I sheepishly shimmied between the others to get a drink from the bar and then to the edge of the dance floor, feeling the eyes of men, including Kevin, on me. Kevin shook his head and smiled as he came to say hello. "Elisabeth," he whispered in my ear as we stood near a tall round table with three men hovering. "I'm going to leave now. None of these men are going to approach you further because I'm here. They know me. But do you need a place to stay tonight?"

"I've had three glasses of wine, two on the house from the theater already, and these men are buying me shots, so there is no way I can drive home tonight," I mumbled in his ear over the loud pulsing music.

"Well, just call me and I'll come get you." He gave me a hug and waved good-bye.

I did want to dance, as I rarely had the opportunity in our sleepy little town. Before long, I was dancing on the dance floor in the pub, eventually dancing with one man, Chip, for several songs. He had started to make romantic advances, and I was growing concerned.

"I've got to step out for a smoke," Chip yelled over the music.

"Okay, I've got to use the ladies' room," I shouted back. My cell phone was in my car. As I walked out of the restroom, I was just starting to worry about how I was going to escape from the romantic dancing partner scene that had overwhelmed me when Kevin appeared with both palms open toward me.

"You ready to go home?"

"Please, you are just in time." My shoulders dropped, and I followed him out the club door without saying good-bye to Chip, purposefully ducking out before he emerged from the men's restroom.

Back at Kevin's beautiful apartment in Ridgway south of Ouray, I began to take a shower to wash away the layers of makeup and dried salt crusts from dancing. I was relieved to be in a safe place. Kevin walked in, pulled the shower curtain back slightly and handed me a bottle of shampoo with a smile.

"Aw." His face melted, he extended his arms and began to move forward to embrace me, while I was naked and vulnerable. I pulled back, tears streaming down my face.

"I can't," I murmured. I was shocked since I had fantasized while rehearsing that I would make Kevin jealous, and I'd seethed with plans for revenge, secretly hoping for just such a longing from Kevin to be close to me again. Thoughts of Drew flashed through my head. I was emotionally hung up on Drew, confused and exhausted. A deep knowing reverberated in me that a transformation was underway for my soul. Freedom was required for me to break free from my career and my old habits and belief systems.

When I woke the next day, I had flashes of Kevin taking care of me sweetly the night before, tucking me into a guest bed with some tender and confusing moments. I stepped out onto his porch that faced the fertile valley and Mt. Abrams above Ouray. Kevin looked up, "Would you like some tea?"

"Sure, that would be great." I took a deep breath and enjoyed the contrast of the crisp morning fall air and the warm sunshine as I sat down to soak up the view.

I'm happy for him. Wow, what a view, even from the middle of this sleepy little town.

Kevin returned with a gentle smile and a steaming cup of tea. He had remembered just the right amount of honey for me. As I blew across to cool the tea and took my first sip, we chatted about my rollercoaster ride with men, and how well he was now doing in his traveling sales job.

"Well, sounds like you can buy a lovely home on your own after all that success. I'm happy for you," I said while holding back the frustration that he couldn't seem to be productive in his career until after our relationship ended.

Kevin looked down and clenched his hands together. "I'm never going to live that long together with a woman without getting married."

I was stunned and let the silence remain for a bit. I held back what I really wanted to ask—why he never asked me to marry him—as I already knew why. Kevin didn't ever pop the question because he refused to have a conversation about his flaws, only mine. While I felt my flaws were deeper than his and now decreasing, it was not a healthy way to grow in relationship.

"Kevin, we would have eventually gotten married if we had stayed together and worked through things," I said as softly as I could. I looked off to Mt. Abrams and took a deep breath, a bit confused but with a surprising calmness that recognized there was a deeper meaning behind the end of our relationship.

After a little breakfast snack together, I hugged him good-bye.

"Thanks for being the sweet, kind man you always are." My eyes started to well up.

"Keep being happy," he replied.

As I drove away, I thought, *Well, that sort of backfired, didn't it? I was hurt more than he was by the entire spectacle that I created last night and this morning.*

Insights and Ruminations: The opening of my root chakra was being expressed in bold red, as Mother Earth energy was pushing up into the center of my heart. I learned this was an expression of the feminine portion of the Divine. This photo demonstrates the strong pitta aspect of my soul, which can push one to spiritual growth. Pitta is one of the three doshas in Ayurveda medicine, a practice I advocate. The Chopra Center states, "Also known as mind–body types, the doshas express unique blends of physical, emotional, and mental

"Hot Lava" stage name, backstage in Ridgway, Colorado.

Root and sacral chakras in artistic expression.

characteristics. Those with a predominance of the pitta principle have a fiery nature that manifests in both body and mind." The predominant prevalence of pitta in my soul was the underlying impetus of my drive in dance, cycling, triathlon, and accomplishments in my career. Dance, extreme exercise, spending extensive hours immersed in raw nature, and the physical practice or moving asana aspect of yoga were the only spiritual practices that quieted my mind at the beginning of this book.

All photos of red dancer are © Dollhouse by Cyllia,
of Cyllia Lynn Photography

Part III:

Ascending to the

Summit of Life

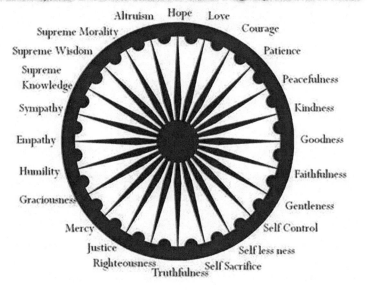

The 24 Spokes of Ashoka Chakra in Indian Flag Represent 24 Virtues

Altruism Hope Love Courage
Supreme Morality Patience
Supreme Wisdom Peacefulness
Supreme Knowledge Kindness
Sympathy Goodness
Empathy Faithfulness
Humility Gentleness
Graciousness Self Control
Mercy Self less ness
Justice Self Sacrifice
Righteousness Truthfulness

*The **Ashoka Chakra** is the twenty-four-spoke wheel depiction of the dharma chakra or "wheel of duty" and appears on the flag of India. The twenty-four spokes represent twenty-four qualities of an individual.*

Source of image: http://bsgtn.blogspot.com/2016/01/national-flag.html)

CHAPTER 20:

Embracing the Mystery

———— •·• ————

*". . . the most important objective in life is to attain the
goal of Self-realization: to know through meditation his
true soul nature and its oneness with ever blissful Spirit."* ∞
—Paramahansa Yogananda

"**A**nnie! Where I can learn about mantras and their meaning?" I
sputtered, dashing into her office. Annie and I worked together,
and she had become a lovely sounding board about healing while
awakening. A warm, open-hearted yogini who taught meditation and
nutrition, Annie was such a lovely soul whom I enjoyed supporting
as her supervisor.

"Why do you ask?" Annie said, smiling.

"We chanted a ton of mantras at Tara Mandala. I want to know
more about what they mean before I chant them anymore," I replied
with a bit of distress. "I'm worried that having chanted *Aum Gam
Ganapataye Namaha* so many times during the Prana Vinyasa yoga
instructor training might have removed obstacles from some of my
desires and accidentally messed with parts of my life I really didn't
want destroyed." I had begun to worry that being unaware of the
meaning of what I was chanting while thinking about frustrating
aspects of my life could cause changes I didn't truly want, since I
wasn't aware of the full impact of my desires.

Annie suggested, "You could receive an initiatory or custom mantra through Blue Throat Yoga, which is kind of an offshoot of transcendental meditation. I know an instructor in Boulder. The training takes a few days."

"A few days to be initiated and learn a new meditation technique? Hmmm. Wow, I don't know. I started meditating earlier this summer, just experimenting with Deepak Chopra and some apps on my phone," I said. "But I've been wondering how else I can meditate more effectively. I've been meditating on simple gratitude—my healthy body, my best friend Mindy, and the sound of the river outside my window in the mornings when I wake."

But I later jumped on the internet and started to read about Blue Throat Yoga, Paul Muller-Ortega, and Neelakantha meditation. I felt a warm vibration emanating across my chest as I read.

The following week in November, I plopped into Annie's office and asked, "What's the purpose of a custom mantra?"

Annie paused and looked down for a couple of breaths.

I blurted out, "Is it so that your divine inner essence can come into full fruition?"

Annie cocked her head and hesitated. "Well. Um. Yes. That's right." Annie raised her eyebrows as she smiled broadly. She seemed surprised by my spiritual answer.

I shrugged my shoulders and smiled back, not knowing where those words I'd said had really come from.

I sent an email to Janet, the instructor Annie suggested. Janet offered to initiate me that weekend before she was to depart for Boulder, so we tried meeting in Moab. But a mid-fall snowstorm was rolling into eastern Utah and western Colorado, and Janet departed before we could meet. We instead set a time to discuss whether Neelakantha meditation would be right for me.

Janet explained, "Neelakantha will help raise kundalini in a safe, more controlled manner. It's the most potent type of meditation technique I have ever experienced."

Sign me up. I need a more stable base to handle these surreal experiences.

It took weeks for us to line up a date, time, and location that would work for me and two other students. At the start of my initiation ceremony, Janet asked, "Do you know the significance of today?"

"Winter solstice and full moon. Seems auspicious."

"It was hard to schedule this, the back and forth. And the initiation is today. You called this in."

There were two other students being individually initiated that evening. When I entered the scheduling equation, only this date worked for all four of us.

I shrugged my shoulders slightly, feeling the power of the coincidence as more than a coincidence.

"And yet, you know we are not in control, right?"

I nodded silently. The universe had been pushing me around to give me lessons at a rapid pace over the previous months.

Insights and Ruminations: Practicing the Neelakantha meditation technique provided powerful healing in my heart over the coming months. During some of the meditation sessions, I set the intention to heal scarring in my heart, which allowed me to move forward into my true Self.

CHAPTER 21:

Continued Normalization of Awakening and Redheads

———— •·• ————

"The moon came to me last night with this sweet question. She said: 'The sun has been my faithful lover for millions of years. Whenever I offer my body to him, brilliant light pours from his heart. Thousands then notice my happiness and the light pointing toward my beauty. Hafiz, is it true that our destiny is to turn into light itself?' And I replied, 'Dear Moon, now that your love is maturing, we need to sit together close like this more often, so that I might instruct you how to become who you are.'"

—Hafiz, Sufi Master, "Faithful Lover," read by Mooji, from Mooji Mala soundtrack

"We should have a glass of wine together one night," I said as I walked by Tabatha. Tabatha's strong, large frame was pumping the stationary bike pedals as we chatted. We had met the previous summer on a hike with a mutual friend. During this early winter, we kept bumping into each other at the little gym in Ouray, and I was curious for the underlying reason. Her gentle, calm energy was very settling to be around.

"That would be nice. Maybe next weekend?" She wiped the sweat from her brow and wisps of red hair.

"I'll be in California then. But let's try to get together after I get back."

"What are you doing in California?"

"Eckhart Tolle conference. I've been having some weird energetic experiences ever since I started experimenting with his techniques."

Tabatha raised her eyebrows and cocked her head. "Hmmm, oh really?"

"Do you know what I mean?" I asked.

"Oh, yeah." Tabatha's facial expression was different than I had ever seen. "We should talk."

I turned the wine invite into dinner and tried scheduling it before I left. But an early snowstorm rolled in, and Tabatha couldn't make it safely to my house. We began to text. Tabatha sent me an article about dimensions beyond the three that basic physics explains.

I texted Tabatha: "Wowzer on the different dimensions. I have felt some of this, but not the level that you have. So much to learn. Trying not to get too cerebral about it though, as I'm wondering if it will extinguish or fizzle the experience or accelerate the process? Being fully conscious and having this experience is more than surreal and eye-opening. I hope I can help others to become conscious in a way that will serve the planet and humankind. And while it seems as if you suffered, I don't feel like I am suffering but instead experiencing something that is meaningful and meant to happen, not just to me but for others so that there is less mental suffering in this world. When one is not suffering mentally, one is way less likely to harm others and the planet."

Tabatha texted back: "It is a very fulfilling experience. I don't really feel like I suffered, but rather I tapped into places where others needed help and unbeknownst to me I shared what they needed. Every enlightening experience has been worth it and gives me a better understanding of why I am here besides the mundane day-to-day routine, which I call the tick-tock reality. LOL. After talking with you, I realize that I have been ignoring the awakening to fit in here. I don't know if that is best for me. I think there is a balance and others might gravitate to us when they are ready to awaken. It's so crazy, but there are parallels to our experience and *The Matrix* movie, just not as extreme, if you really think about it."

I texted back: "Hmmm, I think I get what you mean. I've started to notice that I seem to know what to say to others who are struggling. A couple of friends I'm not very close to have reached out to me with major problems. I'm wondering if that will happen more as time goes on. This is a very cosmic, magical place that we live in. It's only fitting that I'm having these experiences here and have met you. I look forward to seeing you when I return from the Eckhart Tolle conference in California. I may have to take you up on calling you when I'm traveling if I have some aha moments or intense experiences to share, or if I have questions for you. Is that okay, oh awakened new sis?"

Full Moon and Redheads

As the full moon rose over the red rock cliffs surrounding Moab, a fiery redhead named David whom I had met at the hot springs in Ouray pulled up to my campsite. He had found me on the internet after our chance meeting at the hot springs, and his first email to connect with me was about his father's view of reincarnation. Earlier in the summer, after the heartbreaking interactions with Drew, I had met David's best friend who immediately told me David would love me and perhaps we should meet. I had declined saying, "Unless he knows who he is and what he really wants in life, I don't want to meet him." But after meeting David by chance, I felt there was likely a lovely reason to spend some time together.

David's hair extended beyond his shoulders, in a very natural, wild look. He blended in with our surroundings as he hopped from large boulder to boulder around the campsite. With fair yet red-tinged skin in combination with dramatic facial features and his red hair, David seemed like a lovely piece of red earth come to life. He was a wildlife biologist in the desert, and he was very warm and welcoming when I spoke of a few of my mystical experiences. He read Rumi's poetry to me, which resonated deeply in me due to the context of my recent experiences. David made me feel normal and joyous, as I shared my concerns about the experiences that were still disturbing to me and a tiny bit of information about meeting Tabatha. I mentioned that Tabatha's awakening included experiences very different from mine.

"I don't know if I want to have her type of experiences," I muttered with my forehead furrowed in worry.

"What do you mean?"

"Her experiences seem to be dark, sort of scary, and traumatic."

David stepped out of the trailer and looked over his shoulder, "Ancient spirits?"

I paused in silence for a bit. "How did you know?"

"I've been in the area for over thirty years."

I gazed toward him as he walked toward his truck, parked on the red slick rock. I was speechless.

Redheads Continue

As I extended my arms into triangle pose (*trikonasana*), I thought, *Wow, what she is saying really resonates with me. I used to just think her words sounded beautiful. Now, it's more than that.* I had met Kristin, the owner of a yoga studio in Telluride, during a yoga instructor course that I completed a year earlier. Kristin was a visiting instructor in a course in Ridgway.

Over a cup of tea after class, I asked her, "Where did you gain the wisdom you espouse in class?"

Kristin cocked her head, raised an eyebrow, and flashed a humble smile. As she pushed a long lock of red hair out of her face, she said, "I traveled to India and have studied for a while. Why do you ask?"

"It's strange. I think I have had a spiritual awakening, and now your words make sense to me, but I don't know why." I explained some of my mystical experiences.

"I wish I could have some of those spiritual experiences," Kristin replied.

"Um, well. I was stripped down to nothing when it all started. And it's been confusing, and I'm filled with fear from it at times. I didn't really pay attention in that yoga instructor course you helped teach when we were talking about chakras. I didn't want to read the Bhagavad Gita. I thought it was all hogwash. I'm such a rigid scientist and shrugged it off. Eastern religions and spirituality didn't interest me back then. I am really very naive when it comes to spirituality."

"Just because we can't cut into it and look at it under a microscope doesn't mean it's not real," Kristin said. "It's been studied for thousands of years. It's real."

I nodded. "Now, since I am exquisitely aware of my thoughts, I notice that many of them come true. Even those thoughts that don't serve me. So, I'm rather freaked out by it. I really must control my thoughts."

"It's time to make your list of what you want. And be specific!"

I knew what she was talking about. "I don't know if I believe in manifestation or whether it's what I'm experiencing. And I keep meeting men in midlife crises who seem to be wonderful souls, but I then I get hurt."

"Just give it some time. Be specific on your manifestation lists, and it will eventually work out."

Kristin recommended a couple of scriptural books to read during my upcoming trip to Baja, and we hugged good-bye.

Noel Night in Ridgway

As I gulped down my fourth glass of grog, I realized I gravitated toward women who were just the right people to mention kundalini rising to. It was early December, with Noel Night featuring free alcohol, deep discounts, and free live music at some local stores. Upon entering the historic firehouse in Ridgway that now served as a local store, I began to tap on the steel drums there. I glanced up and noticed Alana, the shopkeeper.

"Annie suggested I meet with you," I said. "I'm having some surreal experiences that I'm trying to sort out. She says a *mala* from you might help me." A mala is a loop of beads for keeping count while chanting or mentally repeating a mantra, which helps to clear the mind and is a form of devotion.

Alana pointed to a display of beautiful malas on the counter. "Take a look at the one on the far end. And I'd be happy to meet with you."

I sauntered under the influence of fruit and wine to the end of the display and picked up the mala in question. I loved its colors and texture. It was indeed the one that most attracted me in the entire display. The tag read, "Spiritual Warrior." I froze and then looked in her direction. When her eyes met mine, I mouthed across the store through the gathering of other customers, "How did you know?"

A couple of days passed before I received a text from Alana. "Elisabeth, I highly recommend you get a copy of *The Celestine Prophecy*. It is part of a series that will explain what you are experiencing and more. Know that you are not alone. There are plenty of people around you who have the same stuff happening, and that is nothing to be alarmed about or even to praise. Keep observing it all, as part of the divine play, and the deeper insights will settle in. Keep experiences sacred and to yourself. Stay present, attentive, and relaxed. Reach back out to us if you want."

I texted back: "I drank too much that night, so that's why I started talking about it. It's very reassuring to know that others are experiencing this. Why should I keep it to myself, though? Curious now."

"It is your sacred connection to the Divine," she replied. "You'll dilute its power. But that's just my two cents. Others may say differently. It is so easy to get trapped in the ego when putting too much weight into these experiences. Not to say that they aren't amazing, real, and, valid—because they are—but to build one's story, life, and identity around them gets really sticky if you want to move even further. My recommendations are to purify body and mind as much as possible to receive more insights and to find a lot of stillness to integrate the lessons they bring. As Mooji would say, 'You're in God's oven being cooked like a jacket potato.'"

Insights and Ruminations: I was being blessed with a series of guides who supported me and then sent me on my way to the next guide. Kristin later relayed that rather than wishing for such experiences, she is instead curious about the ecstatic kundalini-rising experiences. She had heard about people who also had these bolt-of-lightning, life-changing experiences of the Divine, but her personal experience was more of a steady current of awakening that included ongoing devotion, introspection, practice, and study.

CHAPTER 22:

Sensing Energy of Passed Loved Ones Revisited

"Wouldn't you expect the dead to be extremely anxious to reach out to comfort and inspire those they love and humanity at large?"
—MIKE DOOLEY

As Eckhart Tolle himself walked onto the conference room stage in November in Huntington Beach, California, and sat down, I felt a spaciousness I'd never sensed before. It was as if my entire body were expanding away from my core to the edges of the room and beyond. My spine elongated on its own.

Not everyone shared my experience. During his second lecture within his conference with other invited authors and speakers, my cousin Stephanie whispered in my ear, "I can't handle it. He looks like a turtle. And each time he pauses for so long, I'm worried he is having a stroke!"

"The pauses are so you can absorb and reflect, Cuz. Just think of him as Yoda from Star Wars."

"If you are here, you have suffered enough," Eckhart was saying.

My eyes welled up. My cousin glanced at me and shifted in her seat. I could not perceive whether she understood on a personal level what he meant, but she sensed I had been through deeper sorrow than she had realized. Of course, she had recently lost her father, Onkel Heinz.

A couple of days later, Stephanie and I were walking on the beach, barefoot on soft sand as the sun glimmered off the waves. Surfers paddled to catch the next wave, and then the next.

"Have you sensed your father?" I asked.

"I asked him to promise to show me some signs," she said. "He shrugged it off, but finally said he'd see what he could do."

I had never been open to believing that one could sense the energy of loved ones who had passed. But my bandwidth for spirituality had changed. Stephanie told me about a moment when her husband picked her up on their first trip together after Heinz had passed. An electrical storm ensued with the headlights of the car flashing, the car alarm blaring, and the doors refused to unlock, all at the same time. She shared that her family's favorite piece of classical music was playing on the local radio after she finished a hard run. After that classical piece that her family listened to at nearly every dinner when she was growing up, the radio announcer stated: "To my wife and child: I am at peace." She felt these instances were communications from her father.

Insights and Ruminations: Over the subsequent months, friends shared stories of sensing the spirit or energy of lost loved ones. Such moving conversations were only possible for me since my awakening.

CHAPTER 23:

Power of Thought or Manifestation?

———•·•———

"Ancient saying: 'When two or more are gathered in the name of the nameless one (the Divine, Oneness, God), manifestation becomes evident.' When you, your body, and your Team (guardians) all align to a particular intention, manifestation occurs."
—ALEYA DAO, *SEVEN CUPS OF CONSCIOUSNESS*

During the trip in California to spend time with Stephanie and attend the Eckhart Tolle conference, I meditated twice daily, consistently, for the first time. Each day, I had simple desires that I reflected on, outside of meditation. No deep wishes, just internal statements such as, "Wouldn't it be nice if . . ."

"Did you convert your van on your own?" A very tan, lean, salt-and-pepper-haired man paused at my campsite on his way back from the showers. We were both camping in vans at Crystal Cove State Park near Laguna Beach.

"Oh, it's just a cargo van with a bed and sink." I smiled back.

"Mind if I look inside?"

"It's not much to look at, and it's sort of a disaster, but sure."

We talked for several minutes and then several times over the next couple of days. Frank was starting the conversion of his cargo van into a camper as well. We exchanged ideas on shaping our vans. After our chat, I packed up to hit the road.

"I'd better start heading south today," I said as I rolled my window down and paused at Frank's site. "I'm not going to use the rest of my shower tokens. Do you want them?"

Frank looked up from his picnic table, "Try to get some money back from them at the gate."

"Okay. I doubt they will give me the money but suit yourself. Nice meeting you. Wish me luck on my crazy love life," I gave him a wry smile. I had shared some snippets of my rollercoaster ride with meeting men in midlife crises over the past few months.

"Nope, we can't give you the money for those tokens. They are your souvenir," the state park ranger said. I turned my Snowflake van around and headed back down to Frank.

"I told you." I extended my hand. "Here, the tokens are yours."

"You should keep them. You might be back." He shook his head as he approached the van.

I slid open the side door and insisted, "I'm not going to be back. Please take them."

"Keep at least two of them." Frank slid his forearm around my neck, pulled me a bit out of the van, and kissed me on the cheek.

"Silly," I said. "Okay, I'll keep just two as a souvenir." I waved good-bye, my face blushing. *That's the third Californian to thank me by kissing me on the cheek. California has been good to me,* I mused as I drove away from the campsite.

A few days later, I was back at the same campground, and Frank was long gone. I had camped at a couple of other areas to the south and found the train tracks too loud for me to sleep through. As I slipped the two coins into the shower timer, I prayed for more time. I was too lazy to go up the many stairs to get more change from the ranger station, and I was out of single dollars and quarters to buy more shower tokens. As I shivered in the cool, moist California evening after plunging into the ocean in late afternoon, the shower kept running and running. I started to push buttons to try to make the shower stop after I was done. It seemed that the shower gods were smiling on me. Heaven. Karma?

When the weekend arrived, the campsite became crowded and noisy. A Girl Scout crew held a birthday party at the site next to me. *Ugh. Wouldn't be nice if I knew someone in the area, whose driveway I could park in? A quiet neighborhood, so that I could get some solid, long sleep.*

The next day, as I drove back to the campground, I got a text from my friend Scarlet. "Hey, how are you? You in Moab this weekend?"

"I'm near Laguna, California! Your old stomping grounds."

Immediately Scarlet called me. "I forgot you were in California. I have so many family members there." Scarlet connected me with her cousin and her family. I spent a few nights parked in front of their house in a quiet neighborhood.

The list of manifestations grew with the addition of a bike ride with a local, practicing kundalini yoga, only three minutes from Scarlet's cousin's home—all within a day of the thought.

As I walked along Reef Point of Crystal Cove, combing through the varied shells, rocks, and seaweed, I had a flash of a dream from the night before. I had dreamed that Drew passed by in his Flipper van in the middle of the night. "There he goes. He didn't stop. I didn't even get to say hello and good-bye for good."

That evening, I was planning my departure from California, still longing for a solid bike ride somewhere mountainous. My plans to ride Mt. Figuero near Ventura didn't materialize due to the devastating fires and resulting smoke. I texted Drew, "I'm leaving Southern California tomorrow, headed to Arizona. Any hilly bike rides along that route that you recommend?"

Drew replied, "Just got to Orange County. Drove through L.A. in the wee hours of morning darkness. Thought of you but also decided that you'd be heading back home by now, sorry. And I could really use a cycle buddy tomorrow! Will probably just putz around Laguna Niguel. I have a super sweet but overpriced campsite near Laguna Beach." The campground was Crystal Cove State Park, one of his perennial favorites.

We made arrangements to meet the next day to ride.

At the start of the ride, I led us to a gorgeous, green nearby park overlooking the ocean so that I could use bathroom facilities.

"Drew, ride a couple hundred yards that way while you wait and look up the slope of the green amphitheater. Look for a red and white sign." The sign stated the following "ATTENTION. Take Note of What It Feels Like to Be Alive, RIGHT NOW."

As I waddled out of the bathroom on my cycling cleats and then clicked into my pedals, Drew rode toward me shaking his head with a huge grin.

Heisler Park, Laguna Beach, California.

Heisler Park, Laguna Beach, California.

Statue which I nicknamed "Trust the Universe," in
Heisler Park, Laguna Beach, California

"Well?" I smiled back.

"Never can have enough reminders."

I sped down the asphalt sidewalk and up the other side of the green hill as I pointed to a mystical statue of a Peter Pan-like man holding a beautiful woman who was swooning and floating horizontally, as if the man were supporting her in moving forward in transcendence and defying gravity.

"Isn't it moving and fitting? This statue reflects how I feel now. There is no plaque providing a title or name of the artist. 'Trust the universe' is my name for the statue."

We caught up on life events as we pedaled through the Laguna hills on fabulous bike lanes. "Why haven't you quit that job and started health coaching yet?" Drew shook his head and smirked.

I shook my head as we road up a hill, "Unfinished business back home. I'm trying to figure out how to leave with lasting changes related to mental health efforts. And besides, I'm still taking courses to prepare myself."

Drew suddenly shifted the conversation to love life.

"Kathy." Drew shook his head as we rode up another hill on our bicycles.

"Yes, who is Kathy and what about her?" I asked.

"I really like her, but she lives in a large town and has young children."

"Sounds like you need to meditate on this. Have you been meditating lately?" I laid my forearm on Drew's back as we rode next to each other, giving him some reassurance as a friend.

"No, I probably should."

"I met someone, too," I said.

"Oh, who is he? Tell me more. Are you making him wear a cap?"

I shook my head, chuckled, and turned red. Drew was referring to an email that I had sent to him, suggesting he protect himself while he plays the field of women. I had suggested he wear "a cap" or a condom as we had discussed in his van in Colorado.

"I'm an authentic lady. He's really great. And I didn't meet him on a dating app. His best friend mentioned him to me this summer and said we should meet. I didn't want to, but we met spontaneously at our local hot springs this fall. He is a cyclist. Is Kathy a cyclist?"

"No, she's not." He frowned.

"David is!" I smirked.

We stopped to figure out where to head next on our quick outing in the rolling Laguna Hills of Southern California.

Drew pulled up a mapping app on his phone.

I gazed at the intersection sign where we paused, "Oh look. The road sign at this intersection says Elisa. That's what David calls me. I was meant to think of David at this moment. And the other road is Mexico. That's where I hope to go next in my van, to Baja. David is fluent in Spanish and has traveled through Baja, so if he goes, I'll have a knowledgeable partner."

"Maybe I'll call you Elisa then."

"Nope, that's only David's nickname for me."

"I can call you whatever I want!" Drew exclaimed.

I breathed deeply, focused on the road sign, and smiled while I thought of David, while Drew looked back down at his phone for a moment.

"Lynn ghosted me." Drew furrowed his brow as we started to ride again and turned a corner. Drew was referring to another female cyclist with whom he'd had relations during the last stages of his marriage.

I looked over my shoulder. "Hmmm. That sounds familiar," I said wryly, referring to Drew's ghosting me in the past.

When we had finished our ride, I waved for him to turn with me. "Let's swing back by my van. I have something to give you."

It was a small but significant little book. "The Tao de Ching! We will do this again." Drew gave me a quick hug and darted away.

I shook my head again. *That was supposed to be a good-bye gift, you silly. I'm trying to let go. Meeting David sure is helping. But I sure would love to ride bikes and spend time with you again, Drew.*

Insights and Ruminations: The old adage is true, "Be careful what you wish for." As I have become more aware of my thoughts and observed the life events of friends after hearing wishes being stated, I have realized that the universe is listening. Some common adages seem to be pertinent on manifesting desires: Let go of what does not serve you, be aware of your thoughts, be specific, and make sure you are ready. The following common sayings seemed to be serving me well in this phase of my life transition and spaciousness: Be patient, listen

to lessons that come your way, listen to your heart, trust your gut, and simultaneously, be fully present. The now, the present moment is a true gift—a present.

As this junction between my old life and my new emerging self, I was learning to not label experiences and to trust the universe. I was also learning I needed to set stronger, healthier boundaries. By not labeling experiences, events may feel painful initially, but if they are surrendered to and accepted, they can open us up to life and future moments of joy and deeper meaning that would otherwise not have been possible. But such a mantra without boundaries, plus the associated misconceptions, can lead to a course not in alignment with how your path is meant to unfold. I find myself repeatedly having to slow my reactions down so I can pause to reflect on a moment or experience and prevent myself from labeling what is transpiring. Our minds try to categorize every moment to make sense of our world, many times to our own disservice. What one perceives is just that: a perception shaped by our mind. In this fast-paced modern world of immediate gratification and rushing from one task to the next, slowing down and questioning our perceptions and reactions can reveal truths and wisdom—an inner wisdom that we all hold, if we learn to listen.

Universal consciousness sends to us specific people and lessons, like a parent with tough love. Because I was trapped for years with a manipulative, narcissistic husband, I was forced to face my own demons and issues. During those years, I was fortunate to have a skilled counselor who supported me in unearthing repressed sexual trauma from more than ten years earlier. That discovery began the healing process of letting go of fear from trauma and beginning anew. Reading and reflecting on how to recover from hidden emotional abuse from more than one narcissist in my life was also necessary for me to let go of fear.

I was moved to practice the Serenity Prayer every day:

God, grant me the Serenity to accept the things I cannot change,
The Courage to change the things I can,
And the Wisdom to know the difference.

CHAPTER 24:

Daily Lucid Meditations

———— •ı• ————

"I feel the air flowing in and out of my nose.
I also feel the movements in my chest and belly as I breathe.
I'm aware of my whole body here in the present moment.
I honor and love myself, just as I am right now."
—JOHN SELBY, FROM *KUNDALINI RISING*

I had mixed emotions. I felt new love for ,David, but seeing Drew again had stirred up my deep fondness for him.

Well, you got what you wanted, I told myself as I prepared for a mountain bike ride in the late afternoon. *You got to see Drew. Just be present, Elisabeth, and be grateful for all of this. You just develop way too deep feelings for everyone you meet and with whom you feel connections.*

As I took my first few pedal strokes up the trails of Crystal Cove State Park, I felt the warm sun on the back of my neck. The night before, I'd read a passage in *Kundalini Rising* that described breathing consciously, and I was trying to do this once an hour, as described by John Selby. *Breathe in and out of the nostrils, feel the chest rise and fall, be thankful for who and where I am.* Another euphoria overtook me. I felt like I was floating again and had a strong tingly vibration running throughout my body. I pondered my proximity to the ocean, the fullness of presence experienced pausing to take in the awe of the scale and power of the unending waves, the sun reflecting off the water, the sounds of the surf. It was no surprise a euphoria happened here, but it was odd it happened on the first few pedal strokes of a bike ride.

Sunset over the Pacific Ocean from Crystal Cove State Park.

The next day, as I finished my run along Oceanside Beach that Frank from the campground, who was from Encinitas, had recommended, I paused to look at the ocean one last time. I saw in the sand, which had dried and hardened from the tide going back out to sea, another spiral, this one drawn by someone who was long gone. I took a few more steps and started to draw my own smaller spiral. A wave washed across my hands as I drew. The tide returned. It was time to leave and head inland to begin my journey back to Colorado. Frank had encouraged me to visit Encinitas, but I didn't have time this trip.

Insights and Ruminations: *I was learning the importance of taking conscious deep breaths to ground, remain present, and improve the quality of my life.*

CHAPTER 25:

Expectations, Devotion,
and Surrender

———•••———

"A person who truly loves you will never let you go,
no matter how hard the situation is."
—ANONYMOUS

I had begun to fall hard for David after a blissful evening together upon my return from California. But David had started to disengage communicating with me when I texted about visiting him in Moab and wanting devotion in a relationship. David shifted from calling me, frequent texting full of emphatic emojiis and attention, to barely responding to texts. When I sensed his distancing, I asked if he were going to be devoted to me. He texted back warning me to watch my expectations and that he preferred freedom.

Then one day, pushing my grocery cart in Montrose, Colorado, around the colorful displays of specialty dried sausages and crackers, I gazed down at my cell phone to review my shopping list, and an email popped up from David. His long, poetic email showered me with praise, but toward the end, I read with shock, "I am pulled in so many directions with my field work and projects at home." The email then went on and on about attachments, expectations, his life changes and transitions, and something to the effect of wanting to fully realize who he was at this stage of life. "This is not a Dear Jane letter. Let's just be friends though. I really want to be with someone who lives around the corner, not three hours away."

Here was another man pushing me back about expectations and evading commitment. It was more than I could take. David used spiritual principles in his correspondence, such as not becoming attached and the impermanence of all things, to evade commitment and devotion.

I took a deep breath. *Why did I have to read this in a public place?* "Ma'am? Ma'am? Can I help you?"

I looked up at a smiling young man behind the deli counter. I looked over both shoulders, as I was quite far away from the deli counter. I shook my head.

He said, "You got this. I know you do. It's going to be okay!"

I tucked my chin in and pushed my cart over to the tea section and started to sob. *Damn empaths. I can't believe how easily he detected that. I had it under control until he had to say something. He meant well, but the timing . . .*

I finished my shopping and sent a furious email to Drew lamenting getting my heart broken again. "You men, do me a favor. Stop using self-realization, attachment, and expectations as an excuse. Until you have figured out what you want, leave me the hell alone!"

I can't believe this is happening again. Well, it's another opportunity to practice stopping my negative thoughts and transmuting negative emotions.

When I arrived home, I threw the groceries into the fridge and then tossed cross-country skis into the back of my vehicle. I ran back into the house to grab a thermos and saw Drew had called, but he hadn't left a message.

That's surprising. He has not been moved to call me in the past after emails. He hasn't called me for months. It doesn't matter. Men suck! I ranted internally as I drove toward Red Mountain Pass. I needed to be in nature to clear my head. As I pulled into the ice- and snow-crusted parking lot, my heart ached, and I felt as if a knife were cutting into the center of it. I reached for my warm mittens, and they were missing.

Darn it! Well I'm going to ski anyway. The sun is setting soon, and I have got to be in nature to handle this pain. I rummaged through the back of the car until I found a thin pair of gloves that I knew would not be enough, but I was determined.

I drew the crisp air in and out of my lungs as I admired the hoar-frost glistening with the last rays of sun. I was using the peace of nature and the present moment to quiet my mind and deal with the pain in my heart. Forty-five minutes later, I was back at the car. My fingers were numb as I loaded my skis into the back. As I blasted the heat in my car, my fingers began to throb with the searing pins-and-needles burning sensation from blood returning to cold tissue. I rocked back and forth, writhing in pain. *The pain in my hands is so extreme it is as if it's pulling the pain away from my heart.*

I glanced at my phone. Drew had sent me a comical but tough love text. "Just called to remind you that if you're feeling pain and resentment that is because you are trying to control events and life with expectations. Try to either accept (in this case), enjoy, or be enthusiastic about everything. What happens and happens next will be better yet, but you will have to let go of what you think you want. David wasn't meant for you (my ego says: that rat bastard, wink). Snow! I miss the snow. But I'm here for a very good reason, even if I don't know yet what it is." He ended with a smiley face emoji.

I called Drew back and left a message with my voice cracking as I fought the tears. "Thanks for the call. I was practicing turning pain into peace in the present moment in the gorgeous mountains and snow here. I hope you are having fun in warm, sunny California." It was nice to know he still cared for me.

A few days later, I met with a local pastor about how to collaborate to help the community. I dropped off a copy of the community health resource guide that my staff maintained, and we discussed ways the county and her congregation could support the health of the community, especially for low-income residents. As I walked out of the church, a large raven was roosting on the large cross, clucking away. My heart was still in pain, but giving back helped soothe my soul.

Surrender. Yes, I know I need to learn how to surrender more. Thanks for the reminder, Jesus.

Insights and Ruminations: *When I reflected on Drew's text later that evening, I felt he didn't understand heartbreak as he had been married to one woman for most of his life. Thus, I doubted he really understood the pain of multiple heartbreaks. My heart was so weary. But as a couple of months passed, I reflected and delusionally hoped that once Drew figured out what he wanted to do next, where he wanted to be, and became settled in the next year, perhaps he would realize how difficult it was to find a compatible partner. In the past, I had experienced men returning with regrets about how they had treated me, months to years later, after meeting other women or being alone for a while. In reality, my ego was playing a trick on me again.*

I later learned David had a history of running the other way whenever a woman treated him well. I had learned of his deep loss in how his marriage ended and sent him healing energy, eventually gifting him a grief recovery handbook to support his heart in healing. My hope was to help him heal so he could accept unconditional love in the future, even if he was not going to accept I from me as his long-term partner. As a friend, David gifted me frequent reminders to have deep gratitude for all the ups and downs of life.

CHAPTER 26:

Sharing the Shift

———•••———

"If you have knowledge, let others
light their candles in it."
—MARGARET FULLER

Sharing Full-Presence Techniques

Deeply focusing as I typed an email at work, I saw my cell phone light up with texts from Cindy, a friend who was visiting me for a few days around New Year's Eve. Cindy and I had met several years prior through triathlons and bonded due to our shared struggles with men.

"I can't stop crying about Steve," she wrote. "I can't get him out of my head and heart."

"Oh, girlfriend. Get outside and on those cross-country skis. Take in some fresh air, feel the crisp cold on your skin, take in the sights of the beautiful fresh snow, and breathe! Try to be fully present and it will all be okay. I'm sorry I can't be with you today. I'll be back at the house tonight, so we can play in the snow together tomorrow. He's not worth all this pain for you, I promise."

Inside, I was furious for her, as Steve had ended their relationship twice, in very unhealthy ways. Cindy had reached out to me months earlier when she noticed on social media that I was struggling. We had been through eerily similar toxic marriages and then had been in similar stages of recovering from heartbreak from subsequent supposedly healthier post-marriage relationships. We had leaned on each other on

153

the phone. It was so great to have her visit so we could continue to help each other heal, in person.

The next evening after walking in the snow at sunrise, with hoarfrost crunching under our feet and glistening in the rising sun, and then venturing on a long cross-country skiing outing together on a frigid afternoon, we curled up across from each other on couches in my living room with steaming cups of hot tea.

"You know," I said, "if the lovemaking was that great, it will take a while to forget him. But when you meet the next man you have great sexual chemistry with, you'll likely be able to let go of Steve in your heart and head in an instant. Trust me."

We both sighed after sharing the anguish of strained communications with men who had broken our hearts. So, a bit of direct humor and reassurance was needed.

"Do you know anything about manifestation?" I asked, shifting the topic.

"What do you mean?" Cindy raised her eyebrows.

"I have to be very careful what I think, as many of my thoughts seems to be coming to fruition rather quickly. I've never experienced it before, and I don't know why it's happening."

Cindy shrugged her shoulder and looked confused, so I changed the subject again.

The next morning, as we drove to town to pick up some groceries, I pulled over as far as I could on the snow-covered dirt road to let a young family who were riding fat bikes over the snow pass in the opposite direction. I recognized Jill, a local woman who leads transformational retreats for women. I waved, rolled down the window, and slowed to stop when she emphatically waved back.

"How are you, Elisabeth?" Jill asked, with a deep level of concern reverberating in her voice.

I suddenly remembered bumping into her on a run along this same dirt road, about eighteen months earlier, when I was in the depths of my depression. "Oh, yeah. I'm better. Thanks for asking. I'm so much better now. In fact, I'm cosmically good!" I waved one hand with fingers pointing to the sky, from my belly upward in a spiral.

"My kundalini rose in 2004 as well. Isn't it like a big orgasm?"

"Umm. Yeh!" I blushed, took a deep breath, and gave a sheepish side glance to Cindy. Cindy is a staunch Catholic, so I had not shared much details on my awakening, as it likely would be shocking and unbelievable to her.

"Some of my girlfriends who have experienced a K-rising, are now experiencing manifestation," Jill said with a joyous smile.

"What are you two talking about?" Cindy asked.

"I need to learn more about manifestation," I said to Jill. "I'd love to chat with some of those women, if they would be willing. My experiences have been so wild that I'm writing a book about it."

"Do you have an editor or publisher yet?" Jill asked.

"Not yet, I'm still writing."

"I have a best-selling book that a wonderful editor helped me with. I'm happy to share her contact info if you like."

"Sure, what's her name?"

"Jane Ashley."

"From Flower of Life Press? That's such a coincidence. I was just looking at her webpage a few days ago."

Sharing the Power of Meditation

Cindy's car battery died, and I could not access the front of the car to jump it with my car due to the depth of the snow on the driveway. I walked to a neighbor's house to ask for assistance. My neighbor Angus was a successful, mostly retired attorney who had moved to the area three years earlier.

"Sure. I can help a damsel in distress. I happen to have a battery that's meant to charge another dead battery. When do you want to get it jumped?"

"No rush, we are enjoying a mellow morning."

"What are your plans in the next couple of weeks?"

"I'm headed to Boulder soon to be trained and initiated into Neelakantha transcendental meditation with a custom mantra."

"My sister has been meditating for years using Joe Dispenza's techniques. She describes these sensations of love that seem to wrap around her. She keeps encouraging me to meditate."

"You should! What's holding you back?

"I don't need it."

"Everyone should meditate. You told me once how you almost got into a fistfight in a bar because of a brief misunderstanding with a fellow patron."

"The people who meditate are the ones who need it. I don't," he said. "And my sister thinks she receives messages from God." He rolled his eyes.

I fell silent and looked at the snow-covered ground.

"What?" Angus asked.

"I don't hear voices, but I do seem to get messages. And my first complete day of wakeful meditation through being on the knife's edge of being fully present created ecstasy for me the next morning."

"What do you mean?"

"It was better than sex."

A large vibration rolled through Angus's spine from his pelvis up to the top of his head. I grinned and walked away as he seemed frozen in the snow.

Insights and Ruminations: *While I don't know if being fully present for a day is why I experienced ecstasy, it was enough to convince Angus. He started dabbling in meditation the next day.*

CHAPTER 27:

Closing a Chapter

—•◦•—

"The sole meaning of life is to serve humanity."
—LEO TOLSTOY

After repeated forays to find my true path, each time I returned to work, I struggled with when to give notice. One midwinter morning, as dawn awakened the sleepy little hamlet of Ouray, I sat down to meditate, running my hands down my mala: *My intention today is to be guided on how to exit this job with grace and lasting impact.* I was worried that much of the work my team and I had done over the past few years might unravel if I didn't tie up loose ends on some grants that built our health department up to better serve the community.

Later at the office, I was transitioning to ensure the staff knew their duties thoroughly before my departure, without telling them I was planning on quitting in the months ahead. As sunlight passed between the blinds onto the pages of the binder in my hands, I flipped through the pages and sighed.

"Anything I can help you with?" Allison looked up from her desk.

"No, that's okay. I just can't find the test kit usage reporting form we are supposed to fax every month to the hospital that gives us the HIV test kits for free. If we don't report that monthly, we won't get free HIV test kits in the future. I made that mistake a few years ago and had to reestablish that relationship."

As I closed the binder I thought, *I hope we have someone come in for STD testing very soon. Allison really needs to practice with a patient while I'm still here. She's only shadowed me once.*

I went for a short walk to the post office and then grabbed lunch to go. As I walked back into the lobby of our office building, a young man walked out into the lobby with Allison. They both looked a bit flustered.

"Thanks for coming in. I'll be in touch," Allison said to the young man as he walked out.

As soon as the front door closed behind him, Allison swung both hands forward from her hips outward with a big exhale, "Ack, you weren't here, and you didn't have your cell phone with you."

"I'm sorry. How did it go?"

"He just wanted to be screened for a couple of diseases, so that's all I did."

"Did you use that questionnaire to assess what else we would recommend he be screened for?"

Allison's face turned red, "Um, which questionnaire?"

"Which box did you give him condoms from? The box to the left of your desk I've been meaning to throw out as they are expired."

"I think I did give him some from that box." Allison's eyes grew wide.

"It's okay. That's my fault on the condoms. We can give him a call. Let's go into your office and go through the forms and educational materials. This is great. You needed practice anyway, right?"

I smiled deeply.

Self-Value

"I think there is a way to get you a raise," my supervisor Cathy said at my next evaluation. "We are going to partner with a neighboring county so that you can direct both health departments."

And with that, she ended the meeting.

My mind was reeling as I drove home. *I wanted some additional income to prepare me for the long break I'm creating for myself. But I can't take more on my plate. I can't share that I'm taking a course to shift my career. And I'm on a spiritual path journey, too. If I take that extra duty on, it will not serve either community if I am leaving soon.*

The next morning, I consulted with my predecessor Cheryl and prepared a letter for my boss explaining how I felt it would be a disservice to the communities in both counties to have one director for both health departments.

A few days later, Cathy called. "Okay, I read your letter. You don't have to worry so much, Elisabeth. That's great you want to help in the interim until the other county can hire someone else. They came to me. They wanted you to reshape their health department. Seems you've made an impression on surrounding communities."

"Thanks for making me feel valued. It really means a lot."

"Of course, you are valued." And the negotiations for additional pay began as I continued in my current role and took on being the interim director for the other county health department, on a minimal level to ensure grants were not lost and for responses to urgent issues.

I swallowed hard. Those words of recognition were so healing to my heart, after losing most of my personal life due to working so hard for the past several years.

Mental Health Matters

My resistance to giving up my role as the health department leader was due to my dedication to leading a three-year federal grant in a six-county region. My staff and public health colleagues were working on mental health and substance abuse prevention in our region through that federal grant and a state marijuana tax-funded grant to reduce substance abuse among youth. Our efforts surrounded reducing stigma around mental illness, such as Mental Health First Aid training for the public and first responders and integration of mental health services within doctors' offices. In Ouray County, we had implemented an employee assistance program as part of worksite wellness. With Annie, I was pushing for mindfulness or quieting the mind in schools. Many colleagues in our region were working on increasing access to mental health and substance abuse treatment resources in rural areas. Now, I had such deep empathy for those facing depression and anxiety that I redoubled my efforts. And I understood on a deeper level how substance abuse is self-medication, as it was tempting to use alcohol to quiet my mind to fall asleep. Because my depression was so incredibly painful, I was doing what I could to help others. In an attempt to make my efforts last, I requested a meeting to discuss mental health training and services for first responders, as well as policy and procedures in hopes such changes would remain after my possible departure. My boss agreed to give me the opportunity to discuss this with the commissioners and scheduled the meeting.

The three commissioners and other county leaders were gathered midmorning as local law enforcement and emergency medical service leaders filed in.

"Thanks for coming, Dustin and Heather." I smiled with deep appreciation.

"Okay, Elisabeth, you have the floor."

"Dustin and Heather and other first responders in our county are being tapped out in response to the mental health and substance abuse calls in our area," I said. "I recommend the county implement a policy to require all county staff take Mental Health First Aid and all first responders take Mental Health First Aid for Public Safety. There's a grant to pay for mental health professionals to ride along or meet first responders at the scene if they feel it's a mental health crisis that may go beyond their abilities. Okay, I'll shut up for a bit and sit behind Dustin and Heather so they can speak for themselves."

Dustin leaned forward, "Mental health and substance abuse calls are the majority of what our officers respond to. My staff are already trained in Mental Health First Aid, but we do have turnover and will need refreshers. And that state grant. I think it's so important that if the county can't take it on, maybe the city could apply, and we could work through an intergovernmental agreement to make it happen for all our agencies in the county."

"Heather," I prodded. "What do you think?"

"Well, I don't know about requiring all county staff to take the more basic training, but it makes sense for my emergency medical staff. I think we should make it a policy for my staff."

One of the commissioners chimed in, "We just attended a meeting for commissioners statewide, and this topic was pervasive. It's very unsettling—the mental illnesses on the rise, mass shootings, the opiate crisis. And the stigma associated with mental illness. We need to work on that more."

"I really would like to see more preventative work, as our partners are trying in our schools and at the youth center," I offered, taking advantage of the figurative door that was being pushed open by the commissioners. "And Crisis Intervention Training for some of the first responders is needed, too, but that's so expensive and intensive. Maybe there is a way we can bring that here one day."

A commissioner named Dan cleared his throat and said, "Elisabeth. I have a request. I'd like for you to create a behavioral health action plan for the county, city, and town. Something that we can implement long term."

I swallowed hard. "Yes, sir, I'll try. I have an idea on something our regional partners created that I can adapt and customize," I said, my voice trembling a bit. "Thanks, Dan."

"I have full confidence in you that you can create something meaningful for us."

I shook their hands. As I walked out into the fresh air and gazed at Mount Sneffels, I reflected, *Wow! My prayers were answered. Now I have more work to do, but this is so cool—long-lasting impact. I hope it's not a sheet of paper or electronic file that just collects dust after I leave.*

Insights and Ruminations: *Manifestation happens most quickly when striving to help others or the earth and when conducting oneself from a place of no ego during collaboration with others.*

CHAPTER 28:

Self-Realization

"The ultimate aim is Self-realization, the realization of man's true Self, the soul, as made in the image of God, one with the ever-existing, ever-conscious, ever-new bliss of Spirit." †
—PARAMAHANSA YOGANANDA

Oh boy, what's this all about? I worried, shifting in my chair.
"We want to talk to you about your vacation request. Do you realize that if you take this vacation you will have no vacation time left?" Cathy said as she closed the conference room door.
"Why yes, I do."
"Do you still like working here?"
I looked down, not sure what to say. Cathy pulled out a chart of my leave time accrued and taken over the past year.
"You have so much sick time accrued."

I was silent for about almost a minute, looking down at the conference room table, feeling trapped and embarrassed. "I was depressed. I almost quit a couple of times. Do you remember that day when you called me and chewed me out?"

"Well, you had quite the outburst," Cathy's tone grew angry.

Samantha leaned back, folded her arms, raised her eyebrows, and listened intently to Cathy.

"I wasn't criticizing you," I said. "I was just trying to get out of the room. I was anxious that day as I had so much to get done and deadlines looming. Anxiety can result from unresolved depression. I was really struggling to function at work but was doing my best. I'm okay now." Tears rolled down my cheeks as I stared at the table.

"I had no idea," said Cathy. "Why didn't you say anything?"

I couldn't speak but was taking deep breaths.

"Well, I guess if it's this hard for you to tell me now, it would have been much more difficult at the time," Cathy said.

"Yes, it's incredibly painful and difficult to explain when you are in the midst of it."

"Well, perhaps you should take sick leave for this trip."

I was very moved by this unexpected, healing gesture. After I returned to the office, I scheduled a three-week trip to drive to Baja in my van.

Baja Bound in January

As Sam and I rounded another curve along Highway 1 and took in the views of the Pacific, he asked to stop near Torrey Pines.

"Sure, no problem. Does this look good?" I asked as I slowed on the next bend.

"Yeah, I'd like to take a photo of the bluff. There are usually paragliders hovering over the ocean due to the strong updrafts along the bluff." Sam jumped back in the passenger seat and then handed me a necklace. "Here, a friend of mine made this. I want you to have this."

A lump formed in my throat. "It's a raven necklace."

"It's a chakra balancing necklace a friend of mine made. With your experiences, I think it's fitting."

I had asked Sam if he wanted to go to Baja with me, as most of my girlfriends had warned me it was too dangerous to travel alone as a woman in Mexico in a van. Sam had experienced so many recent losses. His father and a close family friend had died in rapid succession, and he had lost a job that he enjoyed despite the difficulties of interacting with challenging coworkers. I knew he was likely free, so I thought such a trip would be perfect for him. I was drawn to him as he was another Buddhist cyclist, and he had taught Eastern religion in colleges. I thought perhaps I could learn from him to help put my experiences into context. We had talked about Mooji, Ramana Maharshi, and a few spiritual topics on the initial drive from Colorado, but he told me he was not qualified to interpret my experiences. As I sat in the idling van, I looked over the ocean expanse and promised I would gaze more along our journey through Southern California.

As we proceeded around another curve in the road in Encinitas, I did a double take. "Self-Realization Fellowship Center, what's that?" I asked Sam.

Sam's face lit up with intense joy. "Oh, Yogananda. Elisabeth, you need to read up on him!"

The sign caught my attention, only because I had written a scathing email to Drew a couple of months ago, after David had written me a Dear Jane letter. I had ranted in my email: "Do me a favor. If you are going to use self-realization as an excuse to avoid commitment with me, leave me the hell alone until you figure out what you want!" Thus, I chuckled inside when I saw the sign for the center.

The next morning, I awoke in the van and noticed heavy dew drops on the ceiling, more on Sam's side. I pulled my ear plugs out and glanced in Sam's direction. He turned out to be a snorer, even though he had denied he was earlier in the trip. He was propped up and was drenched in tears.

"Are you okay? What's wrong? Did you sleep?"

"No. I've been crying all night long. I think I may need to sit in once place and cry for twelve days. I don't think I can go. You should unload me. I'll just be a burden."

"Let's get you some fresh air," I said. "Maybe we can find a place to park the van with the door wide open, overlooking the ocean."

"Let's get something at Starbucks," he said. "My treat."

We drove in silence to the nearest Starbucks in southern San Diego. I was overwhelmed with concern for him. After we ordered, we stepped outside onto the patio that faced a cement parking lot. Everything was coated in heavy dew.

"Want to sit here?" Sam said as he wrinkled his forehead.

"Come on, let's head to Torrey Pines."

We drove in silence again.

As we pulled up to the parking lot overlooking the bluff and ocean, we noticed a few homeless people in the lot. I opened the door to the sun and ocean, feeling relieved to be present in some nature again. Sam walked along the bluff and called family and friends.

"Where you two headed?" asked a handsome homeless man, as he tended to a small pot of boiling water on a table behind his car.

"Baja. But I think it's just going to be just me."

"Oh, Baja is wild. It's not a trip to Baja unless you think you are going to die at least once. The roads are not like here. The curves and lack of shoulders will keep you on your toes." He proceeded to tell me stories about his car being taken from him at a military checkpoint, and how he escaped and ran to an airplane on a nearby landing strip, just before it took off, to escape the corrupt military. He threw his hands wildly in the air as he recalled his experiences of Baja.

As Sam approached the van, he appeared calm. "A dear friend of the family lives in La Jolla. I can stay with Janice and then fly back in a few days."

"Okay, if that's what you need. When can we head there?"

As we drove to Janice's, I told Sam of the tales the homeless man had shared, with worry rising in my voice.

"Well, you don't know the full story. Who knows what really happened? I'm sure you will be fine. And I want to give you something I made. Here." Sam handed me the necklace he had been wearing, a spiral he had carved out of bone.

"No, I can't accept it."

"I insist. You and spirals."

I was speechless for a moment. "Well, it is perfect. Perhaps I can have it woven into my mala as the guru bead. Thanks so much."

That evening after dropping Sam off, I sat studying the map of Baja. All the voices of my girlfriends kept repeating in my head. "It's not safe. Please don't go alone."

I texted Sam, "I'm losing my nerve to cross the border in the morning."

"Janice says she would not be comfortable if her daughter was doing what you plan. Go with your gut."

My fingers ran across the gear shifter of my van, and then down to the mala of rudraksha seeds.

As I passed each bead between my trembling fingers, I repeated the Ganesh mantra over and over again, as I tried to overcome fear. *"Aum Gam Ganapataye Namaha. Aum Gam Ganapataye Namaha. Aum Gam Ganapataye Namaha!"*

Maybe I'll just hang out in Southern California again, camp, cycle and see some friends, I thought. *No, I can do this. I've come this far. It was so hard to get three weeks off from work. I'll be so disappointed in myself if I don't go.* I cleared the lump in my throat, took a deep breath, clicked on a Mooji satsang on Spotify on my stereo, started up the van again, and headed back south.

Insights and Ruminations: I had been an advocate for increasing access to mental health services and reducing stigma through my work in public health for three years, but I am not trained in mental health counseling. I tried using a bit of Mental Health First Aid skills that I had learned at a one-day training to assist Sam, but it wasn't enough. He needed time to grieve. I felt I was also meant to experience Sam's grief as a reminder of how painful and frequent loss is in all our lives. Sam quickly figured out that spending time with a family friend who had known him since he was a child was exactly what he needed.

The universe lined up for me to be alone on most of this trip. The exploration provided the opportunity for "secluded isolation for subconscious emptying of my karmic bag," which assists with some dissolution of the ego, as Dr. Shivarpita Harrigan stated during a Buddha at the Gas Pump interview.

According to Paramahansa Yogananda, "Seclusion is the price of greatness." є

I had dozens of books with me to read through, as I was on a search of why the kundalini rising started for me.

CHAPTER 29:

Journey of Recognition

—•◦•—

"In all spiritual teachings, quieting the mind and self-inquiry are required for inner transformation. Radical transformation is possible in freedom from one's conditioned self. Yoga is the process of becoming aware and breaking the bond with suffering."
—RAVI RAVINDRA

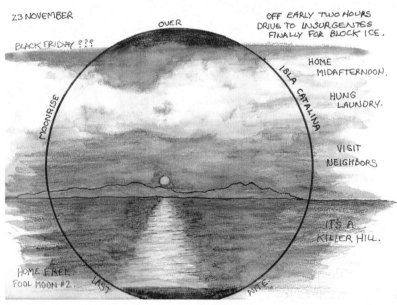

Moonrise over Isla Catalina, Baja;
by "Milt" Miltenberger, wandering artist in Baja

*"Snowflake" takes me to an immensely peaceful
and safe site of solitude in Baja.*

Overcoming Fear and Slowing Down

When I first set eyes the Sea of Cortez and the outskirts of San Felipe in Mexico, the many voices of others were still rattling in my head. A friend at work had told me, "You better try to make it a few hours south of Tijuana or San Felipe if you are going to disperse camp safely in Baja. And whatever you do, don't drive after dark." After consulting with a kind, friendly Mexican American man in a grocery store in San Diego on the morning of my departure, I decided to drive east to cross the border at Mexicali instead of Tijuana. He had told me the law enforcement officials around Tijuana were corrupt. This added distance delayed my arrival at the shores of the Sea of Cortez. As I wound south past San Felipe, the road was less maintained and unpredictable. Two hurricanes and lack of repairs had damaged the roads, making this route more hazardous than roads in the United States.

I gripped the steering wheel firmly as I became nervous about the waning hours of daylight and not making it as far south as had been recommended. I finally hit a stretch of smooth highway a couple hours south of San Felipe. *Yay! I can finally drive at a decent pace to arrive in the safer part of Baja before dark.* As I sped around the next corner, I made out a couple of small pylons. *What's that? Should I go around those two small cones? Oh, my God, the bridge is out!*

As I slammed on the brakes, I saw a rudimentary dirt route open to the right of the cones. With too much speed to stop before the broken-up pavement and now-absent bridge, I cranked Snowflake's steering wheel to the right. The van groaned as I hit the rough dirt too fast for her two-wheeled drive train. *Oh, for heaven's sake. Is this the road?*

I plunged down the road on a steep hill into the ravine, glancing up to see the remnants of the bridge dangling from above. *Well, this is what the bridge was built to go over. Whew, that was a close call!* I steadied Snowflake into a more manageable speed for the rough dirt road. Bridge after bridge was out, providing the same lessons of the necessity of slowing down even when the pavement between bridges was smooth.

Dusk arrived, and my palms began to sweat on the steering wheel. I was not finding a place to camp due to steep, rocky terrain on the sides of the road that Snowflake could not safely navigate. *Please, God. Help me find a safe place to camp that Snowflake can handle.* I took a

few deep breaths, and around the next bend, I spotted a smooth double track on the east side of the road. I slowed Snowflake just in time to make the turn onto the faint route. The double track remained smooth, heading directly to the ocean, with the tallest lupine flowers I had ever seen slapping the underside and sides of the van.

Oh, this is gorgeous. The view across a bay dotted with multiple islands opened up. A half mile later, the double track ended a couple hundred yards from the ocean at a level, secluded campsite, out of sight of the main road. *Thank you. This is perfect.* As the sun set, I rolled out my mat to meditate in gratitude in the quietest spot I had ever experienced in my life. I remained at the site for three days in blissful silence.

Guides Along the Journey

I looked at the intersection and then at the map, repeatedly, scratching my head. I couldn't see the intersection before me on the map, and I didn't know which way to go. I looked across the lower Sonoran Desert. *My sense of direction is telling me, turn right.*

As I crested the saguaro cactus-covered hill, the road became steep and rougher. Without any fixed cabinetry in my partially converted cargo van, items started to fly and crash down.

Argh. Snowflake is not four-wheel drive. "This is getting ridiculous," I muttered and stopped to pick up the strewn bananas and avocados off the floor.

I descended further down the road and was relieved to see a smoother road below me. I came to a T-intersection, studied the map again, and scratched my head. *I don't get it. There is no intersection like this on the map in this area.* I turned left at the intersection, but as I drove, I became confused about which way to go. Just as I was about to turn around, I spotted a Toyota pickup with a slide-in, pop-up camper pulled over. I slowed, rolled the window down, and pulled to the side. A white-goateed gringo turned and grinned as I blurted out, "I think I'm lost."

"Where are you headed?" He smiled. "Do you have a map?"

"Yes, but it didn't help much back there."

"Well, let's take a look together. Want a beer?"

His name was Park. As we spread the map on the hood of his Toyota, he questioned me on where I had come from and where I was headed.

"Oh, you were on the new shortcut," he said. "Wow, that must have been fun in that van. It's a new road and not really done yet. Well, you saved some miles!" He chuckled as his finger ran across the map where there was no line indicating a road.

I sighed with a mixture of relief that I wasn't an idiot on reading maps and that I had found a kind soul who happened to be a seasoned visitor of Baja.

"I've been exploring Baja for the past seventeen years every winter. It's a bit unsettling the first time in Baja. But you'll get used to it. Isn't the remoteness and solitude worth it?"

We joked about how many bridges were out along the route paralleling the Sea of Cortez and the alarming reduction in speed necessary to abruptly turn off from a smooth paved road onto rough dirt detours up and down ravines to keep from flying off the edge of washed-out bridges.

"The hurricane two years ago did most of the damage. The most recent hurricane didn't exactly help. It'll be many years before those bridges are repaired. But let me show you some great spots to visit while you head south."

Hidden Treasures

"I can fill up your van if you like," said a dark, heavy-set man as he extended his hand to the open window of my van. "I'm Jack. What's your name?"

"Elisabeth. Nice to meet you. I just filled up. I'm just panicked because at the last gas station, well, I was distracted when the man started to pump the gas by a lady trying to sell me jewelry. I'm worried he put diesel in when I wasn't looking, and I couldn't find the gas station again. I know that's unlikely, but I worried anyway. Mulege is confusing with all those one-way streets and no street signs."

"Umm. Elisabeth. They don't sell diesel at that gas station in Mulege," he said, his eyes rolling a bit.

"Oh, my goodness. Thanks for calming my nerves. Sorry."

"No worries. Where are you headed?"

"Playa Escondido. A nice man told me to check it out."

"Oh, that's easy to miss for sure. The turnoff is not well signed. Most people fly past it." Jack continued to explain to me what landmarks to keep an eye out for.

Just as Jack had described, the turnoff was easy to miss. I couldn't slow Snowflake down in time, but I recognized the landmarks Jack described, made a U-turn, and turned down the bumpy double track across a hill. When I arrived, there was one spot next to a tan man my age.

"Hello," I said. "Mind if I park on the other side of this hut?"

"Of course. That's fine. Help yourself."

"I'm Elisabeth. What's your name?"

"Rich."

I smiled as I noticed Rich was wearing a tie-dye tank top with a colorful spiral on the back.

"Nice to meet you Rich. How did you find Escondido Beach?"

"I've been coming here for decades and explored all up and down Baja. This is my favorite spot."

As I settled into the beach scene, I met several cordial travelers, many from British Columbia, Canada. I reflected on how I had never seen bioluminescence. *One day*, I thought.

That evening, as the fellow van campers gathered around the campfire near my van, I overheard conversations on favorite experiences in the area.

"Do you remember that night on the beach a few miles south of here? That was the best bioluminescence I've ever seen!"

I had wanted to mellow out in my van alone, but upon hearing that comment, I approached the campfire. "Excuse me, but I couldn't help but overhear about bioluminescence. How frequently do you see that?"

"Oh, you can probably see it tonight, if you paddle out. It's not uncommon," Richard replied.

I had taken a lukewarm solar shower and was finally warm and dry as the coolness of the January evening set in. The idea of getting wet and salty again just before bedtime was not appealing.

"Elisabeth, would you mind if I borrowed your SUP tonight?" Rich asked.

"Of course not. Help yourself. Do you mind me asking why you don't go out in your kayak?"

"I can't sit for long right now. My sciatica is flaring up."

"Well, would you mind if I take your kayak out tonight?"

"Sure, that's fine. Let's head out together if you want. Full moon is rising again."

As we paddled out, we coached each other on borrowed watercraft.

"Okay, that's enough for me. I'm feeling really unstable as it's my first time out on an SUP."

"I understand. May I paddle out further and spend some more time in your kayak?"

"Sure."

As we parted ways, I paddled out into the silence of the bay alone and hit a bright patch of bioluminescence, with each paddle stroke getting brighter. Tingles went up my spine. *Why does this keep happening?* I thought in awe.

Drifting along the water, gazing at the moon reflecting off the top of the smooth water, I took a couple of deep, conscious breaths.

"Pooooooch . . . pooooooch . . . "

What the hell is that? I thought as I gripped the kayak paddle firmly. I heard the water-spout-like noise approaching me. I looked up and saw the backs of three dolphins as they buoyed out of the water to exhale and inhale.

The night was so bright and so quiet that I could hear their air hole breaths echoing off the desert rock cliffs surrounding the bay. Goosebumps rippled across my skin.

The next morning, I rose before dawn to meditate. I followed a local's recommendation for a beautiful place to watch the sunrise at the top of a tall butte that partially framed the cover of the beach. I clambered up the loose, steep, rocky trail to the top of the butte, my headlight guiding me in the predawn darkness. Suddenly my headlight revealed a grotto with a painting of Mother Mary on the rock, surrounded by spirals, angels made of seashells, and a rusted metal cross with a heart in the center, dangling in the breeze. Spirals seemed to be guiding me on my path of transformation. Each meditation seemed to help me heal and ground me more.

Later as the day heated up on the beach, I opened my orange-and-white cooler in my van, and the stench of rotting gray water pushed my head back.

Darn, I thought. *I have got to dump this. Too bad I can't get some cleaner water in this cooler to just have some fluids to rinse the sand from my feet. It wouldn't have to be potable water.*

Thirty seconds later, a large, heavyset man asked as he walked past my van, "Anyone need any clean water? It's not potable, and I want to fill this tank with potable water."

I raised my hand. "Um, wow. What timing. I'd gladly put that in my tank. What's your name?"

"Larry." He quickly poured the water into my cooler.

"Funny, that's the name of a fabulous man I fell hard for years ago. . . who married someone else. I wasn't spiritual enough for him, and that was a deal breaker for him."

"Darn, too bad it wasn't me." He smiled as I blushed.

On my last morning lying in my van in Baja, I read a few pages from *7,000 Ways to Listen* by Mark Nepo. I had purchased the book at the Eckhart Tolle conference—Drew's words that I was not a good listener kept ringing in my ears. I had learned that to be a successful health coach, I had to listen more, with a goal of 80 percent of coaching sessions just listening and not talking—growth that I definitely needed.

The last sentence I happened to read was, "On your journey home, look for signs of what's to come." I closed the book, blushed, and shook my head. *I've already made my manifestation list in different areas of my life and meditated on the lists. I don't want to think or contemplate the future for a while. I'm going to remain in the present moment, as that's how all this started. I'll just trust the universe that what my spirit needs to evolve will happen. So, what I am putting out there to manifest will happen when it's time, even if it might not look like what I envision. It will be what I need.*

Insights and Ruminations: *The trip to Baja alone taught me to overcome fear of the unknown while on my own. The locals were so kind and tolerant, which flew in the face of all the stern warnings I had received from fellow Americans back home*

about safety in a foreign land. Deep reflections only gained from being alone and without the distractions of a blue screen and the internet were necessary for me to understand my sometimes-frightening experiences of the previous several months. This trip gave me the courage to overcome the fear of striking out on my own in my career and away from a secure life.

Return to California

"Hi, Allie. I am crossing the border back into California soon. Can we meet tomorrow at the bookstore?"

As promised, I was reaching out to a former employee from Colorado who had moved back to San Diego. She had mentioned that, because of what I was experiencing, we should meet at a bookstore in San Diego to look for books that might help me on my path. But I received no response from her that evening.

As I approached the border, Drew texted me, asking when I was going to be in San Diego.

So weird. I thought he had ghosted me for good again. I stopped any reaching out a while ago, I thought as I texted a response back. In addition to creating my manifestation lists for my next chapter, I set intentions of meditation on healing my past. I meditated twice a day in Baja, several times with the intention of letting go of pain and trauma from all men in my past to break the bond of suffering.

We made arrangements to meet, but Drew was too sick from a stomach bug to do more than sit in my van at a local grocery store. His demeanor had changed. He beamed with sweetness as he walked up to my van, and he was kind and gentle. He seemed very excited to see me despite how he felt physically. We chatted about adventures in van lifestyle and a bit about my experiences in Baja. Drew quickly said good-bye. We hugged briefly, and he disappeared to go rest.

As I finished cleaning up from lunch in the van after Drew left, I pondered: *Well, the bookstore Allie mentioned is almost around the corner. I'll reach out again.*

Allie finally texted back, "My relationship of five years just ended last night. And my birthday was yesterday. I'm going to go for a walk by myself at the zoo. I'm too crushed to talk or meet. Sorry."

"I'm so sorry Allie. If you need to talk later or change your mind about meeting after your walk, let me know," I texted back. *Okay, I'll go pick up Sam's belongings and prepare to hit the road later today or tomorrow morning at the latest.*

I dialed Sam's friend Janice in La Jolla.

"I'm sorry, Elisabeth. I just received bad news from my doctor three minutes ago. I'm not home right now and can't talk to or see anyone. I'm on the way to the library to see what I can find to give me some help."

"Oh my, Janice. Take your time. Call me whenever you're ready. I don't have to leave until tomorrow morning. Whatever bad news you received, I'm so sorry. I'll pray everything is going to be okay."

I sat in silence trying to decide what to do next. I cranked Snowflake's ignition and drove to the bookstore near the university, where Allie had originally suggested we meet. As I browsed through the mystical section, whenever I had a question in my head, I would pull a book off the shelf and flip open a chapter. The answer seemed to be there waiting for me.

The only book that spoke to me for purchase was *The Mastery of Love* by Don Miguel Ruiz. As I approached the cash register, I paused at the tarot card reader sign. The psychic's name was Lizbeth.

"Is Lizbeth seeing anyone right now?" I nervously asked.

"She is usually booked solid, but she's available right now. How long would you like to see her?"

"What is the minimum?"

"Fifteen minutes for $35."

As I sat down in front of Lizbeth, she gave me a reassuring smile.

"Have you ever been to a psychic?"

"Just one palm reader in Arizona, and she was not very accurate about my current life. She didn't provide much about the future. This is my first time to a tarot card reader."

"Oh, good. I love popping the cherry."

I blushed and started to panic inside a bit.

"Your father . . . " Lizbeth shook her head.

"Umm, yes. What do you mean?"

"He is fu**ed up honey, and he knows it!"

I started to cry. "He just sent me a printed two-page letter criticizing my entire life and glorifying his role in it. And I received that letter just two days after the last man in my life wrote a Dear Jane email to me. My blood pressure went through the roof that day and hasn't come back down."

"He knows you are the light of the family. Look at me, honey. Look in my eyes. Send him some healing energy. Are you the black sheep of the family?"

"Yes. They are all Catholic, and I feel judged by them that I don't practice Catholicism anymore."

"Is your father a surgeon?"

"How did you know?"

"Honey? I'm a psychic." Lizbeth unfurled her fingers with long black fingernails as she extended her arms to the side.

"The thing is—my dad tries to control everything out of fear. He was ninety-five pounds at six foot when he was a teenager during World War II. Many of his friends died of starvation. He experienced moral trauma during his adolescence. So, I'm trying to not take it personally."

Fifteen minutes flew by, and I asked if I could have more time.

Lizbeth slipped out and then back in. "And what's the real reason you are here?"

"I'm so confused by men. My heart keeps getting broken. And the man I just saw. He has been so sweet, then so cruel, and he was just now so sweet again."

"Pick a card."

I did, then Lizbeth picked a card.

"Yep, he is the one. You are a perfect match. You picked Queen of Raphael. I picked King of Raphael for him."

Shocked, I gave her a look of bewilderment and confusion.

"Oh honey. Just let go and let God! You need to read Louise Hay's book *You Can Heal Your Life*. And you really should get charted." She paused, took a breath, pierced deep into my eyes and asked, "Have you found your teacher?"

"I learned a certain technique of meditation from a woman in Colorado, but every time I try to ask a question on the group support calls, I'm muted. And whenever I try to connect to speak or meet with her, it doesn't work out."

"Well, she must not be your teacher then. You know that. Your teacher has not yet appeared."

I walked back to Snowflake, bewildered. *Hmmm. I don't know if that was such a good idea. But she's right on letting go of what doesn't serve me. Each time I do, something wonderful happens, including euphoria or bliss.*

I texted Janice. She replied she was ready. I reached out to Sam.

"What does she like? She just got bad news, and I'm about to go to her place."

"Sushi."

"How about flowers?"

"Sure, everyone likes flowers."

I ran to the store and picked up the gifts.

"Just open the garage, I'll load up and be on my way," I texted Janice to try to not invade her privacy.

"Tell me about your trip," Janice said as I opened the back doors of the van.

"It was amazing. Just what I needed to clear my head and heal. I have something for you."

"I can't accept that."

"Janice, I don't eat raw sushi, it's for you. And that vase will just spill all over the place in my van. Please?"

"But I wanted to host you, and I feel bad."

"Don't feel bad. I understand. It sounds like you are scared. May I come in and use the bathroom when I'm done, though?"

"Of course."

When I entered, an outpouring of her diagnosis of breast cancer came forth.

"My mother was diagnosed with the same at your age," I said. "My father is a brilliant physician and did all the research to reassure us that she was going to have to go through some treatment, but that she was going to survive. And she is alive and vibrant today. I'm sure it's scary as hell, but you are likely going to meet some lovely souls while going through treatment."

We talked about death.

"I know we are more than this flesh. And I think bliss is what's next when we pass." I shared some of my experiences with her. We hugged goodnight. As I reclined in my van in her neighborhood, I realized I was meant to be with Janice that evening.

The next morning, I entered Janice's home one more time to use her bathroom before hitting the road. Janice was cooking, and the flowers were in the center of a nicely set table.

"Time to hit the road for me," I said.

"You are not leaving until I cook you breakfast, and we eat together."

I agreed to enjoy my time in the company of a lovely older soul, and we settled into a leisurely morning together.

"You should go where I took Sam when he was staying with me. It's a meditation place. I don't meditate but I walked the grounds while he was inside. Just lovely."

"What was the name of the place?"

"The name is escaping me at the moment."

I texted Sam, "What's the name of the place Janice took you before you flew back to Colorado?"

"Self-Realization Fellowship Center. Lovely place to sit."

I smiled deeply and looked up to Janice across our shared breakfast.

"I'm running out of time and want to squeeze in a bike ride before the long drive. Drew is texting me a suggestion of where I should ride. Maybe next time."

I gave her one last hug and hit the road.

CHAPTER 30:

Signs

"The universe is always speaking to us . . . "
— NANCY THAYER

The gas gauge needle slipped lower and lower. It was time to get gas before the next large stretch of Utah road with sparse exits and few gas stations on my way home to Colorado. I noticed the beehive symbol base for the Utah highway signs for the first time. *That's funny. A beehive symbolizes universal consciousness to me after Eckhart's profound statements at the conference a couple of months ago. I'm just one of many bees who will bring back the nectar of my experiences to the hive. Ooooh, I wish I had time to check out Great Basin National Park right off this exit.*

Great Basin, that's what I felt I was at the bottom of, when I was depressed. Thank God I'm out of the depths of the basin of hell I created for myself in my head. I checked my gas price app as I pulled to the stop sign at the top of the exit ramp and turned right in the direction of the gas station in Beaver, Utah. I blinked as I pulled up. Spirit Gas Station, with an eagle symbol. As I pumped the gas, I glanced over at another brown recreational sign indicating "Paiute Side Trail." I took a deep breath. *That's the name of the mountain on which Tara slipped to her death. I've heard you repeatedly, my dear. I know, everything is going to be okay. Everything is okay. Thanks.*

As I walked into the gas station, I paused and smiled at the fun photo of three people of varying skin colors hugging each other. I felt the image represented being fully present and that we are all one . . . all in one image. In the restroom, sparkling mirrors in the shape of lotuses decorated the wall. I swallowed and then laughed. One of the manifestation lists I had made in Baja was to continue the journey of discovery in spirituality with the goal of finding more deep peace while trying to lead a normal yet simpler life. The lotus symbol of enlightenment was now before my eyes. The hair on my arms stood up, and I felt a tingling up my spine. I thought of the movie *Bruce Almighty* when the protagonist yelled to God for a sign, and then a construction truck passed, positively loaded with signs. Bruce Almighty wasn't aware of the signs directing him to correct actions. But I was now fully listening to everything in my life, including literal signs on my journey. I sensed God was planting signs for me as well.

While in Baja, I frequently saw huge five-pointed stars. I didn't know their significance at the time, but the spiritual meaning would be revealed later.

CHAPTER 31:

Ineffable Peace and Love

———— •·• ————

*"My life is but a weavin
Between my God and me.
I cannot choose the colors
He weaveth steadily."*
—Grant Colfax Tullar, Excerpt from
"The Weaver" (aka Tapestry Poem)

Self-Love

In the days approaching Valentine's Day, I wondered how I would feel being alone again. On Valentine's Day morning, I awoke worried about work and the direction of my career. *Oh, stop. Just take a couple of deep breaths and clear your mind!* the silent observer in me instructed my mind. And with my second breath, I was completely enveloped in the rapture of love. I lay in bed with a feeling of falling in love for almost two hours. Then my mind kicked in: *Okay, wow, but I need to get up and go to work. It's a shame I can't just lie here and continue to enjoy this heavenly feeling.*

A few days later, I sat with Susan again, this time for charting, based on my exact time and place of birth.

"Hi. Kati gave me a massage yesterday," I said. "So funny. She says you are close friends. What a coincidence."

Painting by Alice Billings.

"Oh yes, isn't Kati wonderful?"

"Yep. And before I left, she had me pull angel cards from her basket. When I pulled one with Drew in mind, the card was patience. Very appropriate as I'm so confused. And for my career, I pulled the healer card."

"Well, we can talk about that after we discuss your charting."

"I'm scared to learn more about my future."

"This isn't predictive. This type of charting is a way of learning more about yourself.

"Your energies are very prominent in your lower two energy centers. You have an intense need for closeness to others, in all relationships . . . romantically, friendships, and family. Your design shows you are deeply impacted by intimacy and that it is an important aspect for you in life."

"That's one reason why I don't feel complete here. It's so stunningly beautiful here in the San Juans, and I feel so grateful I have such a solid job here using my talents. But I have no significant other and no close friends in this valley of only three thousand people. It's so isolating. I work long hours, and I know that's partly why. But I really don't feel like I have found my peeps."

"You'll find them one day. Your circle must be somewhere else. There are other beautiful places, Elisabeth."

"I can't get Drew out of my mind either. He is in California." I looked down and began to cry. My thoughts had raced many times that if I would just quit my job and see him, he would see that I've changed due to his feedback. When I fall for another soul, it's usually due to my deep respect. Thus, I respect their feedback. In each relationship, I grow by listening to feedback on my flaws.

"I know it's painful when you love someone, and that person won't love you back."

"The winters are too long for me here anyway. I have good friends in Arizona and Denver, but I don't want to live there. I'll be so sad to leave here, but I want to be back, maybe just in the summers."

Susan smiled warmly. It was so grounding to be in her presence and with her reassurance.

Wilson Peak near Telluride on Valentine's Day weekend.

Entrance to horse property of Alice Billings,
a Self-Realization Fellowship follower, Ridgway, Colorado.

Insights and Ruminations: *This rapture of love that I felt may have been love from the Divine, reassuring me that quitting my job, taking a break, and starting my own business was what was best for me.*

Ineffable Peace

"It's so funny how you reached out to me. I was just telling a Self-Realization Fellowship friend in Los Angeles that I was wishing I could meditate with a Self-Realization Fellowship follower," Alice responded via text to me one morning.

I met up with Alice a few days later. As I drove up to her little horse property, my skin began to tingle. I had noticed horses in every form kept appearing over the past week.[6] I had petted three horses the day before and opened a bottle of Merlot called H3, with the emblem of a winged horse flying. I smiled at the fanciful horse painting sign welcoming visitors to Alice's property. As I stepped inside, I admired the numerous horse paintings hanging on the wall. I had known she was an artist crazy about horses, but I was now surrounded by her whimsical equine art. We talked about Dennis Weaver's presence in the San Juan Mountains, and his ties to Yogananda and Self-Realization Fellowship (SRF) centers. Dennis was a famous actor and lay minister of SRF who split his time between Southern California and Ridgway, Colorado.

"When I picked up my mala, Alana told me she knew several people who had studied SRF," I said, "but that all were dead except for one. You."

Alice pushed back her large red curly locks with hands arthritis-swollen from too much horse work as she bent over in laughter. "Well, I guess that's true."

"And Cheryl says hi." Alice looked up with a smile.

"I called her to talk to her about my job, since she was once in my shoes. She told me you two used to meditate together."

"Why, yes. Wow, that was so long ago, I had almost forgotten."

"And the Weaver Park by the river. I picked some sage to initiate my mala from Alana. I looked up and saw Dennis Weaver's lovely poem

---

6. At the time the horse symbols kept appearing for me, the meaning of the horse as an omen signified it is time to set your soul free. I needed to overcome fear to set my soul free.

next to the eagle. I got goosebumps. It's just what I needed to read, as I've been worried about the career changes I am planning to make. Starting my own health coaching business is intimidating, and so is this new spirituality for me. Going to Baja on my own helped me overcome fear, but it still feels so daunting at times. After I read the poem and reflected on your connection with the Weavers and Yogananda, I knew I was supposed to connect with you."

We giggled together at the serendipity of realizing we were meant to get to know each other better this way. Alice and I had originally met a few years prior at Wine and Whiskers, a dance fashion show that was a fundraiser for the local humane society. I was drawn to her due to our mutual love of horses.

"And Annie, the nutritionist and yogi at my office, also said that visiting the Self-Realization Fellowship center and attending a retreat . . . well, she recommended those steps." Annie had shared with me how Yogananda brought Eastern spirituality to the West and increased the understanding between the two hemispheres.

"Have you signed up for the lessons?"

"I'm so swamped at work, but I ordered some of Yogananda's books. They are lovely but a bit overwhelming. I want to go on retreat at one of the SRF centers, most likely the one in Encinitas."

"I'm friends with one of the monks there."

"Yes, that's one reason I wanted to meet with you. I'm trying to sort out what I'm experiencing. It's a bit confusing and scary for me. I need to talk to a spiritual person like him."

Alice tried gifting me a couple of lessons.

"Oh, I don't think I'm supposed to get a copy of the lessons except through the headquarters, right?"

Alice smiled. "Well, that's true. You are supposed to fill out an application. Here, this one you can read. It's about higher achievements through Self-Realization."

"Thanks, I'll read it," I said, giving her a hug before departing.

That evening as I wound down at home and read the literature Alice had given me, an ineffable peace came over me that I felt through the night while sleeping and that continued in the morning when I awoke. I texted Alice about the peace.

"Well, I'm not your teacher. But, yes, I think it's an indication this might be your path."

"Aum." I texted back. I had noticed in the intro lesson from Yogananda that the closing was "Aum. Amen. Aum. Amen."

I had pondered, *I've never seen Om spelled that way, as Aum. I wonder why.*

The next morning, I received a text from Alana, with the Om symbol included:

"Full Moon gathering tonight. Join us in an exploration of Aum. Learn about the meaning and inquiry latent within this ancient symbol."

My hair stood up on end. *Oh my. I think I am meant to attend.*

Alana and her husband explained that the dot at the top of the Aum meant *ananda*. I lay on my mat, stunned, and asked, "Does the area around the dot at the top represent your true Self? And does the dot represent bliss or ananda?"

"Why, yes . . . " Alana replied.

I realized that Paramahansa Yogananda provided the path to ananda. *But how did I find it on my own?* I wondered as I drove home in the moonlight between the occasional big snowflakes coming down. I swallowed hard, realizing that it was planned for me possibly due to the introspection and other deep inner work I was doing with the help of so many guides . . . ultimately leading me to a spiritual awakening.

Insights and Ruminations: *Alana later clarified to me that the space behind the symbol is that which is the closest to true Self. The ineffable peace I felt upon receiving a sample of Yogananda's teachings from Alice was a sign that the teacher had appeared for me, in the well-known phrase: "When the student is ready, the teacher will appear."*

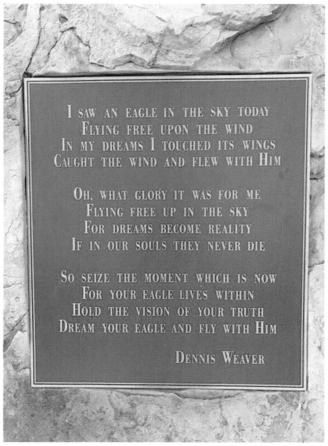

I SAW AN EAGLE IN THE SKY TODAY
FLYING FREE UPON THE WIND
IN MY DREAMS I TOUCHED ITS WINGS
CAUGHT THE WIND AND FLEW WITH HIM

OH, WHAT GLORY IT WAS FOR ME
FLYING FREE UP IN THE SKY
FOR DREAMS BECOME REALITY
IF IN OUR SOULS THEY NEVER DIE

SO SEIZE THE MOMENT WHICH IS NOW
FOR YOUR EAGLE LIVES WITHIN
HOLD THE VISION OF YOUR TRUTH
DREAM YOUR EAGLE AND FLY WITH HIM

DENNIS WEAVER

Plaque at Dennis Weaver Park, from where I picked sage to initiate my custom mala. The message was perfect timing, as I approached the steps to change my career to start my own business.

Eagle in Flight statue at Dennis Weaver Park, Ridgway, Colorado.
Dennis Weaver was a Self-Realization Fellowship devotee.

CHAPTER 32:

Spiritual Home Arrival

---

*"Our spiritual charge is to maintain the wonder
of the singular explorer that each of us is."*
—MARK NEPO

Preparation for Pilgrimage

While I packed my van for another trip to Southern California, I waited
patiently for a reply from Drew. I had sent him a letter asking if he
could be respectful and if we could start over again. Patience is a virtue
I was still working on, which was not easy. Drew had said he didn't
want commitment for a year or two, and a year from that moment
was approaching. Then I paused to meditate, turning to a page in *The
Whispers from Eternity* from Paramahansa Yogananda in preparation:

> *"The caravan of my prayers is moving toward Thee. It has
> been delayed now and then by blinding sandstorms of despon-
> dency. As I lead the sacred procession I glimpse afar an oasis
> of Thy silent encouragement. My spirits revive; I redouble my
> efforts to reach Thee. May I dip my thirsty lips of faith into
> Thy bliss well and drink deep!∞"*

I texted Alice about the serendipity of the passage.
"Well, you are blessed . . . " Alice texted back.

"And that photo of Paramahansa Yogananda on the cover. His eyes are like the Mona Lisa's eyes. His eyes are so loving yet piercing and seem to follow me."

A few days before, I had run into Kevin and had murmured, "Most people go to India when they experience something like I did." I didn't have time or enough money to go to India. But this trip seemed right for me somehow, anyway.

Arrival in California

As I finished loading up my van after riding the Malibu Gran Fondo in March, I opened an email from Drew. His response was that he only wanted to be cycling buddies or friends. I had included in the email that if he didn't want to try to date, perhaps we were to be soul friends instead as described in John O'Donohue's book *Anam Cara*. And then he ghosted me even as a friend. I was crushed, cried on the phone for a while with my dear girlfriend Gale, and then drove to the coast to try to find camping. One campground after the next was full or closed due to the recent fires. As I drove further north, away from the Self-Realization Fellowship Centers in Los Angeles, the evening wore on. I turned around and headed back south, as I didn't want to be too far away come morning, and I was growing so tired.

Maybe someone will not show or cancel, I thought, noticing it was already almost ten o'clock and the gates would soon be closing. I pulled up to the original campsite I'd tried, the closest public campsite to L.A. on the coast. It was 10:01, and the gate was still open.

"Any chance someone canceled?"

"Why yes, someone just did. You have the last spot."

I looked in the rearview mirror. Another car pulled in behind me, looking for a site as well.

I was so grateful and drifted off to sleep quickly.

The next morning, I awoke to a surprising amount of grief. As I meditated at dawn facing the ocean, waves of grief went through me. *He was so disrespectful to me. I don't deserve that, anyway. I deserve someone who cherishes and respects me. Why can't I just realize I need to let go and know there is a greater plan? I'm being so ungrateful.* I shook my head as I tried to meditate through the tears. As I walked along the beach, I added stones to the round prayer stone mounds along the shore, and only saw seaweed among the rocks and sand.

As I neared the van, I paused and reached down. *What's this?* I picked up a broken toy as a few tears were drying on my face, and I took a deep breath. *It's just a broken toy,* I thought, but as I started to let go, I noticed it was a little brown plastic horse. I flipped it upside down and read "Just play" on the underside. *Oh my,* I started to cry. *Okay, I hear you. I am here for spiritual reasons and to make a fresh start on my own, not for a man. I know there is a greater plan for me.*

I wedged the little horse into the vents on my dash as I drove down the coast toward the SRF centers.

Insights and Ruminations: *My grief was partially based on a delusion that Drew, a strong man in the health industry, would help guide me in launching my own health and wellness business. As insights set in, I realized that all the heartbreak and travel to discover and heal were part of the divine plan to wake me up, find my spiritual path, and allow me to find peace, sovereignty, and my true Self. The meaning of the horse changed for me during my awakening and eventually represented one of the five horses symbolic of the five senses as explained in the Bhagavad Gita.*

Finding My Path

I called my friend Scarlet to pick her brain on Southern California, as I had such an open schedule alone to explore. When I crested the hill near a Self-Realization Fellowship Temple, I joked with Scarlet, "Maybe we knew each other in a previous life in California. It seems strangely familiar to me here."

"Yes. I agree. You know how when you meet some souls for the first time, there is just a knowing when you look in their eyes that you already are familiar with them?"

"Oh, I don't know if I believe in reincarnation. But I've always wanted to learn more about the concept. It keeps coming up in conversations. Okay, I'm at the temple. It's time for me to run in. I'm a bit late."

As I made my way into the temple, the seating and lighting appeared so welcoming. The topic of the sermon was on reincarnation. The hair on the back of my neck stood on end, as the entire sermon made sense.

As I sat in the service, the hour sped by. I was stunned. Tears of joy came down my face during the sermon and at the end. It seemed as if the brother's speech was custom-made for me. *I have found my spiritual home!* I thought as I wiped the tears of surprise and joy from my cheeks. Memories of feeling trapped in Catholic Masses passed through my head, and how this was the complete opposite. I was in shock. As I walked out of the temple, I thought, *Oh, my God. I believe in reincarnation.*

As I drove away from the Glendale temple, I became stuck in Los Angeles traffic and thought, *I've never been to Los Angeles, and yet I feel comfortable here.* I had a lump in my throat as I sat in bumper-to-bumper traffic mulling over the talk given by the wise brother at the temple. *In the next life, I hope I don't fu** it up like I must have in the past and in this life. And not being attached to the fruits of your labor? What about the labor and hopes to help others? Shouldn't we strive for the fruits of such labor?* I had so many questions and was eager to learn as much as I could.

I called Scarlet back and immediately blurted out: "Reincarnation is real. Holy cow! I have found my spiritual home. Well, what am I supposed to do? I can't live in L.A. I am a country pumpkin. I need peace and quiet." I knew the Self-Realization Fellowship lessons could be mailed to wherever I was living, but I wanted to be close to others on the same path and near a community of truth seekers.

"Go to Ojai. I think you might like it there. I'm looking at a mug given to me from a relative. Funny, there is a horse on the mug." Scarlet knew the horse was a significant symbol in my life for overcoming fear and, at this juncture, spiritually as well. My favorite horses in my life were the ones that learned to overcome fear, which was based partly on building trust. One horse had taught me to overcome fear as well. But Scarlet had no idea Ojai was a spiritual place.

"Kevin mentioned I'd like it, too. I've been wanting to go there for a very long time, and I'm not sure why." And yet another friend, a professional counselor who experienced a spiritual awakening while coming out of depression, responded on the phone, "Yes, Ojai. I've never been there. But I think your tribe might be there. And enjoy the serendipities of learning on the spiritual path ahead of you." I swallowed hard. I had listened to John O'Donohue's *To Bless the Space Between Us* on the drive to California. Within the chapter on belonging, John lyrically stated in his Irish accent, "You are on your way to your tribe." I felt as if John were speaking to me from the ether.

That evening, I read a small booklet from the Self-Realization Fellowship temple on the guru-disciple relationship. I was becoming weary and started to enter "the" into Google's search engine to look for the name of a yoga studio on my cell phone, and Jiddu Krishnamurti's name auto-populated. I was shocked. I hit return. I reviewed some Krishnamurti's quotes that resonated with me. *Hmmm. Well that was nice to read, but I'm not sure why that happened.*

As I awoke the next morning in my van in a campsite next to a lake outside of Ojai, I was in tears. *I'm scared. I'm changing every aspect of my life, alone. Should I move to Southern California to make a fresh start? I want to use my many years of experience in the health and wellness field and this awakening to best serve others while I nurture myself and heal . . . But I need a quiet place to rest and ensure that what I'm doing is best,* I thought as I put my mala around my neck. The night before, I was reading Paramahansa Yogananda's *Auto-biography of a Yogi* as I cooked dinner in my van. The importance of meditating twice a day, as I read in the book, seemed to echo in my head that morning; I needed to calm myself. I walked out to a lush, clover-covered field next to the lake with the hills draped in an early morning fog. As I meditated, I heard the honking of a pair of Canada geese. I peeked as the geese flew in a couple of circles above my head and then landed about twenty feet from me. When I had finished my meditation and opened my eyes, the two geese were staring at me. One goose at a time honked as I sent emails to two women in California with whom I wanted to collaborate to build my health coaching business. After a few minutes, the geese flew off across the lake, in the direction of town.

I walked across the meadow back to Snowflake as a bank of clouds rolled in. After breakfast, I sipped on some tea, listened to rain pitter-patter on the roof of the van, and looked up the meaning of a goose as a spiritual omen: "You are not alone. You will no longer be elusive when it comes to your spiritual truths, and this will open up a whole new meaning for your existence." I began to cry. An invisible, loving force seemed to be telling me that I was not alone and was being cared for. Birds kept appearing at critical moments during changes in my life. As I wiped the tears from my face, I promised to meditate twice a day and logged onto the internet to create the limited liability corporation for my business on the web. As I was typing away, a large white egret slowly walked in front of the open side door of my van, stopped and stared at me for a time, and then slowly walked away. *I'm doing it. Finally starting my own business. This is way overdue*, I thought as I swallowed hard. A Google search of the meaning of an egret as an omen resulted in "the importance of learning to stand on your own two feet, to become independent and self-reliant."

The next day, the sun returned, so I cycled from camp and became enamored with the beauty of the Ojai valley. Because of a fire over a year before, followed by a very wet winter, the landscape was lush and verdant. My soul felt good here. I decided to stay for several days to explore, but I needed some local insight. I attended a class at Hamsa Yoga Studio. The instructor was friendly, so after the class, I asked him what he recommended to do if one was considering moving to Ojai.

"Go help harvest at the local community-supported agriculture fields. Sulphur Mountain is magical to cycle up. And Ecotopia . . . go soak there," he suggested with a warm smile.

"Hot springs too? I was just thinking that's the only feature that's missing from the area."

I followed his advice, and the following morning was pulling turnips that were almost popping out of the ground, as a light sprinkle of rain misted the back of my neck.

"This land is so fertile. I've never put my hands into such wonderful soil. And on the first day of spring . . . thanks for letting me help."

"Ojai is pretty special."

As the clouds drifted, the eight-thousand-foot peaks shimmered with a fresh layer of snow. I was stunned by the contrast of the green hills and snow-capped peaks so far south in California.

"Do you think I could help out on a farm or ranch in exchange for living there in my van?" I asked as I wiped some dirt off my brow.

"Everyone wants that in Ojai. I have a buddy who's been searching for years," said an earthy compadre helping to pull carrots.

"Well, I'm a former large animal vet. Maybe that will help me win over someone's trust."

"Good luck, honey. Maybe," said a lovely dreadlocked young hippie as she grinned and wiped some sweat from her cheek.

"Isn't the moon going to be full tonight?" I asked. "Where is a good place to watch it rise?"

"Lake Casitas."

"Oh good, I'm camped there. Thanks."

After the harvest, I drove my van to the outskirts of town to prepare a meal and enjoy the views from the open side door of the van.

My phone rang.

"Hi, Sis! Where are you? Mom and Dad are worried, you know? I told them that you are going to be just fine."

"Hi, Heidi. I'm great. I've fallen in love with Ojai, and I'm thinking about moving here."

"What? Oh, I have heard so much wonderful things about Ojai. I've always wanted to check it out. But isn't it really expensive? Why Ojai? What is the main economic driver? How are you going to make a go of it there? That's not where unhealthy people live. You need to be in an area where people really need your help to be healthy, don't you think?"

"Oh, Heidi. I'd be in my van. I don't know exactly why Ojai. My soul feels good here. I'm done with the cold winters of Colorado.

And I want to be close to the temple of the spiritual path I'm starting on. Heidi, it was so beautiful. The service was an hour but felt like five minutes. Isn't that wonderful? And the people are so nice there."

"Alright, let me know how it goes. Please call Mom and Dad."

"I don't know if I can handle talking to Dad. But I'll try. Thanks for your concern, Sis."

After cleaning up after the meal, Heidi's words kept echoing in my head. I rolled the side door closed, revved up Snowflake, and drove back into town. As I walked into the Visitor Center and peered across the fliers and free maps of trails, a woman with a stern face raised her eyebrows.

"Hello. How may I help you?"

"I'm just browsing through your information. I'm thinking about moving here."

"You know it's rather expensive to live here. And besides, you should visit the Chamber of Commerce instead. This is for tourists," she said as she scanned me up and down.

"Oh, I'm starting my life over again, by just living in a van. I am going to try to find a farm or ranch that might need some help in exchange for me parking on their land."

"Good luck. I've been trying to find that for almost three years," she retorted with frustration on her face.

"What's your name?"

"Nancy."

"Nancy, thanks for your help." I smiled and waved as I walked out the door.

I shook my head as I walked to the museum section of the same building.

Wow, that's an appropriate name . . . Ms. Negative Nancy. She doesn't seem to understand what phase of life I'm in. The universe is being so kind to me right now, and I'm still not sure why. I'm not going to let her pessimism affect me, I thought as I opened the door on the opposite side of the building.

The museum included information about the history of the Ojai Valley. The most prominent plaque was titled "Spiritual Seekers" with a description of many significant spiritual sites. Mouth ajar, I read the sign. There displayed was Krishnamurti's name that had auto-populated in my phone when I clicked on the Google search app just two nights before. I looked over my shoulder, still dumbfounded.

"You should go to the Krotona Institute," suggested a very friendly museum staffer with a wide smile.

"I should?"

"Yes, it's not far. It's such a peaceful and special place."

"Great, how do I get there?"

Visit to the Krotona Institute Later That Day

While visiting the Krotona Institute, my spiritual emergency transformed into insights, where interpretations of scriptures became a path to connect with divinity for the first time in my life. And I began to gather pieces of the puzzle of why my awakening occurred. During my first week in Ojai I learned the importance of being in a community of fellow spiritual searchers. I sensed that the Krotona Institute was an excellent place for discernment of interpretations of spiritual teachings during the start of this new chapter in my life.

During that week, I emailed my spiritual counselor Laura, "God works through Google." I knew that visiting the Krotona Institute had been divinely arranged for me.

After attending a couple of days of Ravi Ravindra's series of talks on "The Journey of Transformation," I pondered whether to attend another session that morning as I opened *The Whispers from Eternity* before meditating in my van. I turned to a passage that seemed to be encouraging me to continue to attend the lectures.

Coming Full Circle

Turning my bike into the parking lot of a campground a few miles to the south of Ojai, I found the lot was empty except for one car. I wanted to try a cheaper campsite and a different setting than Lake Casitas, but each time I drove to this site in the early evening, I found the gate closed. I pulled a payment envelope from a metal box to use as a note for the camp host who was not at his camper. No pen in sight. I rode over to the one car. The woman in the car was on her phone.

"Hi, so sorry to interrupt, but would you happen to have a pen that I could borrow? I want to leave a note for the campground host."

"Hold on a second, John," she said to a friend on the phone. "I know, he's hard to catch. Here's a pen."

I rode back over to the empty RV, scribbled a note asking when he closes the gate, included my cell phone number, and rode back over to the woman in the car.

"Thanks. I appreciate it. I'm gonna try to come back in my van. Camping is getting expensive if I'm going to do this long term while I start my life over. I'm looking for a farm or ranch to help out on, so I can find a quiet spot to live in my van."

"I'm Jennifer," she said, extending her hand warmly.

"Oh, that's the name of my best friend from vet school. I'm Elisabeth. Nice to meet you," I said as we shook hands.

"Elisabeth, my middle name is Beth. I'll remember that. Want to live on the farm I live on? It's called Full Circle. Ojai is a great place for grounding."

As the days unfolded, I learned that Ojai is a spiritual place and immediately felt at home. Jennifer and I became friends after I visited the farm. Despite discouragement from some locals that it was nearly impossible to make a fresh start in Ojai unless wealthy, I naturally made connections, through seemingly serendipitous moments, for my fresh start in a spiritual place not far from the United States headquarters of the next step on my spiritual path. Repeated chance events and meetings of other souls appeared as my new guides, including the Krotona School of Theosophy in Ojai.

I decided to stay in Ojai for a week and return to another service in Los Angeles, this time at the Lake Shrine to ensure that this feeling of spiritual home wasn't a fluke. On my drive to the Lake Shrine, George Frederic Handel's *Messiah's* "Hallelujah Chorus" began to play on Spotify, as if angels were singing a celebration of my soul's progress.

Brother Satyananda's talk included how "God works through Google." He included many messages about taking one step at a time when making major or daunting changes in one's life. I began to cry again, as I realized that those messages may have been meant for me.

I stopped in the gift shop by the lake, still stunned by the serendipities. Everything in the gift shop was appealing to me. I wandered over to the large selection of incense, where a beautiful Indian lady was also browsing.

"It all smells so heavenly. What do you recommend?" I asked.

"Oh, these are from India. Very special," she smiled warmly as she handed me a package.

"I was so moved today in the service, that I think I might move here. I've never wanted to live in California. I'm sort of in shock." I blushed as she turned to face me.

"Oh, I sense that you and Yogananda are karmically connected. He arranged this for you. He made this possible. I wish I could do the same, but I must remain in Texas with my family. You will not regret this. You must return for the convocation in August. It's so lovely. What's your name?"

"I'm Elisabeth. Lovely to meet you. What's your name?"

"Bindu. I'm so happy for you. There is a reason why we met. You must come back in time for the convocation!"

"When is the convocation again?"

"Early August."

"Hmmm. Wow, I don't know if I can wrap up my life in Colorado that fast."

We chatted for a bit and I felt a warm connection to her. When it was time to say good-bye, we hugged. I felt so welcomed and so encouraged by our conversation.

Guidance to Gita

After attending the service that Sunday, I decided to attend a kirtan (call and response chanting and singing) and meditation at the Lake Shrine that evening but wanted to find a natural site to work on my book. I entered Malibu Creek State Park into Google Maps and began the drive. I slowed to turn into the parking lot of my intended destination and was stunned to look up at a Hindu temple.

Fine, I thought. *There must be a reason I was sent here. I'll walk through this temple. My experiences seem to be best explained through Hinduism.*

Over the preceding months, many of my Google searches resulted landing on web pages that had nothing to do with what I was searching for but were exactly what I needed to read. And on my way through Utah on my last trip, a Google Maps search had taken me to a Christian church instead of a thrift shop.

I opened the side door of the van and admired the beautiful carvings in the white marble as I prepared lunch. As lunch simmered in the pan in the van, I remembered how just two days prior in a campground near Ojai, I had begun dancing to live music playing while I was taking a shower. I had rushed outside to find out where the beautiful music was coming from and met some locals who said it was a Hindu celebration. I now smiled while I ate my lunch, remembering how much I had enjoyed the live Hindu music.

When I walked through the courtyard of the temple, I found a Hindu man explaining the Bhagavad Gita to a fellow Caucasian female visitor. I stood nearby and eavesdropped, thinking, *Why does everything he is saying make complete sense to me?*

I waited patiently for my turn.

"I think I have answered enough questions for you today. I think you have enough to consider," he said, sighing, and she walked away.

"Do you need a break? I gather that you spoke to her for a long time, and it's getting into early evening. I'm sure it's been a long day for you."

"Yes, may I help you?" he said with a bit of frustration on his face.

"Google Maps brought me here instead of a local park."

"Ah, Krishna sent you!" he said with a huge grin.

"I experienced kundalini rising and then a bright flash of light here." I pointed to the point between my eyebrows. "Perhaps that's why I was guided here?"

His face went limp, he backed away from me with a bit of shock on his face, held his finger up motioning me to stay, turned and ran away.

A couple of minutes later, he ran up to me with a copy of the Gita.

"Here. You should have this. It is the nicest version I have left. It's nicer than the one I gave her."

I asked for his name and thanked him.

"Namaste! I am so appreciative." I placed my hands in prayer in front of my chest and bowed slightly to him in the gesture of *pranam*.

I drove to a nearby field and parked the van in the shade. There I Googled his long Hindi name, which translates to bee, which in my mind is a symbol of a miracle. I lay down on the bed in my van and took a deep breath.

This is starting to feel like "The Twilight Zone," I thought.

Insights and Ruminations: *Laura and I spoke while I was camped at Casitas Lake near Ojai. I expressed how sad I was that Drew had rejected me again via email just a few days earlier, but I was so thankful that in a weird way he had drawn me out to California, where my spiritual home seemed to be. She replied, "He was not the island but instead the raft to get you out to California to find your path." My primary desire had been to see Drew again, but I had told myself that if it didn't work out that way, then I wanted a spiritual growth trip, and that is what came to be.*

Scarlet, Kevin, and Lynn had no idea that Ojai is known as a place for spiritual seekers when they encouraged me to visit there. As the weeks passed, I uprooted my old life so I could enter the new, vastly different life that was unfolding for me. I learned to recognize the Divine trying to show me that various entanglements had prevented me from following my path in the past. Having spaciousness in my life allowed me to find my spiritual path. And as my new life unfolds, the space is allowing me to become who I am meant to be in all aspects of my life and purpose.

I believe I was guided and given the Gita to show me that Kriya Yoga, the ancient scientific meditation techniques of God-realization, was to be my path. These techniques have been known for millennia to the yogis and sages of India, as well as to Jesus. After visiting the Krotona Institute again, I sensed that I should read Yogananda's interpretation. I had been required to read a different version of the Bhagavad Gita for a yoga instructor course that I had completed three years prior to this moment. I had tried reading it, but it did not resonate with me at the time.

I greatly enjoyed interacting with others at the Krotona Institute, which is a branch of the Theosophical Society. The Theosophical Society's emblem declares: "There is no religion higher than truth."

"Uniqueness is manifestation of oneness.
Be open to whatever comes and be willing to be surprised,
which requires releasing from feelings of 'me.'

Allow something else to intervene . . . make room.
All spiritual development is spiral in nature."
—RAVI RAVINDRA

THREE TRUTHS

» *The soul of man is immortal, and its future is the future of a thing whose growth and splendour has no limit.*

» *The principle which gives life dwells in us, and without us, is undying and eternally beneficent, is not heard or seen, or smelt, but is perceived by the man who desires perception.*

» *Each man is his own absolute lawgiver, the dispenser of glory or gloom to himself; the decreer of his life, his reward, his punishment.*

These three truths, which are as great as is life itself, are as simple as the simplest mind of man. Feed the hungry with them.

Quote on the plaque in front of Krotona Library Garden, from
The Idyll of the White Lotus, *by Mabel Collins © 1884. This material was reproduced by permission of Quest Books, the imprint of The Theosophical Publishing House (www.questbooks.net).*

Labyrinth at Krotona Institute, Ojai, California.

*Shiva in Joshua Tree National Park, leading a group
to meditate and pass through a "birth canal" in a rock formation,
just days after my spiritual counselor Laura said that I was going
through a birth canal of transformation.*

CHAPTER 33:

Spiritual Return to California

Preparations for Another Journey

Upon returning to Colorado, I immediately started planning my next trip to California. I had more paid vacation leave to burn before my final weeks in my role as public health director, and I knew I'd need another break. It was difficult adjusting to the lower vibrations, cold, and snow in Colorado after the spiritual moments in sunny, warm, and friendly Southern California. A local massage therapist yogi from Ridgway had mentioned the musician M.C. Yogi to me and that he played at big yoga festivals. And a friend had mentioned Bhakti Fest in California in the fall. M.C. Yogi was scheduled to perform at Shakti Fest, the sister festival in May. I eagerly registered to attend Shakti Fest put on by the same organizers, held at the Joshua Tree campground, north of the national park. My typical fiery, pitta brain was envisioning the simple fun of taking many vigorous yoga classes and dancing to live music. At the time I registered for the yoga festival, I had no idea what the word shakti meant. I was also returning in part because several cyclists I met on the prior trip kept asking whether I planned to attend the Tour of California, a professional cycling race that was fun to watch. I had originally envisioned watching the Tour with Drew, but now I knew that was not in the cards. I was constantly learning not to project and envision any future events in my head, as it seemed to cause so many disappointments.

Feminine Energy Challenges

As I continued to tie up loose ends after giving my three-month notice at work, my root and sacral chakras began flaring up again. I arranged another counseling call with Laura.

"It can be healing to have sex at this time," Laura reassured me. "Just don't get entangled and emotionally attached. You should not be in a relationship now. I have another book for you to read; it's called *Healing Love through the Tao* by Mantauk Chia."

I ordered the book and waited eagerly. I was confused. Emotional connection and attachment are automatic for my soul when sharing such touch and energies. When the book arrived, I opened the package on the counter in the tiny Ouray post office. The provocative drawing on the cover created a rush of feminine energy in me. I ran out to the car, jumped in, shut the door, and hyperventilated as I gripped the steering wheel. I slowed my breath and flipped through a few pages.

Oh, for heaven's sake, now I feel like I need to go home to take care of myself, but I must go back to work. This is maddening. I can't do this. There has got to be another way to handle this! And a Theta Healer wants to counsel me on past life regression, which scares me. I'm getting a bit overwhelmed.

That night I searched on the internet for counseling that specialized in kundalini rising. I stumbled across Patanjali[7] Kundalini Yoga Care. There were only a handful of counselors out West. I visited the website for each counselor, and the one who resonated most for me was in the town that Drew had just moved to.

Universal consciousness has a sick sense of humor with me again, I thought as I tapped my chin. I emailed the counselor who called me the next day.

"I'm glad you found me," she said. "From what you described, you have your antennae up. It's vital to be discerning, especially now because you're vulnerable."

We scheduled a full appointment on the phone and one in person during my next trip West.

---

7. Patanjali was a Hindu sage who is thought to be the author of the Yoga Sutras.

Buddha Nature

As the weeks passed after my first visit to Ojai, I reached out to Drew from the deepest Buddha perspective that I could muster within me. I decided to send him an email before my next trip out to California with ample warning ahead of time that I was coming to his town.

"I'll be in your town briefly and want to warn you, so you don't freak out if you see me. I am so sorry about three things:

1. assuming you ever had any negative intentions.
2. overreacting to you wanting to be friends only.
3. making you feel guilty; that was not my intention. I was hurt.

I did experience trauma and abandonment—before and again after I met you—that I'm recovering from. That's why I overreacted. I am a very strong woman but was extremely vulnerable when we met. That's one reason I was afraid to meet you at the time . . . a year ago. Then I was confused for months after an intense awakening, in some part due to you. But my soul cannot handle friends with benefits.

Please don't ghost me to protect me. The ghosting is not protecting me but instead disturbing my peace in a completely different way.

Friends? I am now friends with Kevin and David. Hard but immensely healing.

I'll be seeing a spiritual counselor who is helping me navigate how to integrate the experience into my life. She keeps telling me it's a gift. I'm very excited to meet her in person, as I've just talked to her on the phone thus far. It's an extremely strange coincidence that she is in your town (yikes!).

So, don't freak out if you see me or Snowflake . . . like our mutual shock when we bumped into each other in Telluride.

And I care for everyone, even if they hurt me accidentally. I worry when I don't hear back.

Blessings to you."

About a week later, I was once again packing my van, and I had not heard from Drew. I had prepared a gift bag for him, including a stuffed dolphin as a meme for his van, a copy of *The Awakening* by Mark Nepo, and a draft copy of the book you now hold. I thought it was doubtful that I would see him, but I cared for him and prayed to have the opportunity to thank him in person for his role in my awakening. I had delusions of just bumping into him and handing him the gift bag while in his town to see the spiritual counselor. I rolled my eyes at myself and told myself to stop obsessing about him.

Spiritual Return to California

As I drove up in the dark to the campground north of Joshua Tree National Park, I was waved down by an intense but friendly soul.

"I think you went too far. Did you pay for camping?" he asked with a weary tone. I would later learn that he was the Shakti Fest organizer.

"Yes, sir, I paid online. Sorry, where should I go?"

"Make a U-turn here and head back one row, that way. You'll need to get a pass to hang from your rearview mirror first thing in the morning. Everyone's gone to bed. Nice van. Sleep well."

"Thanks, and sorry I'm rolling in so late. It took me two days to get here."

The next morning, I awoke into ineffable peace.

Whoa. Again. Why is this happening here? This is the same peace I felt when I first read the introduction to Yogananda's teachings. Well, I don't want to leave my van, but I need to get the rearview mirror tag for camping.

Over the next hour and a half, I remained in the state of ineffable peace while I walked the grounds, meeting new people, carrying on lengthy conversations with so many warm souls, and picking up my tag, schedule, and wrist band from the registration booth. It was the first time I had experienced one of these blissful states while interacting with others. As I walked back to my van, I pondered why now and why here.

On the second day of the festival, one of the yoga classes morphed into an ecstatic free-form dance to live music. A sweet yogi man grabbed me by my waist and swung me around in circles. I was so moved by the positive vibrations, I leaped over to grab my cell phone to record a few seconds of the festivities and glee.

Drew had just emailed, inviting me to stay with him. I smiled and covered my mouth. He did seem to reach out or respond whenever another man touched me.

Oh, thanks, Buddha, for your example. I am so touched Drew trusts me to visit, I thought as I smiled and glanced back across the crowd dancing on their yoga mats.

Later that day, as I cooked lunch in my van, my father texted: "I sent you a long email," ending with a heart emoji.

"Is your message judging and criticizing me? If it is, I am not going to read it."

"*No!*" he replied.

I took a deep breath and opened my email.

"By nature of your personality, you are the most lovable of our children. This is felt by your siblings as well, sometimes with some level of envy. You have always tried your best and accomplished much in your chosen endeavors." The rest of his email went into deep brooding and worry about my choices, outlining the challenges only with little faith in my plans.

My throat tightened. I didn't believe the tarot card reader months ago when she described how my father felt about me. His worry wasn't going to help me on my path, but I knew it was normal. I was somewhat shocked at the sweetness of his email, as I had finally unleashed decades of frustration of his constant display of disappointment in his children, which had resulted in my never feeling like I measured up, no matter what I did with my life. Just a couple of months prior, my father had repeatedly tried to control me, attempting to force me to take high blood pressure medication. I had yelled at him that his letter in the fall and my feelings of never being able to measure up to his expectations were some of the underlying reasons for my high blood pressure.

After deep reflection, I typed: "Most lovable? Aw. I know you love each of us equally, which is the way it should be." The rest of my email response was written with the intention to decrease his worries.

That Sunday of the festival was Mother's Day. I had grown tired from so much moving yoga on the mat and dancing and retired to my van for a break. I called my mother via FaceTime. I mulled over how to reassure her that I was spiritual before time ran out. My parents are elderly, and they were very disappointed that I was not a practicing Catholic.

"Hi Mom. Happy Mother's Day. I'm sorry I can't be with you today. I just came from a yoga class where we prostrated into a hundred and eight *pranams*, which are full body prayers. We were giving thanks for Mother Earth and all of our mothers. See, my mala has a hundred and eight beads. It's similar to your rosary beads for praying."

My mother was touched and began to cry.

During the last morning of the festival, I decided to attend the morning meditation guided by an Ayurveda health and wellness expert. I hurried to the lotus-shaped tent, with just a couple of minutes to spare.

"It's rather packed in there. Leave all you can outside the Lotus Belle tent so there is room," said a friendly volunteer.

I tossed my bag down outside and eyed the only place that seemed open enough for me to squeeze in, smack dab in front of the presenter.

I was moved by his spiritual presence, and Drew vanished from my head for the rest of the festival.

"Now envision your teacher, your guru."

He listed many sages.

"Some advanced yogis see the five-pointed star at the third or spiritual eye."

I suddenly remembered seeing many large five-pointed stars on billboards during my trip in Baja, immediately after reading the statement "look for signs of what's to come," in Mark Nepo's book on how to listen.

At the end of the meditation and lecture, he asked if there were any more questions.

One woman thanked him, "This is what I really needed at this festival instead of the vigorous yoga classes."

He smiled wryly and replied, "Those classes are the candy to get you to come for the yoga inside."

After a moment of silence, I shyly raised my hand.

"May I ask who your guru is?"

"Yogananda."

I nodded and swallowed deeply. Much of what he said prior to the start of the meditation felt like it was directly to me from Yogananda. The guidance was about how important it was to slow down and to not push oneself so hard.

I walked outside to a table where a woman was handing one of the presenter's books to a customer.

"Is that the last book?"

"Why yes. But you can buy it online."

"What's your name?"

"Elizabeth."

"Of course. Hi. I'm Elisabeth. Nice to meet you."

I sputtered a few comments about discovering Yogananda, the spiritual symbolism of the horse toy I found during that trip, and the strange sense I had from the presenter just moments ago.

"Oh, he would love to hear that, Elisabeth. You should email him. I think he would find that lovely."

"Well, my blood pressure has been sky high for the past six months, and I've been wanting to see an Ayurveda expert anyway."

"He is a master. If you have time, you should see him."

I reached out to him via email and set up an appointment.

That evening was the last of the festival. There was not a single negative vibration felt the entire four days I was there. I had not experienced so many open, positive, welcoming people since my days at a fine arts high school. But this was even more special. I met a couple of women who shared their very different but equally shocking kundalini rising stories. At the last night's concert, I was interlocked in one huge embrace with fellow yogis, swaying to the spiritual beats under the open sky. Tears of joy rolled down my face. A fellow yogi saw my emotions and rubbed my back and gave me a reassuring glance. I smiled and nodded. I had found my peeps, as had been promised.

After a post-intensive session by Shiva Rea the next morning, which I signed up for as a last-minute decision, we drove separately away from the festival grounds and toward Joshua Tree National Park for meditation in pure nature. I thought, *Wow, it is so strange that I feel so comfortable with such spiritual yogis, Hindus, and Buddhists after growing up in a Catholic family.* I approached a stop sign and put my blinker on to turn left as I noticed a man holding a cross and a sign on my right, but I couldn't make out the sign. A fast approaching car from the left honked his horn as he thought I was going to pull out in front of him. The man holding the sign turned to face the blaring honks from the passing car, revealing the large sign, "I am the light and the way! —Jesus Christ."

I hear you. I know that Jesus is part of this, too, I thought as I smiled and turned left.

A few days later in Ojai, the well-respected Ayurveda expert greeted me softly.

As he gathered some materials for our meeting, he gently spoke, "Your kundalini rising occurred because God was telling you that you were headed in the wrong direction."

I remembered how he had mentioned at Shakti Fest that the physical asana practice can serve as "candy" to draw souls to the spirituality that yoga can provide. That was partly how my transformation began as well.

A few minutes later, he tapped away on his laptop without looking up.

"You have been pushing yourself too hard for too long. You need to cut down your exercise by fifty percent."

I shifted in my seat, "Yes sir. I know I need to slow down and take a break."

"Your cardiovascular and nervous system have been through too much. Your intense need for exercise is partially due to ego."

I knew that my ego was fortunately decreasing as a result of the awakening, but this was still hard for me to hear.

"You need to meditate and be devoted." He continued by recommending breath work and meditation, at least ten to twenty minutes per day. He suggested that I concentrate deeper in my spine, especially at the heart region.

"I plan to attend a 'how to live' retreat at the Self-Realization Fellowship Temple in Encinitas."

"Yes. Good. The new lessons that have just come out have been beautifully shaped. And you are to find your true purpose to serve in this lifetime."

"Yes, I want to be a health and wellness coach. I want to learn more about Ayurveda so I can incorporate that wisdom in what I will offer. There is a little bit included in the course I'm taking now, but I need to finish that course first."

He nodded.

But so many more ideas swirled in my mind and heart. I wanted to help women who have been traumatized by men, to heal through trauma-informed yoga and meditation. And Dr. Chalam at Shakti Fest had blurted out during a brief one-on-one interaction about which deity statue I should purchase that I am to be a transformational coach for executives, in perfect reflection of what Jane Ashley, one of the editors of this book, predicts as well. I sensed that my spiritual path would guide me to best serve others with my knowledge, skills, talents, and high energy.

"May I ask you how you found Yogananda?" I asked as he reached for a scoop for his herbs.

"I've known him for many lifetimes."

Ganesh picks up chocolate in my van at Shakti Fest,
just before departure to visit Drew.

"What do you mean? How do you know that?"

"You know. There is a familiarity with him," he said with a sidelong glance as if to say that I likely sensed the same.

As I said my good-byes, I told him that I was going to see a Patanjali Kundalini Yoga Care counselor.

"But she hasn't replied on whether she will respect my current spiritual path," I said with concern.

"Babaji[8] initiated Patanjali in Kriya Yoga. So, it's from the same root. It should be fine."

I gave him a hug and waved good-bye.

Visiting Drew

A few days later, I drove north away from Joshua Tree and Ojai toward Drew and the spiritual counselor. I had started to realize how spooky it was to know the divine play of it all. Even though I had fallen so hard for Drew, I knew that we were only to be friends. But Drew had drawn me to California as each trip I had hoped that I would get to see him. I shook my head and said to the universe, *I know what you are doing. You've been using him this entire time for my spiritual development. This is brutally hard on my heart. I don't know how much more I can handle. But it's all to help me grow spiritually.*

You can do this, Elisabeth, I thought as I gripped Snowflake's steering wheel.

As I drove north, I became excited to share with Drew how I had learned how to quiet my mind, was slowing down, and had deepened into my transformational process. I hoped to spend enough time with him to show him that I was changing. His words about my fast-paced body and mind that eventually repelled him echoed in my head. I listened to my thoughts as a silent observer: *He meets all the criteria of what I was looking for in a man: an intelligent, joyful, playful, successful, healthy cyclist. And we had such strong attraction and chemistry initially. I hope I can show him that I'm mellowing out like he predicted might happen. I know it takes a long time to get to know someone, and we got involved too quickly.*

---

8. Mahavatar Babaji is the first in a line of contemporary gurus in the spiritual lineage of Paramahansa Yogananda. This lineage is described on the Self-Realization Fellowship website, which provides highlights that the SRF teachings are founded upon the teachings of both Jesus Christ and Bhagavan Krishna. Yogananda embraces all paths to the same truth, which so resonates with me.

As I opened the door to Drew's new home, he grinned, walked and reached with outstretched arms toward me.

"My hands are covered in pizza dough but come here."

Drew's face was filled with beaming, exuberant joy. He extended his fists high up into the air and wrapped his elbows over me. I was stunned by how much warmth he showered over me.

"Can I help?" I smiled.

"I've got it under control. How was the drive?"

"Beautiful. It's fun exploring a new area. I have a gift bag of goodies for you."

"I'll open it later. Something to look forward to."

I place the gift bag on the far end of the dining room table. We bantered as he swirled around the kitchen. Drew loves to cook and seemed excited to entertain. I was struck by the simplicity of his house, furnishings, and the small town he had chosen. Nothing hung on the walls yet, and there was a modicum, an eclectic smattering of used furniture. He had done such a good job of shedding material things, and it seemed as if he were reluctant to acquire them again.

A cold rain had settled into the evening.

"The hot water heater is out. I can boil some water for you and pour into the tub."

"That sounds like a lot of trouble. But I rode this morning with a new friend and have a chill on me. Thanks."

I had been on a date with another Libra cyclist from Fitness Singles that morning, but once again, I didn't feel the same connection as I did with Drew.

The evening quickly slipped away. Drew gave me a tour.

"You sleep in here," he pushed on the mattress. "This is the most comfortable bed."

"Drew, this is your bedroom. I was planning on sleeping in my van, but it's parked on a slant. I could sleep in the guest bedroom."

"No, no. You sleep here." He smiled, shook his head and walked away. I was so touched. Sweet man again.

The next morning brought more cold rain. I was feeling achy from a cold that had started and wanted to chill out.

After relaxing for most of the day in his bedroom and working a bit on writing this book, I unfurled my yoga mat.

"I'm going to plant some trees," he said.

"Okay. I'm not feeling that great. I want to help you, but it's so cold and wet."

The raindrops grew larger as he dug holes in the yard and easily inserted several fruit trees. My root and sacral chakras started raging again as I repeated sun salutations.

Oh no, not again, I thought as I bent over and touched my toes.

That evening, we talked about dating.

"On those dating apps, you can't ask the woman if she has a big butt," Drew said, smirking.

"Well, you should fall for her soul."

"There has to be an initial attraction. And I want a woman with whom I can discuss the important stuff. I don't know what I'm gonna do about finding the right woman."

I swallowed sadly and wondered why he didn't realize those criteria were met in me.

I decided to shift the conversation.

"May I ask you about spirituality?"

"Sure."

"You said you were 'Buddhish.' What else are you willing to share?"

"I don't think you can wrap your little head around it!" Drew said with a cocked head and one raised eyebrow.

I sat quietly for a moment, then replied softly, "Try me."

"I'm connected to the cosmos," he boldly stated with a haughty air. I sat silently.

"How much death have you experienced?" Drew asked, while jutting his lower jaw to the side, looking slightly down his nose at me.

"Yes, some recently. My uncle. A close friend. Why?"

He nodded and became very still.

"Susie."

"Who is Susie?"

"She was stillborn."

I took a deep breath. "Oh, Drew, I'm so sorry. I had no idea."

Drew looked off in the haze, then down slightly, his face dropping.

Noticing his bleary eyes, I was cautious about whether to ask more. I assumed it was a daughter many years ago in the early stages of his marriage.

I gently prodded, "Did you sense her?"

"Yes, for many years."

"Yeah, I sensed my uncle and my friend, too."

We sat still for a moment.

"You know, you are one of the reasons I had an awakening." I raised my eyebrows.

"It wasn't me, Elisabeth. It was all you."

I explained how I had continued using Eckhart's tips and the resulting first euphorias. Drew was quiet.

"My spiritual counselor said that I've been experiencing ananda on occasion," I stated as I waved one hand upward in front of me and up to the ceiling. "I'm not sure why, but I think it was partly because of quieting the mind and practicing full presence. I was trying to stop my internal suffering after a series of mini traumas, including you."

"Yeah," Drew nodded, seeming to agree that he had caused me some pain.

"Then I experienced pure consciousness bliss, which is making contact with God."

Drew shifted in his seat.

"You don't like the word *God*?"

Drew shook his head and tensed up, remaining silent.

"Remember how Eckhart mentions God only briefly, and instead speaks of the universe, universal consciousness, and divine intelligence? Remember how he said that was to cut through the layers of the ego, so that our ears remain open?"

Drew nodded slightly and remained quiet.

"There's more. I don't know how much I should tell you." I was partly thinking of how hard I had to dig deep to forgive him and how it unearthed so much past trauma that I had to heal from.

Drew looked curious but remained still.

"I haven't told anyone but my spiritual counselor. It's in the draft book in your gift bag. You are in the book a lot. I hope you read it."

Drew shook his head sternly, "I'm not going to read it. I won't, Elisabeth."

We fell silent, as his anger intimidated me from asking why he didn't want to read it. I became frustrated, searching for a reason to make him interested enough to read my book.

"I had a beam of light come across the earth and blow me back . . . then into me."

"Well! You were hallucinating," Drew shot back, raising his eyebrows in fear.

"I wasn't hallucinating," I said defensively.

Our conversation turned into a bit of banter about reincarnation as we started to clear the dining room table.

"Depending on what you do in life, you can be reincarnated to a lower life form in a subsequent life . . . possibly as low as a group of mosquitoes," he said.

My mouth went dry. Ravi Ravindra had shared the same statements even down to the mosquitoes at his talk at Krotona Institute.

Drew then mentioned Steve Jobs, as he had during our previous time spent together. I smiled, as I had placed a copy of *Autobiography of a Yogi* into his gift bag only an hour before hearing back from him at Shakti Fest. I had jotted on a sticky note on the cover of the book how Steve Jobs was a devotee of Paramahansa Yogananda. Steve Jobs had gifted a copy of *Autobiography of a Yogi* to all who attended his own memorial service.

I told Drew that I had found Yogananda as my spiritual guide, and that finding Yogananda was in part due to him.

"Why do you need a path? Are you trying to repeat an experience?" Drew asked with a tone of judgment in his voice.

I paused in silence for a few moments before asking, "Wouldn't you want to experience God again?"

We both fell silent as we cleaned up in the kitchen.

I cocked my head as we stood next to each other busy with our kitchen tasks and gingerly asked, "Why did you think I wouldn't be able to handle what you shared on spiritual matters?"

Drew looked down and sheepishly smiled a little. "Well, I guess I shouldn't have assumed."

We discussed that I needed to just *be* for a while, and he encouraged me to let go of the land near Ouray as well. "Just let it go," he said.

"But I want to shape it into a place for meditation and hopefully one day help women who have been through severe trauma."

As I waited silently for a response from Drew, memories darted through my mind that each time I panicked about money and felt I should sell the land while I started over, I would meet yet another woman who shared her trauma and pain from sexual assault.

He shrugged his shoulders.

I knew it would take me years to ensure I had the funds to create such a space for healing and meditation.

As the night wound down, we prepared for slumber. As I passed him lying in the guest bedroom with his door open, I paused and pondered on how to explain.

"You know, we are supposed to help others and not just be."

"True. We are all in this together."

We smiled at each other and I settled into the other bedroom. The doors to both bedrooms were open all three nights. I wanted so much for him just to lie next to me and hold me. But I was so grateful that he welcomed me into his home and seemed to enjoy taking care of me a bit while I recovered from traveling to visit with the spiritual counselor.

The next morning over breakfast, the conversation turned to the irony of my presence in California.

"Do you remember how mad I was when you changed your mind about moving to Colorado and decided to move to California instead?" I grinned.

"Yeah. It's a little scary you are going to be in California. And I could have ended up in any town," Drew said softly as he glanced down at the food on his plate.

"I know. And this one spiritual counselor is in your town. Do you know what that is called?"

Drew shrugged.

"Divine play or *lila*. Well, the joke is on me. And I'm shocked that I found my peeps and spiritual path here in California . . . " I shook my head.

"Well, I'm glad you like Ojai."

"It's nirvana for me. It's a spiritual place, and the cycling is amazing. I cried when I arrived again last week. My soul feels good there. You should go for a bike ride with me there one day."

"Maybe," Drew whispered.

I shared with him my inability to completely let go of the San Juan mountains. He encouraged me again to let go to free up finances and attachments so that I could just be. Drew knew that my soul needed a break from a demanding career.

After I packed up my things in the van, we quickly said good-bye with a halfhearted hug from him, and he didn't look into my eyes.

I knew he hated long good-byes, but it made me a bit sad, as I had no idea when or if I would see him again. I took one long look over my shoulder at his van Flipper, in which we had first met in Moab late one night in the desert. Each time he ghosted me, I worried that he had flipped off the road in Flipper since he had so many adventures alone. I stepped into Snowflake and began the short drive to my appointment.

Insights and Ruminations: *I had purchased a Ganesh statue from Dr. Chalam at Shakti Fest to help me cut through negative emotions surrounding Drew and to help give me strength and guidance as every aspect of my life was changing with so many long-term goals looming ahead. I thought many times that Drew was just like most men; if the chase was over too soon and they'd had a bite of the apple, the interest in that woman was lost. I had become determined to show him that there was more of me to love than he realized. The Divine was definitely using Drew for my spiritual development. I would whisper to Ganesh to give me strength to overcome my obstacles. I had offered flowers and chocolate to Ganesh. On the journey to visit Drew, the jostling of the van allowed for Ganesh to pick up and hold onto the chocolate that had been placed near him.*

I had wanted to spend more time with Drew to get to know him as a friend and to show him how I had changed based on his constructive feedback. I knew it took a long time to truly get to know someone and that starting a relationship with a man as a friend was best on so many levels. I was so worried the entire time that he would find another woman before I could make it out to California to get to spend more time with him. I had been reminded in my sessions with my psychotherapist Susan reviewing my chart that if he and I were really meant for each other, it would all eventually work out. My prayers to see him again were answered so I would understand why we were possibly not a good fit for each other.

As I reflect on some of the conversations with Drew during the visit to his new home, it felt like we were in a comical spiritual competition. I was trying to convince him to read my book so he could understand my positive transformation that began with him rejecting me. My search for answers to understand my spiritual experiences had been in part to try to slow them down, not to experience more. My statement on experiencing God again was based partly on pride, in hopes of impressing Drew. That statement obviously backfired.

Kundalini Care

"Oh, Elisabeth. He doesn't have the framework to handle that," the counselor in Drew's small town explained. "Why would you want a man who doesn't want you in all your splendor?"

I shrugged my shoulders as I sat on her couch.

"You aren't supposed to share this energy with a man, anyway. This is just for you."

I looked up, confused.

"Elisabeth . . . " her eyes ran up and down me.

"Yes?"

"You were made for Kundalini Shakti Ma."

"What do you mean?"

"Kundalini Shakti Ma is going to keep moving around and working on you until you become devotional. She won't stop working on you until you focus on your spiritual growth. You are not supposed to take care of anyone else but yourself. No helping others for a while."

I shifted in my seat, uncomfortable with that thought.

"What do you mean? That doesn't sound very spiritual. Aren't we supposed to serve others? It makes me feel good, too. And that's the intention of this book I'm working on . . . to help others."

"Not right now. The feminine Divine wants you to just *be* right now."

"Hmmm. I sensed earlier in this trip that this is a special time in my life."

"Yeeeeesssss. This is a very sacred, special time. From what you told me during our last session on the phone, you were already looking for spirituality. You are karmically ready in this lifetime."

"What should I do next?"

"Yogananda is the real deal. Move forward on this path."

It felt so good to hear another validation of the path that had been gifted to me.

As I drove away to journey back to Colorado, I was brimming with gratitude for seeing Drew and all the gentle spiritual moments. I realized that I was being redirected to my teacher, according to the common saying: "When the student is ready, the teacher will appear." Chills went up my spine as I drove across Nevada with this and other insights setting in.

～

Insights and Ruminations: *My search for answers on why this spiritual awakening was happening for me and the desire to slow down or stop the uncomfortable aspects of my awakening led me to a spiritual path for which my soul was not prepared. Divine intelligence kept pushing me back to the teacher and path that had been selected for me. A talk at the Krotona Institute earlier in the spring brought up the importance of having a teacher or guru in the flesh. Some doubts about Paramahansa Yogananda had entered my mind due to that statement, as I felt I needed discipline and devotion taught by a living teacher. Yet another trip to California was required for wise spiritual guides to redirect me to the Self-Realization Fellowship lessons.*

CHAPTER 34:

Desires and Answered Prayers

———— •‑• ————

Our Heavenly Father does answer prayers in
His own time and in His own way.
—THOMAS S. MONSON, FORMER PRESIDENT OF
THE CHURCH OF JESUS CHRIST OF LATTER-DAY SAINTS

After returning to Colorado, I began the daunting process of letting
go of material objects by purging my belongings—to start my
life over. One day in early April, I stopped by Kevin's house to drop
off some of his belongings. I had planned on slipping into his garage
without notice since it was still painful to see him, but he happened
to be organizing his car.

"Oh, you are in town," I said with a lump in my throat. "Here are
a few more of your things. How are you?"

Our conversation turned to our past. It went from good times to
his feelings on why it ended.

"You always assumed that I would do the same to you as your
ex-husband did," he said with anger. "Baggage. That's what your
brought into our relationship." Kevin was in part referring to my
lack of trust in a partner related to finances.

"You still haven't forgiven me. I've changed. You men. Always
hurting me. I'm so sick of it."

I cried without saying good-bye, ran out to my car, and drove
home instead of back to the office. I texted Vivian, one of my staff

members, "I'm a mess. I had an interaction with Kevin that tore me up. I'm not coming back to the office. I still have to pack and drive to Denver tonight."

Vivian text back, "I'm sorry. I understand."

I slipped into my bed fully clothed and began to sob as I held *Whispers from Eternity*, which I read each morning before meditation.

"Please send someone to me who won't hurt me," I cried.

After releasing the sorrow for thirty minutes, I slowly rose from the bed, grabbed my cell phone, took a deep breath, and muttered, "Okay. Shake this off. I've got to pack and drive for almost six hours."

A message appeared on my phone from a mindfulness dating app, and I clicked on a message from Sean, a handsome younger man on the Kriya yoga path. I had not included anything about Kriya yoga, Yogananda, or Self-Realization on my profile, so it was a funny coincidence. I had given up on fitness-related dating apps, as I realized that I would want to be with a man who is deeply spiritual, conscious, and who meditates.

"What made you reach out to me?" I typed back.

"I noticed you changed your profile to Ojai, California. I have family in Southern California and am toying with moving there."

Oh, my goodness. He's handsome, a little younger than me, and is a devout practitioner of Kriya Yoga. Wow, I think my prayers have been answered, I mused as I loaded my car.

Sean kept me company on the phone the entire drive to Denver. We tried meeting on that trip to Denver, but a blizzard prevented the meeting from transpiring until a few weeks later. We talked and texted enough for me to understand that he was devout and had been on the path for more than twenty years. We arranged for me to visit him on his farm in northern Colorado on my next trip to the Front Range, which included getting a deck built on top of my van. As the weeks passed, I grew eager to meet him.

Upon my arrival, I opened the side door of my van and peered across the lush green, rolling hills of his farm. Sean stepped out the back door of his house and immediately waved me over.

"Come here, Elisabeth. Let's sit down on the grass."

He took a deep breath and looked at me a bit nervously.

"You can tell I need grounding, huh?"

"Yeah," he said sternly. "Take some deep breaths. This is where we have had a few healing Tibetan Buddhist fire ceremonies, on this exact spot."

We chatted for a bit as the sun set, and he invited me in for dinner. We both immediately and mutually sensed that there was no romantic attraction, but that our meeting was for another purpose. He prepared me a lovely meal with prayers and blessings in Sanskrit. Sean told me his story of discovering Kriya Yoga, how he spent three years in an ashram, and how the path had transformed him and his family.

"My discovery and changes thus far have not been by choice," I said. "It's been hard, but I love what I've read so far, as the teachings are so beautiful."

"That's because it comes from a place of zero ego."

Over the coming months, Sean was the best sounding board over the phone on the intense experiences that unfolded for me during meditation and adjusting to how my relationship with my family was changing.

"Occasionally, when I come out of a beautiful meditation, it's difficult for me to function in the three-dimensional world," I said. "And then . . . eerie experiences when I'm out of meditation."

"Elisabeth, you really should consider living in an ashram. You are open and very vulnerable right now. And with what you are describing, you probably were on this path in a previous life."

"I can't right now. Too much of normal life to wrap up. But I'm isolated, so I think I will be okay while I'm here."

Sean connected me with two women who had had similar experiences. Those subsequent phone conversations reassured me that I was not alone.

Insights and Ruminations: *My prayers were being answered— in the way that I needed most at that time rather than the way I had hoped and prayed for. My desire for a compatible long-term partner was once again being used for my spiritual growth, but this time in a gentle, supportive way. And wise people were telling me that I was going through a tremendous amount of change and should avoid a relationship with a man.*

CHAPTER 35:

Diving Deeper to Find the Light

"One day He did not leave me after kissing me."
—RABIA, *LOVE POEMS FROM GOD:*
TWELVE SACRED VOICES FROM THE EAST AND WEST

While I continued to tie up loose ends in Colorado, my root and sacral chakras began to throb again. The Patanjali Kundalini Yoga Care counselor's words echoed in my head: "Kundalini Shakti Ma will not leave you alone until you become devotional. You have been given a path. Yogananda is the real deal."

This is a sacred time. I need to dive deep into Yogananda's lessons, I thought as I picked up the blue-and-white booklets to renew my efforts on this path.

As I began the Self-Realization Fellowship lessons, I was brought to tears by the pure teachings from Yogananda on Christ and Krishna. My chakra experiences softened.

"Why me? What did I do to deserve this beautiful gift?" I wondered as I rocked back and forth, wailing in joy and shock, in a patio chair in front of the rental house in Ouray, in the same spot where I had sat a year ago, depressed and hopeless. Others seek this type of truth, but I had been forced onto this path. I continued to sob uncontrollably as I realized the kindness of an intelligent force.

A few hours later, I had sent a couple of texts to Drew, as I had accidentally left a pair of shoes with my valuable custom orthotics. He had become silent again. Over a week after my return at the end of May, I received a short, scathing email from Drew: "What a fu**ing pain in the ass. Please send me $35 for shipping. I have so much to do."

A few days later, I opened the box and felt the immense anger within. I took a couple of deep breaths and told myself to not take it personally. Most of the contents of the gift bag, including the draft book into which I had poured so much love, were dusted with dirt and wood chips from the shoes. He had rejected most of what I had included. I was heartened to see that he had chosen to keep the copy of Yogananda's *Autobiography of a Yogi* that I had inserted in the gift bag just prior to his initial email reply. I thought he might enjoy the teachings since he and his wife had swapped faiths of Christianity and Buddhism during her awakening and their divorce. Drew had switched from Christianity to Buddhism, and his wife had shifted from Buddhism to Christianity. And he kept the dolphin-themed gift for his van Flipper. But I was also once again so confused. I grew angry that the Divine had used Drew and my thoughts of Drew for my spiritual growth yet again. I muttered that I couldn't take it anymore. The divine play felt more like a dirty trick.

Drew's ex-wife had written a book, partially on her spiritual awakening that had begun during their divorce just a couple of years ago. I had read it, and we had started conversing. I now reached out to Drew's ex-wife via Facebook messenger.

"You didn't give him a copy of your book, did you?" she said. "I told you he wouldn't be able to handle it!"

"Yes, I gave him a copy, but he refused to read it and returned it to me."

"Forgive him and forget him. I know it's hard. He is really not that great."

"I *have* forgiven him many times. What do you mean?"

"He is bipolar."

I almost dropped my cell phone. It all made sense now. Sweet, cruel, ghosting, sweet, repeated ghosting, sweetness, followed by intense anger again. I had become concerned that I had fallen for another narcissistic Libra, as I had many years earlier with my ex-husband. A matchmaking service had reminded me of the narcissistic patterns of love-bombing, disrespecting, and discarding. But all the times he had suddenly lashed out flashed back. His statement about protecting me from him and the eerie sidelong glance almost a year ago echoed in my memory. I had mentioned just before he was supposed to visit me in Ouray that I was a mental health advocate in my work, and that he was safe to share any such concerns with me. Drew had quickly retorted, "I laughed out loud when I read that message from you. There is nothing wrong with me." And yet I sensed he was trying hard to not hurt me. I mentioned in early emails to him that I am emotionally very sensitive and struggle with that sensitivity but was learning my best to not take actions from others personally. I had asked him a couple of times if he remembered those moments of lashing out or statements of grandiosity, and he didn't seem to remember them. He frequently dismissed it by stating he must have been smoking pot. I had never smelled any marijuana on him, and I started to realize that he was most likely not aware of those moments, or perhaps it was a cover, denial, or both.

I wrote back to Drew's ex-wife: "I wish I had known. It would have been easier to forgive him. But digging deep each time to forgive him made me grow and was also part of my awakening. So sad. Has he ever tried medications?"

"I said he has signs of bipolar. He has never been diagnosed. I don't believe in psychiatrists or such medications."

I cried and prayed that night for his soul, with sadness that he and his ex-wife hadn't tried to seek professional care. Unfortunately, I was familiar with the elevated risk for suicide in souls struggling with bipolar disorder. The significant other of one of my family members was bipolar and had taken her life many years before. The stigma surrounding mental health challenges that I had been fighting in my professional work was facing me once again in my personal life. I knew Drew had a very tender soul under those confusing moments of his lashing out immediately after being so loving. Reflecting on the empathy of the exquisite pain of depression from my recent experience, I began sending him healing and loving energy from afar, in alignment with a Buddhist metta meditation of benevolence and loving-kindness. Flashbacks of his emphatic comment against medications for my depression the previous summer entered my mind, and I knew he was a very natural man.

After speaking to two counselors about bipolar disorder, I learned that the resistance to treatment is common due to the enjoyment of euphoria and high states of energy during the up phases. And the depression in many souls who have bipolar disorder does not respond to medications. During my last visit with him, he could not remember some of the hurtful statements toward me, which I also learned is typical of bipolar disorder.

And yet despite all of the ruminations on the possibility of being bipolar, I've learned that such diagnostic labels include stigma and may not be accurate. I would have completely accepted him into my life and loved him fully, label or no label.

I was sad that it was unlikely for me to have the opportunity to ask Drew more about feeling one with the cosmos, a similar concept as described on my spiritual path. I emailed Drew a link to one of Paramahansa Yogananda's free online guided meditations, which mentioned sending peace to the cosmos. In my own experience, meditation is natural medication for the mind, even if not used for spiritual purposes. Then I followed up with a humorous *Saturday Night Live* video clip on Chris Farley as an inspirational speaker living in a van and visiting a spin class, in hopes of lifting Drew's spirits. I set the intention of being his friend no matter what. But I sensed his role in my spiritual growth was over. I sighed with relief. The Divine had indeed been trying to protect me all along.

Regardless, Drew ghosted me again. Perhaps I scared him with what I shared about my awakening or due to his aversion to the use of the word *God* in conversation. I will likely never know.

The next day, I rode my bike from Ouray up and over Red Mountain Pass late in the afternoon. Insights always seem to sink in deeper whenever I spend quality time alone in the mountains. By the time I returned to my van, my mind was clear, but I was wet from sweat and becoming chilled in the early evening air.

"Hello. May I ask you a question?" a woman wearing all red walked around the back open doors of the van as I secured my bike under the bed in the van.

"Oh!" I yelled and leapt off the pavement in my bike shoes. She startled me as I hadn't heard her approach over the nearby Uncompahgre River raging from early summer runoff from the massive snowpack that was finally melting.

"Sure, what do you want to know?"

"That church. I sense I've seen it before, but this is the first time I've been here. I am having a déjà vu."

"Well, do you believe in past lives? I didn't until just a few months ago."

"Why yes, I think I do."

"Well, perhaps you have been here and inside that church in a past life. A recent spiritual awakening is making me open to such ideas."

"Oh, this conversation is God-arranged. You are so strong. May I talk to you about cycling? Can you help me to get fit like you?"

I offered to help her as a health and wellness coach but explained that I wasn't quite ready yet and had to finish writing this book. "But it's all going to change based on what I just learned."

"What do you mean?"

I explained the disturbing information I had just learned about Drew.

"Oh, honey. Did his ex-wife tell you to ruuuuuunnnn?" she crooned in a sweet, thick Arkansas accent.

"Sort of. She told me to keep writing, keep searching, and that I wasn't ready for a man yet, anyway."

"Let me tell you, honey. I fell the hardest ever for a bipolar man. They are the sweetest souls, but they will tear you to shreds."

"He kind of already did, but I'm trying to just be a friend to him."

We hugged, and I realized that I was benefiting most from this not-so-coincidental meeting.

A couple of days later in early June, as I lay in bed, I Googled the biblical meaning behind the true names of the men in my life over the previous years. I was stunned. The irony. God had been using men to try to awaken me all along. I hoped it wouldn't continue now that I was awake and spiritual.

I shook my head and looked at a photo of Yogananda.

Okay, I just need to let go of fear, have faith, and trust more. I'm so sorry I didn't trust you. I know that you and the Divine are looking out for what's best for my soul. I know you are sort of doing it again. Just when I have started to realize how much I am changing and how much I want a grounded, deeply spiritual man and a kind soul to support me on this new path, I have met a man who intrigues me in that way. Divine intelligence is pushing me again, but in a much more beautiful way and hopefully without so much pain this time. I sense that all this change is not just for me. Perhaps I'm being shaped for a special soul partner who is waiting for me. Even if one of the men I have already met isn't the next sweet soul to help me grow, I know you will look out for me. I fully let go of previous frustrations and smiled as I sat down to meditate that morning with a Self-Realization Fellowship lesson laid on the floor in front of me.

I let go of all fear and began repeating a mantra of faith and trust, as I started meditating.

Then . . . rapture of deep, sweet, unconditional love, just when my soul needed such love the most . . . as I had no such love from a person in the flesh. The more that I surrendered, the more my heart was filled with love, as if my heart were exploding like a volcano. (For the reader to sense the love that I experienced, it is recommended to pause and listen to "Nur Allah Nur" by Sean Johnson and Wild Lotus Band, sung by Gwendolyn Colman https://www.youtube.com/watch?v=3hUk-KzSSCg). The following poem captures the essence of the moment for my soul.

> *Thereupon wouldst though,*
> *With divine rapture,*
> *Experience true spiritual attraction,*
> *Lay down thy life in the path of the Friend,*
> *And sacrifice thy soul in the wilderness of His love.*
> *This indeed is the meaning of stillness in flight and*
>   *flight in stillness . . .*
> —BAHÁ'U'LLÁH

I blurted out at the end of one meditation session, "I want other humans to experience this divine love." It was a love that was more beautiful and explosive than any I had felt for or from a human. I began to understand the definition of yoga as union with the Divine. I had no idea that I was going to experience divine love, let alone have expectations of it.

The timing of feeling that divine love was also just a couple of days after I had sent an email to my sister lamenting that I had tried to share unconditional love with all those who became a part of my life, but for some reason, it was so hard for me to find unconditional, long-term love in return, at least from a man.

Transition into a New Life

A couple of weeks later, while lying in bed, enjoying the aftereffects of the intense divine love and joy from meditation, tears welled up in my eyes. I realized that my soul was likely being shaped—not for my own enjoyment but likely for a soul who has been praying for a spiritual woman, and I had no idea who it might be. That belief about being shaped for another soul stemmed from conversations with an awakened, spiritually wise friend in Ouray. "Please protect and guide me," I prayed.

Just a month before my departure for California, planned for late July to be close to a concentration of souls on the same spiritual path, my parents arrived in the San Juan Mountains for their annual summer stay. My father gave me two gifts from my older brother. One gift was a framed print of a cowboy kneeling on a hill overlooking a herd of cattle, with a rosary dangling from one hand. The second was a rustic yet elegant wooden framed poem:

For Doctor Spatz
(Spatz is an abbreviation of a German nickname meaning
    little sparrow, which my family calls me)

Sermon to the Birds
By Saint Francis of Assisi, Patron Saint of my new path,
    unbeknownst to my brother.

*My little sisters, the birds, much bounden are ye unto God,
    your Creator, and always in every place ought ye to praise
    Him, for that He hath given you liberty to fly about
    everywhere . . . sisters, beware of the sin of ingratitude,
    and study always to give praises unto God. (excerpt)*

As I read the footnote of the poem, which read "The History Place, Great Speeches Collection," I choked up and wiped tears from my face, unable to speak.

My father glanced at me and then down into his suitcase as he continued to unpack. "Your brother talks about you a lot. He's worried."

My brother and I were not emotionally close. Thus, this was so unexpected and sweetly thoughtful that I was overwhelmed. And this was not the first time that my family had bestowed a gift related to St. Francis of Assisi. At the site where I was married in an aspen grove in the San Juan Mountains, my parents had placed a large statue of Saint Francis of Assisi, as a remembrance of my wedding, but also as an offering to God, as they were upset that I did not have a wedding in a Catholic church.

As I departed in my van from Colorado, I thought, *Well, my home is anywhere I am. Not just this van, or in this body, but in the long run, in this spirit or soul.*

Insights and Ruminations: *The most difficult challenges in the subsequent weeks were letting go of my steady, secure job and the tedious and daunting task of letting go of most of my belongings in time for the Self-Realization Fellowship convocation. But even more heart-wrenching was being around my parents who did not understand my changes, displayed disappointment in me, and doubted me instead of supporting me. I dug deeper into faith of my new emerging Self and the path that had been presented to me so I could start my life over. It took two years of steady effort to heal my relationship with my parents after my awakening began, which pushed me to heal all relationshipsd. Despite the exquisite, raw, natural beauty of the San Juan Mountains of Colorado, from which I drove away in tears, my soul yearned to be with other truth seekers on the same or similar paths. But I could not completely let go of that intense and raw nature of southwestern Colorado and vowed to return to split my time between the beauty of those mountains and the rich community of similar truth seekers of Arizona and Southern California.*

It was not until my journey through California that I learned that St. Francis of Assisi is the patron saint of my spiritual path. And when Google Maps took me to the San Juan Capistrano Catholic mission instead of my intended destination as I entered Southern California, I was reminded of the deep devotion and sacrifice for which Catholic saints are known. The story of Father Serra's journey across the Atlantic, leaving his family to never see them again in act of service by establishing missions, put my small journey in perspective. According to the placard in an old chapel on the grounds of San Juan Capistrano, "Some of Serra's social views, which were common to most eighteenth-century Europeans, are not views we hold today. But in the context of his life, he was a selfless and self-sacrificing visionary who brought an abiding zeal to his work as president of the Catholic missions."

I was so naïve about divine love and the path. I didn't realize the true purpose of being guided to write this book until those moments of divine love, and my realization of the desire for other humans to experience the love, joy, and peace available to all souls who are karmically ready and open.

Lotuses floating at San Juan Capistrano,
Catholic Mission in Southern California.

CHAPTER 36:

Spiritual Family Gathering

————— •◦• —————

". . . the path will become visible. Once on the way, you will
meet other wayfarers, who will advise and guide you as to the
path. Your job is to muster whatever strength you have to get
underway—thereafter help is assured."
—ANANDAMAYI MA

In the midst of travel to and upon arrival in California for the
Self-Realization Fellowship World Convocation, the divine play
was intense, personal, and delivered in a way that reminded me that I
needed to become deeply devotional. I asked Paramahansa Yogananda
whether such devotion would likely lead me to my primary remaining
unmet human desire: a strong, grounded, kind, spiritual man who
would not hurt me.

One morning, preparing to meditate in my van before attending
the first few days of the convocation in early August, I began laughing
hysterically at the inside jokes of the divine play of birds, songs, books,
and meeting people to make me more devotional, and then blurted
out, "Okay, Okay! But it's not funny anymore. I'm scared. It's as if
all my thoughts are being read and responded to. I know I need to be
more devotional." I began to cry. "It's almost not fair at this point. I
promise to be devotional."

I wiped tears from my cheeks and prepared to attend the convocation that day. I prayed to continue to be shaped and led to a partner with whom I could collaborate to serve as a vessel for our purpose of helping others, to continue reverently on the Self-Realization Fellowship path with devotion, and to ultimately be with a partner where we can mutually support each other on our individual paths. I hoped that such a man would support and help me find the way to be deeply devotional, but in a gentle way. Cycling was now off my list of top desired traits of a future partner.

As I sat next to a young woman from India before a talk at the convocation, I asked her a couple of questions and was moved by her wisdom.

"It's a bit scary how much Yogananda can read my thoughts," I whispered to her.

"Guru won't hurt you," she reassured me with a gentle smile, the typical Indian sing-song and endearing bobble of her head. "He is here to help you."

When I walked into the large conference room, I was feeling stereotypical Catholic guilt for having any desires. I took a few deep breaths in the presence of these lovely souls and vowed that I would now direct my energies in a more powerful way to serve others.

Later that same day I watched the closing remarks of the movie *Glimpses of a Life Divine* being played at the convocation. Sri Mrinalini Mata explained how at the end of meditation one day, Yogananda began laughing intensely. As his infectious laugh spread through his disciples and devotees, Yogananda was asked why he was laughing. Yogananda expressed that a joke is being played on us all. And then he began to cry with compassion and love . . . and said he felt sorry for all humans.

I swallowed and wiped tears from my face. I realized that Yogananda only wants me to stop suffering. It's what he wants for all of us. Yogananda wants all humans to stop suffering. Yogananda is encouraging us to go beyond our five senses and the three-dimensional world to open to the world of Spirit.

The rest of my experiences in the subsequent days, weeks, and months shall remain between me and the Divine, despite the potent, profound power of those moments. Suffice it to say that I entered into a relationship with my new spiritual path . . . that I pray will last my entire life. My next journey would be the start of a honeymoon with the Divine that I had never dreamed of in this lifetime.

I feel blessed beyond words.

Insights and Ruminations: *Upon joining the large gathering of other souls on the same spiritual path, I felt that I had finally found my peeps and a new family.*

CHAPTER 37:

The End . . . Or Is It?

---·•·---

"We are born to learn how to die."
—LINDA LANCASTER, N.D.

My loss, grief, and awakening began due to my tendency to push myself too hard and to my lack of gratitude for all the wonderful aspects of my life. I had a wonderful, loving, kind partner in Kevin, had a rewarding yet over-demanding career, and lived in a lovely house in my favorite part of the world. Meister Eckhart von Hochheim, a German theologian and medieval Christian mystic, imparted the following wisdom: "If the only prayer you ever say in your entire life is thank you, it will be enough." And earlier in my life, I had stated to nonspiritual friends that it didn't make sense to criticize spiritual people as long as they weren't hurting anyone else. I would mutter, "Don't you notice how much better spiritual people can handle the tough parts of life? I wish I had a strong spiritual side to me." Well, the universe was listening.

This memoir is a portion of my spiritual emergence, which turned into a spiritual emergency. "Spiritual emergence is the process of personal awakening into a level of perceiving and functioning, which is beyond normal ego functioning. The process may at first include one of the following phenomena: out-of-body experiences, occult phenomena, precognition, clairvoyance, astral travel, and perception of auras. At its peak, spiritual emergence is the experience of the ultimate unity of all things, a mystical experience, a merging with the Divine which transcends verbal description. Among the positive effects of this process are increased creativity, feelings of peace, and an expanded sense of compassion." (Emma Bragdon, PhD, paraphrased from a longer explanation.) A spiritual emergency is a rapid awakening with stages of a "profound psychological transformation that involves one's entire being, including sequences of psychological death and rebirth," as defined by Christina and Stanislav Grof.

My tumultuous personal transformation from a fast-paced mind and body to a place of outer and inner stillness was a foreshadowing of the COVID-19 pandemic forcing the masses to become still and find inner peace at home. Stillness of the mind and body is essential in spiritual growth, as reflected in "Be still and know that I am God!"— Psalm 46:11. I was guided from tapping into all senses to quiet the mind as Eckhart Tolle teaches, and using other techniques to stop thoughts, to a spiritual path where one must also still the body, mind, and breath and then disconnect from all senses to connect one's soul with the "Great Spirit." Ceasing identification with the senses allows one to identify with the awareness of the soul.

In the midst of this spiritual emergency, I simultaneously worked to affect community mental health and shed previous unhealthy interpersonal conflicts so I could fully heal and blossom. As my "spiritually transformative experiences" and challenging relationship lessons intensified after the end of this storyline, I promised myself that if I survived and blossomed on the other side, I would publish this book to help others by including a list of books, counseling and coaching contacts, and tips for those who may experience a spiritual emergency, as well as learning opportunities for mental health care professionals on the interrelated aspects of spirituality and mental health and how to recognize spiritually transformative experiences in their patients. "Spiritually transformative experiences" was coined by Yvonne Kason, MD, who is the cofounder of Spiritual Awakenings International. There is a great need for more mental health professionals to increase their capacity to support each soul in their healing through awareness of the client's spiritual views, practices, and experiences.

I was then led to a course to be a Spiritual Emergence Coach®, which fostered the inclusion of many resources that I became aware of through Emma Bragdon.

My introspection through awareness of every thought and emotion became deeper as I evolved through this awakening. My fast-paced mind and body was no longer tolerable for my soul. Stopping each negative thought before it could become an emotion and transmuting negative emotions became my practice. At the time, I didn't realize that the method to stop my suffering while isolating myself further was a spiritual practice.

While many have told me that I am not supposed to know why these experiences happened for me, I began searching. As a rigid scientist who had helped others for years, I had learned how to search for answers. I was on a search for why I touched ananda multiple times and why a kundalini rising occurred for me. I was given those experiences so that I would search for the answer of why until I was given my spiritual path. I was frightened and wanted the experiences to stop. While searching for those answers, I was brought to a spiritual path for which I was not prepared, and which intensified my experiences. The experiences were disorientating, and the truths provided on the spiritual path were in stark contrast to my upbringing and Western scientific mind, turning my entire world upside down.

I was also led to courses in Ayurveda (holistic health wisdom and practices based on the Vedas), life, spiritual, and somatic coaching. According to the Strozzi Institute, somatic coaching is "a transformational process that empowers individuals to more effectively fulfill their commitments, to work more skillfully with others, and to embody new, generative ways of being . . . " and which "moves the center of learning from the head into the body, giving . . . access to all aspects of your intelligence—intellectual, emotional, and physical." Through an Ayurveda course from Mas Vidal, I learned further from David Frawley's book *Yoga & Ayurveda: Self-Healing and Self-Realization* about my spiritual experiences, progress, why I was brought to Kriya Yoga, and how Ayurveda supports yoga of the mind and spirit in a way that complements Paramahansa Yogananda's teachings. Certain Kriya Yoga techniques help open the *sushumna* or central channel, through which *prana* or life force must enter for the kundalini to rise upward and pierce through the chakras, which are perpendicular to the *sushumna*.

For souls who may have unexpected, disorientating, or intense spiritual experiences, it can be difficult to find the right wise person to help understand what one is going through, integrate the experiences, and ground oneself. Thus, I've included within the list of resources some reading, training, and names of counselors and coaches who may be able to provide that type of support.

I had to be violently shaken out of my old lifestyle, relationships, thought patterns, career, family influences, and geography in order to be led to the spiritual path that was designed for my soul in this lifetime. Those spiritual experiences were not all my own doing. Nothing in life is ever all our own doing. There were divine interventions repeatedly along the way, at critical moments. While searching for a certain version of the Gita by Paramahansa Yogananda in a used bookstore in Ojai, I stumbled across a possible, simple explanation on why I may have experienced ananda. According to Robert Beer, author of Hindu Altars, "The path of knowledge is the direct non-dual method of self-liberation through philosophical introspection, whereby the 'being-awareness-bliss' (*sat-chit-ananda*) of the Supreme Self (*paramatman*) is realized purely through intensive self-inquiry." However, I am not liberated . . . not even remotely close.

Mas Vidal shared, "Just because someone experiences kundalini rising doesn't make them spiritual. Some turn away in fear. It will keep happening in future lives until their soul is ready for spiritual growth." I believe that the Divine sent my counselor Laura to me at one of the most critical moments to reassure me of the beauty of the experiences and to calm my fears. And just because someone is spiritual and on a sound, well-respected path doesn't mean they have addressed their core personal work.

The beauty of the breadcrumb trail left by the Divine, the frightening divine play, and the pain that intensified and then was removed during truth-seeking and meditation was leading me to a strong connection to Kriya Yoga. Self-Realization Fellowship and Kriya Yoga International are not cults, and Paramahansa Yogananda's teachings are not a new age belief system but include the purest available interpretation of Jesus's teachings and the Bhagavad Gita (Song of the Lord). While I had been practicing and teaching the outward, physical aspects of asana yoga on the mat for twenty years with little inner, spiritual change, I was led to yoga of the mind and spirit through meditation, *pranayama* (life force or breath control), mantra, *pratyahara* (withdrawal of the senses), *dharna* (concentration) and additional aspects of Kriya Yoga . . . and led from despair to deep wisdom. The physical yoga practice helps me prepare for meditation and has helped me with healing the nervous system from trauma in combination with other somatic therapies, especially when taught with a trauma-sensitive approach. The Universe, Higher Power, Spirit, Divine Intelligence, the Divine, aka God felt like my soul was ready for deep wisdom that is still hard for me to handle. Perhaps it was to help me anchor before the world crises began, as I was already frequently dismayed and disillusioned about how we treat each other and how humanity treats Mother Nature.

It is no coincidence that I was in a stage of being shaped by Shakti when I attended Shakti Fest and then in a stage of increasing devotion as an ambassador for and attending Bhakti Fest in 2019. As I entered my new chapter of life in my van, I was exhausted from the entire process and prayed for gentleness. My decision to live in a community of truth seekers and Self-Realization Fellowship devotees was exactly what I needed. While on retreat at the Self-Realization Fellowship's ashram in Encinitas, I've never been moved to tears so many times in a week, as I began to understand Paramahansa Yogananda's selfless commitment, purpose, and love for humanity, due to certain spiritual experiences, readings, and interactions that were designed for me.

The more I search for answers and truth, the more I learn, the less I realize that I know. Simplified scriptures, the specific spiritual path to which I was guided, and certain coaching courses provided the answers on a deeper level that I could not find in other books. The humbleness I feel as I learn more is reflected well in a statement from a fellow Self-Realization Fellowship devotee, "I am an ant at the base of the Himalayas." Paramahansa Yogananda's lessons and his interpretation of the Bhagavad Gita humble me beyond measure.

I was wrong about why I was being shaped so quickly. I was not being shaped for a spiritual man who was waiting, but instead for my own soul growth, so I could write and gift this book to readers with whom this resonates, and to add spiritual emergence and life purpose coaching to my skills. As I finalized this book, the lessons did *not* slow down but instead sped up. A rapid-fire delivery of extremely harsh, humbling, and sometimes frightening lessons about my desires and love in the three-dimensional world was followed by additional spiritual experiences meant to help heal me. We really are here to work through our desires and attachments. I had to lean on many modern teachings on self-love and deep self-care in order to survive the strange sequence of events, and turned to reading the compassionately toned wisdom teachings of Paramahamsa Prajnanananda, the current spiritual leader of Kriya Yoga International.

My sense is that my desire for a partner is being used to force me to quickly resolve past life karma. Each time I meditate, I want a partner less because what I experience is all-fulfilling. I'm trying to remain open-hearted to all I meet. I've learned to not trust others until I have known them for a long time.

I wrote this book in the midst of my awakening and resulting transformation. Thus, my interpretation and understanding of my experiences will likely shift over the coming years. An open heart is what led me to my experiences and path. My mind initially fought against being led. That resistance only delayed me from an immense mountain of Truth and wisdom. Without the space in my life at the time of my awakening, I would not have found my path for spiritual development and personal growth. And as my new life unfolds, this space is allowing me to become who I am meant to be on all levels of my life, stepping back into deep gratitude, joy, and wholeness.

"Kundalini Shakti is the divine presence within every human soul. It motivates and guides yearning and intention and makes it clearer to us what we need to do to cooperate with the spiritual source within us to get deeper and deeper to the source."
—JOAN SHIVARPITA HARRIGAN, PhD,
FROM *BUDDHA AT THE GAS PUMP* INTERVIEW

After the dust settled from the fear associated with such a rapid awakening, I took time in isolation in the mountains of Colorado to ground firmly on my own two feet and to find my own sovereignty and strength. By taking care of the Divine within, my true purpose to serve others and how to merge into service of the world is being revealed. I trust that the greater Divine will take care of the rest.

While I was recovering from the stripping nature of my spiritual emergency, the pandemic began. A former public health official prior to my awakening, I worked for decades in the fight against lethal infectious diseases and helped prepare for such a world event as the coronavirus pandemic. I worked so hard in public health that my personal life fell apart. I had done my best to serve and love, but it was not enough. When all that was important in my personal life fell away, I worked even harder to serve, but even such service was not enough to soothe my soul. And then I was quickly led to a spiritual path and a completely different view of life, death, relationships, and nature.

My coaching clients were sharing their struggles with how the pandemic was affecting them. I felt anchored by the meditation practices from Self-Realization Fellowship and conversations with a fellow devotee. I supported my clients to take the opportunity of being forced to become still at home to assess what was most important to them, to tap into or develop spiritual practices they had to go deep within, to take steps to design their life to be nurturing for themselves and their loved ones, and to reflect on how they could channel their frustrations with the outer world to do what they could to serve others in their community.

I prayed for all those who were suffering and could not help but observe how the rest of the world seemed to be going through what I had just gone through in my personal life. The severely narcissist president reminded me of how I too had been fooled by narcissists earlier in my life, but how that allowed me to heal from trauma, work on myself, help others, and awaken to Truth. World crises were being intensified by a narcissistic president and other unconscious leaders, which pushed many kind souls to figure out what they could do in their own life and within their own community to make a difference. I began working part-time and remotely in public health, helping interview people who had become ill with coronavirus. I was able to hear firsthand about the devastation that the virus was having in people's lives through losing work, losing loved ones, and losing their health and hope. While it was not a surprise to me, their sharing was in stark contrast to those I would hear making statements belittling its impact. And I was reminded once again how hard many governmental employees work to help individuals and communities.

While I was finalizing this book, the pandemic resurged, interracial tensions and violence in the States intensified, unprecedented wildfires spread in the western US, and the election created rifts between Americans. The modern culture tendency toward greed, selfishness, racism, and lack of respect for Mother Nature created these turbulent times. The dark times and events will continue to push us into brighter, more loving and spiritual times, especially for American due to our greed-based economy. This is long overdue.

I hope sharing my experiences with raw, self-deprecating honesty will inspire you to live in full presence and to meditate. I hope this book will help calm souls going through a spiritual emergence or emergency in the future and encourage them to not turn away in fear.

I hope readers will learn to perceive the true divine essence within, the divine essence of others, and all of nature, that when undisturbed by man are expressions or manifestations of the divine essence of God or being.

I wish that you, the reader, find your true purpose, and feel the true love of light, of Truth.

We are all one.

You are never alone.

I am no longer fearful of death.

As the Prophet Muhammad stated: "Die before you die."

As many wise souls have stated: "Death of the body is the end of an illusion."

Namaste

Intertwining of Mental Health, Core Personal Work, Spiritual Growth, and Relationships

———— •• ————

"We turn to the dharma to feel better, but then may unwittingly wind up using spiritual practice as a substitute for facing our psychological issues.
—John Wellwood, Psychotherapist,
Teacher of Integrated Psychospiritual Work

B lessed and cursed to be aware of the stigma associated with mental health challenges and the lack of awareness of the types of experiences being delivered to me, I had the wherewithal to not share much of my spiritual experiences with traditional mental health professionals in my region. I had a healthy fear of being institutionalized. During a Spiritual Emergence Coach® course from Emma Bragdon, PhD, I learned that being treated with pharmaceuticals in a foreign environment could very well have prevented the best possible transformation for me. My counselor Laura is a true godsend into my life, as she has the perfect blend of traditional western psychotherapy training, a few personal experiences similar to my journey, and deep spiritual wisdom that was delivered in the most respectful, sacred space to honor and support my process.

During Emma Bragdon's course through Integrative Mental Health for You, I heard several stories of souls who were not as fortunate as I in being led to such a counselor and were instead hospitalized and treated with medications in a way that halted their potential positive transformation. This observation of my good fortune and the misfortune of other souls spurred me to include the list of the learning resources for mental health professionals interested in expanding their awareness and skills in this arena.

Integrative Mental Health for You (imhu.org) states, "A Spiritual Emergence Coach® is trained to recognize psycho-spiritual phenomena and support those who are challenged by the ups and downs these unusual phenomena can create. Examples of the phenomena include psychic opening, near-death experience, and kundalini awakening." A Spiritual Emergence Coach® recognizes that assessments by medical and mental health professionals can be valuable and necessary. In a group format, the coach facilitates individuals sharing stories and resources in a supportive environment. The group thus provides encouragement and support for further personal and spiritual growth. A spiritual emergence or emergency can cause a shift of personal values into a yearning to help others in a new way or to find a new life purpose. Sharing with others in a group can assist in finding meaning and direction in the experience. Meeting personally with a certified life coach with spiritual emergence coaching skills can deepen this experience. If one is going through a spiritual emergency, counseling is recommended in place of or in combination with coaching.

Despite the professional counseling support from Laura, I still felt very alone, as the spiritual experiences and painful interactions with others were delivered at an alarming rate. The universe was watching. Resources on core personal growth were flying at me during the entire spiritual awakening. It was as if the universe were informing me, "No spiritual bypassing allowed." While I conducted searches on the internet, the search results repeatedly landed on pages that had nothing to do with what I had entered in my search engine. Once I noticed that pattern, I slowed down, read the search results, and realized that the articles and webpages revealed the exact core personal work wisdom that I needed to better understand both my role and the role of the person with whom I was interacting, to tease out what was causing the misunderstanding or conflict. The timing of interactions with wise souls, finding books, and receiving podcasts also mirrored this divine timing and intervention. This created an immense amount of compassion for me and the other souls, as all souls are doing the best they can at their level of consciousness. Thus, while I was being rapidly led to a spiritual path that had been picked for my soul, I was being partially forced into addressing my own personal core work on remaining emotional issues. It's as if the universe were telling me, "You are going to have to face all your unresolved personal issues and grow, in order to be able to handle embarking on this spiritual path at the same time."

Spiritual growth through understanding scriptures, praying, devotion, practicing meditation techniques, and attending *satsangs* (spiritual discourses or sacred gatherings) will take one only so far in interpersonal relationships and to excel in the world. The phrase "spiritual bypassing" was coined and defined by John Wellwood, a pioneer in integrating psychological and spiritual work for the past thirty years, as "a tendency to use spiritual ideas and practices to sidestep or avoid facing unresolved emotional issues, psychological wounds, and unfinished developmental tasks."

During the timeline of my experiences within this book, Sounds True founder Tami Simon launched a series of e-newsletters sharing free interviews of leading spiritual authors and free live webinars expounding the exact personal and spiritual wisdom needed to complement my growth. The Sounds True mission is to "wake up the world" and to "disseminate spiritual wisdom" in a practical and accessible way. This includes delivering spiritual and personal wisdom to some of the most marginalized populations, including "survivors of violence, at-risk youth, prisoners, veterans, individuals with disabilities, and those in developing countries."

Relationships and Unconditional Love

Every relationship has taught me to introspect my flaws. During my past two years of core personal work, mental health counseling, and my specific spiritual practices and path lessons, I gathered nuggets on unconditional love that can be applied to romantic relationships with conscious souls who have an open heart and an open mind, and are ready to grow with you:

1. Establish healthy boundaries and understand the healthy boundaries of your partner.
2. Be curious about the other soul; hold a deep longing to understand the other soul.
3. Observe without judgment; accept and appreciate the other soul, exactly as they are.
4. Trust the other soul.
5. Keep an open heart for forgiving.
6. Be compassionate when your partner makes mistakes. We all have unconscious moments.
7. Hold sacred space and time for the other soul to express, share, and grow.
8. Shine a light on each other's blind spots in the most loving, respectful manner, and be willing to receive the same in return.

When both partners give unconditional love, the strongest friendship, loyalty, trust, commitment, and devotion are developed, aspects that are vital for a relationship to successfully weather the ups and downs of life in this world. The sanctuary of creating such reliable love provides safety, connection, and dignity for both souls to grow and flourish, and a steadfast companionship that can stand the crashing waves of forces outside of the relationship. You are usually attracted to qualities in a partner that you are lacking. Recognizing those qualities and being open to learning from your partner's example can stimulate growth in those areas, which then builds a stronger relationship.

While being coached by Master Match Makers in the middle of this story, the head coach delivered a mass of articles to increase my awareness on my romantic relationship issues, which was based on surveys and three one-hour intensive interviews on my history, to reveal my unhealthy patterns and to help me establish healthy habits. My favorite article that I had clipped years prior happened to appear in the mass of articles: "Every Successful Relationship Is Successful for the Same Reason" by Mark Manson, "Author. Thinker. Life Enthusiast": https://markmanson.net/relationship-advice. Mark is not a psychologist, but his article is based on the results of a survey of over fifteen hundred couples who reported being in a happy relationship for over ten years. I highly recommend printing the article and handing it to your partner to discuss.

For readers who want to delve deeper into the topic of this epilogue, I once again highly recommend tapping into John Wellwood. He left a legacy of wisdom on the "psychology of awakening, relationships as a transformative path, and embodied presence." His areas of expertise and related books such as *Journey of the Heart: A Path of Conscious Love,* and *Perfect Love, Imperfect Relationships: Healing the Wound of the Heart* are listed on his webpage titled "Integrating Western Psychology and Eastern Spiritual Wisdom" at http://www .johnwelwood.com/index.htm.

The most powerful explanation that I have found of what unconditional love means in the interface of human love, self-love, and divine love is within Quatrain 32, "There was a Door to which I found no Key" and in the addendum titled "Omar's Dream-Wine of Love; a Scripture of Love," in Paramahansa Yogananda's *Wine of the Mystic,* his spiritual interpretation of The Rubaiyat of Omar Khayyam, published by Self Realization Fellowship in 1994. It would be an injustice to quote only a portion of such wisdom.

Personal and spiritual growth take courage and grit. Pepper that growth with humor, and it will be accelerated. Laughter is proven to support learning and bonding. My favorite couple in my life is my late Uncle Heinz and surviving Aunt Johanna. They constantly laughed together through good and bad times. He was the masterful, witty storyteller, and my aunt has been described as having the ability to "see a silver lining around a pile of poop." Enjoy the wild ride together and look at the world through a lens of humor.

View of Wilson Range and Wilson Mesa near Telluride.
Photo by Matthew Landon.

To Maxwell

"It's not our path, but it's your happiness and that honestly is what I wanted all along."

Your wish came true, Maxwell. Happiness arrived for my soul in a way that I never imagined.

Parting Prayer

Spiral shell centers next to the mural of
Mother Mary in a Grotto, Baja.

*"You are a Christian because you believe in Jesus, and you are
a Jew because you believe in all the prophets including Moses.
You are a Muslim because you believe in Muhammad as a
prophet, and you are a Sufi because you believe in the universal teaching of God's love. You are really none of those, but
you are all of those because you believe in God. And once you
believe in God, there is no religion. Once you divide yourself
off with religions, you are separated from your fellow man."*
—MUHAMMAD RAHEEM BAWA MUHAIYADDEEN

This quote was shared within *Illuminated Prayer* by Michael
Green, whose art enhances *The Illuminated Rumi.* Michael sat
for ten years with the enlightened Sufi master Bawa Muhaiyaddeen.
Green brings this marvelous little revelation: "It was one of the most

important things I ever heard His Holiness say—It could bring peace to our planet."

I bow reverently to the ultimate teacher for my soul: Paramahansa Yogananda, who seemed to provide reassurance and encouragement through the ethers at critical moments of my life unfolding in a new direction, including through his book *Whispers from Eternity*. Even my logo creation was timed in alignment with my reading of a passage from *Whispers from Eternity*. It was a long, wild ride to find you. I surrender to your continued guidance.

> *Your acts of kindness are iridescent wings of divine love,*
> *which linger and continue to uplift others long after your sharing.*
> —Rumi

> ***Lokah Samastah Sukhino Bhavantu***
> *May all beings be happy and free, and may the*
> *thoughts, words, and actions of my own life contribute in*
> *some way to the happiness and freedom for all.*

Resources

I. Mental Health Hotlines & Resources

    a. Crisis Text Line 741741: https://www.crisistextline.org/texting-in

    b. Mental Health First Aid. Take a course to be there for someone you love.

    c. Evryman: an interactive behavioral curriculum for men to connect with other men about their emotions, Evryman is not therapy or guru worship. https://www.evryman.com/

    d. Man Therapy ("A mustache is no place to hide your emotions."): https://www.mantherapy.org/

    e. National Alliance on Mental Illness: https://www.nami.org/

    f. United States National Suicide & Crisis Hotlines: http://suicide hotlines.com/national.html

    g. Guided Meditations from Paramahansa Yogananda: https://yogananda.org/guided-meditations

    h. Article by David Frawley, "Yoga and Ayurveda's View of Depression and How to Overcome It": https://www.vedanet.com/yoga-and-ayurvedas-view-of-depression-and-how-to-overcome-it/

    i. Integrative Mental Health for You (IMHU), a nonprofit established by Emma Bragdon, PhD. IMHU contributes to improving mental healthcare through online and live educational presentations and certifications for wellness seekers and healthcare providers. https://imhu.org/

    j. *Integrative Mental Health Care: An Introduction to Foundations and Methods (Alternative and Integrative Treatments in Mental Health Care)* by James Lake MD. This book is the first in a series on alternative and integrative treatments in mental health care. The other books in the series cover the following mental health problems: Alcohol and drug abuse, Anxiety, Attention-deficit hyperactivity disorder (ADHD), Bipolar disorder, Dementia and mild cognitive impairment, Insomnia, Post-traumatic stress disorder (PTSD), and Schizophrenia.

II. Grounding Resources & Tips

a. Mother Earth . . . plant your bare feet and hands into the earth every day.

b. Surround yourself with grounded, wise, spiritual humans, preferably those who have been on the same path for decades. Avoid spiritual teachers who want to charge you large sums of money. They are not enlightened.

c. Practice discernment to find truly enlightened teachers or "masters" and institutions with good reputations. There are very few truly enlightened teachers in the flesh.

d. Ayurveda Wellness Counseling such as: Dancing Shiva (dancing shiva.com), David Frawley (Pandit Vamadeva Shastri), American Institute of Vedic Studies (https://www.vedanet.com/), or another practitioner who is a member of the National Ayurvedic Medical Association https://www.ayurvedanama.org/

e. Articles on the positive effects of grounding: https://earthing institute.net/research/

f. *Earthing: The Most Important Health Discovery Ever?* Clinton Ober, Martin Zucker, and Stephen Sinatra, Basic Health Publications, 2010.

g. Receive massage or bodywork, to reconnect with your body and heal. Consider receiving bodywork specifically designed for healing from trauma.

III. Books to support healthy transformation and grounding during a spiritual emergence:

a. *Grounded Spirituality*, Jeff Brown, Enrealment Press, 2019.

b. *The Call of Spiritual Emergency: From Personal Crisis to Personal Transformation*, Emma Bragdon, PhD, Lightening Up Press, 2013.

c. *The Source Book for Helping People with Spiritual Problems*, Emma Bragdon, PhD, Lightening Up Press, 2006.

d. *Farther Shores, Exploring How Near-Death, Kundalini and Mystical Experiences Can Transform Ordinary Lives*, Yvonne Kason, MD, Author's Choice Press, an imprint of iUniverse, 2008.

IV. Counseling with Spiritual Aspects and Spiritual Emergence Counseling:

a. Laura Wade Jaster, MA, NCC, eRYT, Spiral Center for Transformative Practices: https://www.spiralwellness.com

b. Roberta Godbe-Tipp, PhD, Clear Mind Counseling, Transpersonal Therapy and Couples Counseling, including psychotherapeutic methods drawn from Western psychology, Eastern meditative traditions and nondual therapy, https://www.clearmindcounseling.com/. "Transpersonal therapy is a type of therapy that doesn't focus on a person's body and mind, but on the health of a person's spirit. This type of therapy puts an emphasis on a person's spiritual path or spiritual enlightenment during his life." www.careersinpsychology.org

c. Don and Martha Rosenthal, counseling couples and individuals, offering workshops on "relationship as a spiritual path . . . learning to live with an open heart": https://www.awakeningtogether.com/

d. Spiritual psychotherapy and counseling associated with Patanjali Kundalini Yoga Care; individualized spiritual guidance: http://www.kundalini-science.ch/en_index.html): http://kundalinicare.com/affiliates/

e. Spiritual Emergence Network: "Much of our transpersonal (psycho-spiritual) directory is online for self-referral. If you don't find a self-referral that works for you, you can leave a message at 415-634-5736. We will usually be in touch within twenty-four hours with other potential referrals and/or ideas for finding the help you need." http://www.spiritualemergence.org/directory/

f. Spiritual Crisis Network: https://spiritualcrisisnetwork.uk/

g. American Center for the Integration of Spiritually Transformative Experiences (ACISTE). ACISTE was established in 2009 to support people who have spiritually transformative experiences. https://aciste.org/

h. American Center for the Integration of Spiritually Transformative Experiences article on "Common Challenges Following a Spiritually Transformative Experience": https://aciste.org/about-stes/common-challenges-following-an-ste/

V. Spiritual Emergence Coaching:

a. Reach the author via ElisabethLava.com or http://beetrueyou.com/ or select a coach who resonates with your soul from the lists below:
b. Directory of Spiritual Emergence Coaches®: https://imhu.org/coaching/directory
c. American Center for the Integration of Spiritually Transformative Experiences Support Directory: https://aciste.org/support-directory/aciste-certified-life-spiritual-coaches/

VI. Spiritual Emergence Peer Support

I recommend getting some counseling and/or coaching in addition to these support groups.
a. Visit American Center for the Integration of Spiritually Transformative Experiences for free online peer support groups: https://aciste.org/support-directory/support-discussion-group-list/
b. Spiritual Emergence Anonymous: https://spiritualemergence anonymous.org/

VII. Spiritual Awakenings Awareness Groups:

a. Spiritual Awakenings International (SAI): https://spiritualawakenings international.org, cofounded by Yvonne Kason, MD MEd, CCFP, FCFP. "SAI's mission is to spread awareness globally of Spiritually Transformative Experiences. Spiritual Awakenings International (SAI) is a nonprofit worldwide network of individuals and groups who are interested in collaborating to raise awareness, network, and share personal experience relating to diverse types of Spiritually Transformative Experiences, "STEs," to raise global spiritual awareness. SAI is multi-faith, multicultural, nonaligned, and open to anyone peacefully seeking a higher understanding."

b. Emerging Proud (https://emergingproud.com/about/) is a non-profit, grassroots social movement aimed at: reframing "madness" as a catalyst for positive transformation.

VIII. Training and Books for Mental and Primary Care Health Professionals on Spirituality and Mental Health

a. Spiritual Competency Resource Center is approved by the American Psychological Association to sponsor continuing education for psychologists: https://spiritualcompetency.com/

b. "The ACISTE [American Center for the Integration of Spiritually Transformative Experiences] Cultural Competency Guidelines are available for mental health and other professionals working with clients who may present issues related to their spiritually transformative experiences." https://aciste.org/competency-guidelines-for-professionals/

c. The American Center for the Integration of Spiritually Transformative Experiences provides an excellent summary of "Common Challenges Following a Spiritually Transformative Experiences," based on near-death experiences, which will be updated as more information becomes available: https://aciste.org/about-stes/common-challenges-following-an-ste/

d. Integrative Mental Health for You (IMHU); Improve Mental Health by Learning More about Spirituality: https://imhu.org/. IMHU's mission is to contribute to improving mental healthcare through online and live educational presentations and certifications for wellness seekers and healthcare providers. Integrative Mental Health for You free course, "Spiritual Emergency: What is it?" https://imhu.org/product/spiritual-emergency-3/

e. *Spiritual Emergency: When Personal Transformation Becomes a Crisis*, Stanislav and Christina Grof (eds), Penguin Publishing Group, 1989.

f. *Spiritual and Religious Competencies in Clinical Practice*, Cassandra Vieten, PhD and Shelley Scammell, PsyD, New Harbinger Publications, 2015.

g. *The Call of Spiritual Emergency: From Personal Crisis to Personal Transformation*, Emma Bragdon, Lightening Up Press, 2013.

h. *Spirituality and Narrative in Psychiatric Practice: Stories of Mind and Soul*, edited by Christopher C. H. Cook, Andrew Powell and Andrew Sims, Royal College of Psychologists Publications, 2016.

i. *Spirituality and Psychiatry*, edited by Christopher C. H. Cook, Andrew Powell and Andrew Sims, Royal College of Psychologists Publications, 2009.

j. *Religion and Spirituality in Psychiatry*, Philippe Huguelet and Harold G. Koenig, Cambridge University Press, 2009.

k. *Spirituality in Clinical Practice*, a quarterly peer-reviewed academic journal published by the American Psychological Association covering research on the role of spirituality in psychotherapy: https://www.apa.org/pubs/journals/scp/

Bibliography

1. Tolle, Eckhart, *The Power of Now: A Guide to Spiritual Enlightenment*, Namaste Publishing, 2004.
2. ☺ Yogananda, Paramahansa, *Sayings of Paramahansa Yogananda*, Self-Realization Fellowship, Los Angeles, 1980.
3. The Holy Bible Containing the Old and New Testaments in the Authorized King James Version, Good Counsel Publishing Company, 1960.
4. Tolle, Eckhart, *Stillness Speaks.* New World Library, 2003.
5. Myss, Sharon M., *Anatomy of the Spirit: The Seven Stages of Power and Healing*, New York: Harmony Books, 1999, Audiobook, live recording of speech.
6. Khalsa, et al., *Kundalini Rising: Exploring the Energy of Awakening*, Sounds True, 2009.
7. Taylor, Steve, *The Leap: The Psychology of Spiritual Awakening*, New World Library, 2017.
8. Mercier, Patricia, *The Chakra Bible: The Definitive Guide to Working with Chakras*, Sterling, 2007.
9. Prophet, Elizabeth Clare, *Your Seven Energy Centers: A Holistic Approach to Physical, Emotional and Spiritual Vitality*, Summit University Press, 2000.
10. Kefala, Zeffie, *From Root to Truth: A Journey into the Energy Centers of the Body*, CreateSpace Independent Publishing Platform, 2014.
11. Nepo, Mark, *The Book of the Awakening: Having the Life You Want by Being Present to the Life You Have*, Conari Press, an imprint of Red Wheel/Weiser, 2011.
12. ∞Yogananda, Paramahansa, *Whispers from Eternity*, Self-Realization Fellowship, Los Angeles, 2008.

13. Dhalia, Heitor, *On Yoga: The Architecture of Peace,* documentary with Michael O'Neill, photographer, 2017.
14. Dao, Aleya, *Seven Cups of Consciousness: Change Your Life by Connecting to the Higher Realms,* New World Library, 2015.
15. *Ŧ* Yogananda, Paramahansa, *God Talks with Arjuna: Bhagavad Gita,* Self-Realization Fellowship, Los Angeles, 2001.
16. Dooley, Mike, *The Top Ten Things Dead People Want to Tell You,* Hay House, 2016.
17. *€* Yogananda, Paramahansa, *Man's Eternal Quest,* Self-Realization Fellowship, Los Angeles, 1982.
18. Yogananda, Paramahansa, *The Yoga of the Bhagavad Gita: An Introduction to India's Universal Science of God-Realization,* Self-Realization Fellowship, Los Angeles, 2007.
19. Kramer, Michael, *St. John of the Cross, Dark Night of the Soul,* Christianaudio.com, 2008, Audiobook.
20. Nottingham, Theodore J., *The Journey of the Anointed One: Breakthrough to Spiritual Encounter,* Theosis Books, 2013.
21. Barks, Coleman and Michael Green, *The Illuminated Prayer: The Five-Times Prayer of the Sufis,* Ballantine Wellspring, 2000.
22. Harrigan, Joan Shivarpita, *Kundalini Vidya The Science of Spiritual Transformation: A Comprehensive System for Understanding and Guiding Spiritual Development,* Patanjali Kundalini Yoga Care, 2006.
23. Uru Hu, Ra. Jovian Archive was founded by Ra Uru Hu and his family in 1999. Jovian Archive holds the exclusive copyright to the Human Design System.
24. Ladinsky, Danie, *Love Poems from God,* Penguin Publishing Group, 2002.
25. Beer, Robert, *Hindu Altars: A Pop-Up Gallery of Traditional Art & Wisdom,* New World Library, 2007.
26. St. Francis of Assisi, *Sermon to the Birds.* http://www.historyplace.com/speeches/saintfran.htm
27. Lipski, Andrew, *The Essential Sri Anandamayi Ma; Life and Teachings of a 20th Century Indian Saint,* biography of Alexander Lipski, words of Sri Anandamayi Ma translated by Atmananda; edited by Joseph A. Fitzgerald, World Wisdom Books, 2007.
28. Frawley, Dr. David, *Yoga & Ayurveda: Self-Healing and Self-Realization,* Lotus Press, 1999.

Acknowledgments

---◆◆---

I have deep gratitude for the guidance and counseling from Laura Wade Jaster, MA, NCC, eRYT, of Spiral Wellness, who was told by the Divine to approach and introduce herself to me during a transformational workshop led by Shiva Rea at Tara Mandala in Colorado.

I bow to the expert writing coaching by Jane Ashley, MA, of Flower of Life Press, who also utilized transpersonal counseling to help me to understand my experiences and to put those experiences into a greater context to share with others.

I thank Shiva Rea for her guidance during the transformational workshop in the fall of 2018 and for her yoga teacher training, a path without which I may never have come to understand the spiritual awakening. Thanks also to Katie Graves and Monica Mesa Dasi for bringing Shiva's Prana Vinyasa instructor training to Ridgway in the San Juan Mountains of southwestern Colorado. I would not have realized what I was experiencing without those connections.

I am grateful for the encouragement from my cousin Stephanie to write this book, sparked partly by a poetry request from my family in honor of my Uncle Heinz, Stephanie's father.

Thank you to my parents who encouraged me to write a book, although the topic is vastly different than they would have ever dreamed of coming forth from their daughter.

To Ashley Slater of AG Creative Studio for cheering me on during my transition and for her conscious creativity in my logo development for Bee True You and Lava Bee Well, LLC.

To Hansa Devi for her expert mala creations and sharing her

wisdom in Ridgway, Colorado: www.vicharainspiration.com, email: vicharapublications@gmail.com

To Ted Steinhardt for the impeccable timing of our conversations of that loving presence, the *Twilight Zone* moments, and so much more during my final days at the health department.

To Scott Salzman of BrightSpot Solutions (http://mobilemeditator.com/home) for his encouragement on the Kriya Yoga path, guidance, and for hosting me at a critical stage of my awakening.

I have deep gratitude for Jennifer Cummings, LMT and bad-ass healer, who welcomed me to Ojai and provided encouragement and a bit of guidance on the initial shaping of this book.

I am honored to have so many lovely souls who opened up to share their spiritual experiences, especially with stories of sensing energy of passed loved ones. Only two stories are included here, as I honor the sacred privacy of such experiences.

I thank Brady for helping me integrate my experiences, modeling strength, seeing the beauty of and the growth from the events in the months after this storyline ended, and being my cheerleader in stepping into my new purpose.

I thank Self-Realization Fellowship leaders for running such a responsible organization with the utmost intentions to preserve and promote Paramahansa Yogananda's teachings, vision, purity, ideals, and devotion.

I would not have survived my experiences without my interactions with the leaders of the following organizations related to Kriya Yoga outside of Self-Realization Fellowship, who expressed gentleness, compassion, humility, kindness, and provided divinely timed, wise guidance and support:

- Kriya Yoga International
- Swami Vidyadishananda and his staff members of the Self-Enquiry Fellowship
- Ananda Village

And most prominently, I bow reverently at the feet of the ultimate teacher for my soul, Paramahansa Yogananda. A hundred years prior to the writing of this book, your auspicious arrival in the United States was a gift to the World. Aum. Peace. Amen.

Made in the USA
Columbia, SC
15 June 2021